Mastering Sass

Create interactive and responsive cross-browser apps with
Sass and Compass

Luke Watts

BIRMINGHAM - MUMBAI

Mastering Sass

First published: August 2016

Production reference: 1230816

Published by Packt Publishing Ltd.

Livery Place

35 Livery Street

Birmingham B3 2PB, UK.

ISBN 978-1-78588-336-1

www.packtpub.com

Credits

Author

Luke Watts

Reviewer

Bartosz Skupień

Commissioning Editor

Amarabha Banerjee

Acquisition Editor

Prachi Bisht

Content Development Editor

Onkar Wani

Technical Editor

Shivani K. Mistry

Copy Editor

Safis Editing

Project Coordinator

Ulhas Kambali

Proofreader

Safis Editing

Indexer

Rekha Nair

Graphics

Kirk D'Penha

Production Coordinator

Melwyn Dsa

About the Author

Luke Watts is a web developer and digital artist from Galway, Ireland. He started learning web design in 2012 after many years working with AutoCAD in the manufacturing industry. In 2014 he set up his own web development agency called Affinity4 (`http://affinity4.ie`) in Galway, Ireland. He is an Oracle Certified MySQL Developer, and an Adobe Certified Associate (Photoshop and Dreamweaver).

Luke has a keen interest in learning and teaching others. He has written articles for many websites, including his own blog, on a wide range of subjects such as SEO, WordPress Development, SVG, Sass, Jade, OOP, Git, Silex, MySQL, and PHP.

Luke is also an accomplished artist, both in traditional mediums (mostly pencil and ink) and in digital painting. When not building websites or writing code he will most likely be working on a digital painting on his Wacom tablet using Photoshop or creating a 3D model or scene in any number of 3D modeling applications.

I'd like to thank Gareth Milligan, who, from the very beginning showed me what web design had to offer, not only as a career, but also as a hobby. His advice, encouragement, and support in those early days of learning web design and when setting up my own company, helped me greatly. I'd also like to thank Marc Patterson, who helped me get through the difficult MySQL exams and who started me on my journey into PHP and programming.

To my friends, and colleagues who helped me stay positive and focused while writing this book. I would not have made it this far without each of your support. Also, thank you to my family who have always encouraged me and given me the courage to take on such a challenge. To my mother and father, this book is mostly dedicated to you. I miss you both terribly.

I'd also like to acknowledge the web design community. It has always been welcoming and open to newcomers. Designers and developers are always eager to share their knowledge and hard work with the community others. It's that open spirit which keeps this industry going and makes it the most exciting and rewarding industry to work in.

Finally, I would like to thank Packt, who gave me this amazing opportunity. Thank you so much! I've enjoyed working with you all immensely and hope it won't be the last time.

About the Reviewer

Bartosz Skupień is highly motivated interactive developer with a good technical knowledge and open mind for all frontend technical news. Pixel perfection and a good eye for any kind of design are his strong abilities. He is eager to learn new skills and competencies, and is not afraid to make mistakes but able to draw conclusions. He is a team person, always willing to contribute own experience and best practices to make improvements. Creative Engineer who likes working in big global projects putting in force the latest styling trends and solutions. Currently working for a global company helping enterprises deploy digital solutions that transform their business.

www.PacktPub.com

For support files and downloads related to your book, please visit www.PacktPub.com.

eBooks, discount offers, and more

Did you know that Packt offers eBook versions of every book published, with PDF and ePub files available? You can upgrade to the eBook version at www.PacktPub.com and as a print book customer, you are entitled to a discount on the eBook copy. Get in touch with us at customercare@packtpub.com for more details.

At www.PacktPub.com, you can also read a collection of free technical articles, sign up for a range of free newsletters and receive exclusive discounts and offers on Packt books and eBooks.

https://www2.packtpub.com/books/subscription/packtlib

Do you need instant solutions to your IT questions? PacktLib is Packt's online digital book library. Here, you can search, access, and read Packt's entire library of books.

Why subscribe?

- Fully searchable across every book published by Packt
- Copy and paste, print, and bookmark content
- On demand and accessible via a web browser

Free access for Packt account holders

Get notified! Find out when new books are published by following @PacktEnterprise on Twitter or the Packt Enterprise Facebook page.

Table of Contents

Preface

The Web is moving fast! Since its boom in popularity in the late 90's to the early 2000's, web technology has begun to move at breakneck speed. However, while programming languages such as JavaScript, PHP, Ruby, Python, Java and others were developed to be quite well suited for their purposes on the Web, one of the core languages was holding everyone back…CSS. For almost a decade, developers and web designers had to devise numerous clever hacks and workarounds to make up for the shortcomings of this simple language. That's right! CSS is meant to be simple! A very conscious decision was made to omit variables, functions, loops, and conditional statements from CSS. This was to make it simple for beginners. When the W3C even started to *consider* introducing variables into the CSS specification it was met with opposition by many who felt it would make it too difficult for non-programmers and beginners.

The revolutionary movement that sparked the debate (and subsequent introduction) of CSS variables was started by one of Hampton Catlin's projects called Sass. In 2006, Hampton created Haml. The goal of Haml was to simplify writing HTML by removing the need for closing tags, instead using nesting and a Ruby-like syntax. Around the same time, he released Sass, which was a very similar idea, but for CSS. While Haml has not been as successful perhaps, Sass has quickly become a favorite, if not an industry standard among designers and developers. Yet the original indented Sass syntax was still a turn-off for many designers. It was perhaps too far removed from the familiar curly braces and semi-colons of CSS for many to embrace.

However, when the SCSS syntax arrived, Sass exploded into life. You couldn't read a web design blog, watch a tutorial, or go to a conference without Sass being at least mentioned. This surge in popularity was largely because with the newer SCSS syntax you could write plain old CSS if you wanted and work in the other features at your own pace. It was *relatively* easy for beginners to get on board with it, once they got passed working with the command line.

So why all the excitement about Sass in the first place. Well, Sass as you probably know by now, gives you access to variables, functions, loops, conditionals and many other features which allow for code reuse. Things which CSS lacks. These are things which, once you've started using them to write CSS you'll begin to wonder how anyone writes CSS without it.

Regardless of what stage you're at with Sass, this book aims to show you what it is truly capable of, using working examples and real-world situations. We'll work through setting up projects, we'll look at Compass, sourcemaps, using Sass with NodeJS, Gulp, and Susy. We'll also talk about writing good CSS and some useful best practices and methodologies to know, such as SMACSS, OOCSS, and BEM, which will help you organize and manage large projects. Then after all that, we'll put it all together to create a mobile-first homepage for an e-commerce website.

What this book covers

Chapter 1, *Requirements*, covers the software and libraries which will be used throughout this book. Here, we'll discuss more than what you'll need installed, we'll also look at some required knowledge too, such as the commonly used command line/terminal commands and some HTML and CSS examples.

Chapter 2, *Sass – The Road to Better CSS*, will cover setting up a Sass project and taking control of the CSS output. We'll also be writing mixins and functions to create some baseline typography styles. We'll then look at using the !default flag, lists, nesting, loops, and error handling and debugging to create more robust, usable code.

Chapter 3, *Compass – Navigating with Compass*, will look at creating a project using Compass. We'll look at how to take control of the default options through the command line, including what directories Compass creates by default, and where. We'll look at the many functions and mixins Compass has.

Chapter 4, *CSS and HTML – SMACSS, OOCSS and Semantics*, will talk about some CSS and HTML concepts which are vital to a good Sass workflow, such as OOCSS, SMACSS, BEM, and Atomic Design, and also why you should convert to using HSL instead of RGB or HEX color codes.

Chapter 5, *Advanced Sass*, will look at some of the more advanced features of Sass. We'll dive into the nuances of variable scope, using extends and mixins for better code resuse, the @content directive and maps.

Chapter 6, *Gulp – Automating Tasks for a Faster Workflow*, will start working on our final project. We'll look at installing and configuring Gulp, and installing various plugins and setting up tasks to automatically watch our project for changes and compile Sass and sourcemaps, and then reload the browser. All in one keystroke!

Chapter 7, *Sourcemaps – Editing and Saving in the Browser*, what source maps are and why you should care. We'll look at setting up sourcemaps to work in Firefox and Chrome with a few short examples of how this can be really useful when designing in the browser.

Chapter 8, *Building a Content-Rich Website Components*, will continue with our final project. We'll use many of the functions and mixins we wrote before to create reusable, configurable components as the core of our design.

Chapter 9, *Building a Content-Rich Website – Layout*, will install and set up Susy through bower. Once that is done we'll create a complete mobile-first grid system using breakpoints and the built in Susy mixins.

Chapter 10, *Building a Content-Rich Website – Theme*, we'll conclude our design, by giving it some color and style. We'll work out what fonts to use to best match the brand indentity of the project, and we'll add some eye catching elements such as dropcaps, tag clouds and stylish title underlines.

What you need for this book

To follow along with the examples in this book you will need Ruby version 2.1.7 or greater. You will then need the latest Compass and Sass gems. The Compass gem will install Sass also. You will also need NodeJS and npm. Npm will come built in with NodeJS. Any version after 4.2.1 will do. Finally, you will need Bower which can be installed through npm.

Not to worry…in Chapter 1, *Requirements,* we will cover installing Ruby, Compass, Sass, and NodeJS.

Who this book is for

This book is aimed at those who know CSS3 and HTML5 quite well and who've built a few small-to-medium-sized websites from scratch using Sass and Compass.

Conventions

In this book, you will find a number of text styles that distinguish between different kinds of information. Here are some examples of these styles and an explanation of their meaning.

Code words in text, database table names, folder names, filenames, file extensions, pathnames, dummy URLs, user input, and Twitter handles are shown as follows: "We can include other Sass files through the use of the @import directive."

A block of code is set as follows:

```
@import '../../bower_components/susy/sass/susy';

$susy: (
    columns: 12,
)

$breakpoints: (
    sm: 480px,
    md: 768px,
    lg: 980px
);

@each $size, $value in $breakpoints {
    @media (min-width: map-get($breakpoints, $size) {
        @for $i from 1 through map-get($susy, columns) {
            .col-#{$i}-#{$size} {
                @include span($i);

                &-last {
                    @include span($i last);
                }
            }
        }
    }
}
```

When we wish to draw your attention to a particular part of a code block, the relevant lines or items are set in bold:

```
[@import '../../bower_components/susy/sass/susy';

$susy: (
    columns: 12,
)
$breakpoints: (
    sm: 480px,
    md: 768px,
    lg: 980px
);

@each $size, $value in $breakpoints {
    @media (min-width: map-get($breakpoints, $size) {
        @for $i from 1 through map-get($susy, columns) {
            .col-#{$i}-#{$size} {
                @include span($i);
```

```
                    &-last {
                        @include span($i last);
                    }
                }
            }
        }
    }
```

Any command-line input or output is written as follows:

```
$ sass --update assets/sass/main.sass:assets/css/main.css --style=expanded
```

New terms and **important words** are shown in bold. Words that you see on the screen, for example, in menus or dialog boxes, appear in the text like this: "Clicking the **Next** button moves you to the next screen."

 Warnings or important notes appear in a box like this.

 Tips and tricks appear like this.

Reader feedback

Feedback from our readers is always welcome. Let us know what you think about this book—what you liked or disliked. Reader feedback is important for us as it helps us develop titles that you will really get the most out of.

To send us general feedback, simply e-mail feedback@packtpub.com, and mention the book's title in the subject of your message.

If there is a topic that you have expertise in and you are interested in either writing or contributing to a book, see our author guide at www.packtpub.com/authors.

Customer support

Now that you are the proud owner of a Packt book, we have a number of things to help you to get the most from your purchase.

Downloading the example code

You can download the example code files for this book from your account at `http://www.p acktpub.com`. If you purchased this book elsewhere, you can visit `http://www.packtpub.c om/support` and register to have the files e-mailed directly to you.

You can download the code files by following these steps:

1. Log in or register to our website using your e-mail address and password.
2. Hover the mouse pointer on the **SUPPORT** tab at the top.
3. Click on **Code Downloads & Errata**.
4. Enter the name of the book in the **Search** box.
5. Select the book for which you're looking to download the code files.
6. Choose from the drop-down menu where you purchased this book from.
7. Click on **Code Download**.

Once the file is downloaded, please make sure that you unzip or extract the folder using the latest version of:

- WinRAR / 7-Zip for Windows
- Zipeg / iZip / UnRarX for Mac
- 7-Zip / PeaZip for Linux

The code bundle for the book is also hosted on GitHub at `https://github.com/PacktPubl ishing/Mastering-Sass`. We also have other code bundles from our rich catalog of books and videos available at `https://github.com/PacktPublishing/`. Check them out!

Errata

Although we have taken every care to ensure the accuracy of our content, mistakes do happen. If you find a mistake in one of our books-maybe a mistake in the text or the code- we would be grateful if you could report this to us. By doing so, you can save other readers from frustration and help us improve subsequent versions of this book. If you find any errata, please report them by visiting `http://www.packtpub.com/submit-errata`, selecting your book, clicking on the **Errata Submission Form** link, and entering the details of your errata. Once your errata are verified, your submission will be accepted and the errata will be uploaded to our website or added to any list of existing errata under the Errata section of that title.

To view the previously submitted errata, go to `https://www.packtpub.com/books/content/support` and enter the name of the book in the search field. The required information will appear under the **Errata** section.

Piracy

Piracy of copyrighted material on the Internet is an ongoing problem across all media. At Packt, we take the protection of our copyright and licenses very seriously. If you come across any illegal copies of our works in any form on the Internet, please provide us with the location address or website name immediately so that we can pursue a remedy.

Please contact us at `copyright@packtpub.com` with a link to the suspected pirated material.

We appreciate your help in protecting our authors and our ability to bring you valuable content.

Questions

If you have a problem with any aspect of this book, you can contact us at `questions@packtpub.com`, and we will do our best to address the problem.

1
Requirements

One of the hardest things to overcome when learning any specific web development topic is what I like to call *the void*. The void is that place where most of us get when we've covered all the essentials and beginner stuff. We've watched all the beginner videos and read the essential books and we're confident we're past being a *beginner*, but we're not quite an advanced user. We're in the void that sits in between those two states.

You know you're in the void because all the beginners stuff is too easy, but all the advanced material seems to start a step too far ahead, almost like they start on step 3 and you're missing steps 1 and 2. I think we fall into the void because somewhere after being a beginner we all continue on very different paths, no matter what we're learning. We pick up different tools and tricks to make our daily task quicker and easier.

This chapter's goal is to try and *avoid the void* by quickly going over what I personally use and will be using throughout this book. I'm not just talking about the stuff you'll need installed, I'm also talking about some required knowledge too.

We will cover the following topics:

- Installing Ruby, Sass, and Compass
- Updating Ruby, Sass, and Compass
- Installing or updating Node and NPM
- Required HTML, CSS, and programming knowledge
- Basic command line/terminal knowledge

Ruby, Sass, and Compass

If you've used Sass and Compass before, then you already have installed them. However, I'd like to ensure your versions of Ruby, Sass, and Compass are all what they need to be to follow along with the examples I'll use later in the book. Many of the topics will use the very latest features of Sass and Compass.

Ruby

Sass and Compass run on a language called Ruby. Ruby became very popular in web development by offering clean syntax while still being very powerful. It achieves this power and simplicity by being strictly object oriented. In simple terms, everything from a single letter to a full class is treated as its own object in Ruby, meaning you can treat everything in Ruby much the same way. There are no second class citizens in Ruby.

In this book, we won't be working directly with Ruby; however, you do need it installed for Sass and Compass. So let's look at getting set up.

Ruby installer for Windows

I'm currently working on Windows. Yes, you read that correctly, I'm one of those weirdos who is actually more productive using Windows than Mac. So, for those of you on Windows, you'll know we don't have Ruby on our systems by default. It's not a big issue. You just go to `http://rubyinstaller.org/downloads/` and you'll find a list of all available `.exe` installers for the stable Ruby versions.

What version should I use?
I like to always be one step behind on this one. What I mean by that is, at the time of writing, the current stable release of Ruby is 2.2.3. The previous stable release was 2.1.7. So I have 2.1.7 installed. The reason I choose to do this is gems are more likely to have been updated to work with at least 2.1.7.

Updating Ruby for Windows

I also have Ruby 1.9.3p551 installed on my system, and updating wasn't as straightforward a process as installing was. So, let's quickly explain how to install multiple versions of Ruby and switch between them if you need to.

The following method will allow you to have multiple Ruby versions installed but will require editing your **PATH** manually to switch between versions:

1. To start with, simply download and run the installer as normal. The RubyInstaller executable creates a separate folder for each Ruby version so you don't have to uninstall or overwrite your current version.
2. Select your language and read and accept the **License Agreement**.
3. Next, you'll be asked what directory to install Ruby into and also whether to **Install Td/Tk Support**, **Add Ruby executables to your PATH**, and **Associate .rb and .rbw files with this Ruby installation**. You can keep the defaults here, as shown in the following screenshot:

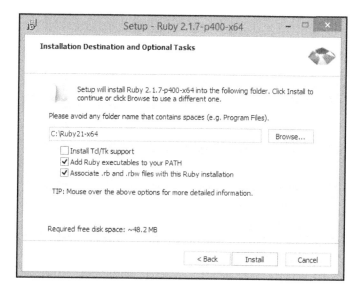

Installing Ruby on Windows

4. Next, you may need to update your system Path manually to use the newer version of Ruby. To check this, simply open the **cmd.exe** (WinKey + *R*, then type cmd and hit *Enter*). Then, type the following command:

   ```
   ruby -v
   ```

   If your version is incorrect, you'll need to update your PATH variable manually. I'll also explain why this happens, seeing as it's actually a common problem with some applications.

After you've switched to a new version of Ruby, you'll need to install your gems again for that version. To see what gems you have installed you can run `gem list`.

5. To update your **PATH** you'll need to open up your **System Properties**. You can do this by going to your Windows start screen and typing `System Environment Variables` and selecting the first option, **Edit** your system's **Environment Variables**.

6. Next, select **Environment Variables**.

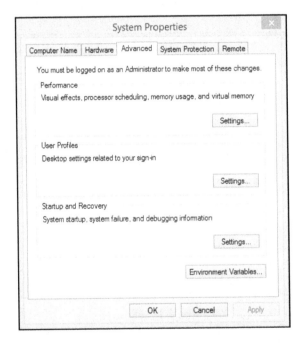

System properties

7. Then you'll need to set your **System variables | Path** value. The installation process will update the **PATH** variable for the user account but not the global path variable.

Setting the System Variables path

8. Replace the incorrect version of Ruby with the newer version you wish to use.

 The correct format is `C:\Ruby21-x64\bin;`, with no trailing slashes, and *do not* include the `.exe` executables.

9. To check everything is working, open `cmd` again and type `ruby -v`. You should see the correct version.

Updating Ruby for Mac

There are many more options for installing/updating Ruby for Mac. Depending on your OS version, you'll already have either 1.8.x or 2.0.x installed on your system by default. However, if you haven't updated, you may want to update to 2.1.7 or later. To do this, you can use Homebrew to easily update to the latest release with the following command:

```
brew install ruby
```

If you wish to have multiple version of Ruby on your system, you may want to look into a package manager such as **Ruby Package Manager** (**RVM**). You can learn more about RVM from their website at `http://rvm.io/`.

Sass and Compass

This one is easy. I'm using the most up-to-date versions of Sass and Compass, Sass 3.4.19 (Selective Steve) and Compass 1.0.3 (Polaris). If this is your first time installing Sass and Compass or you recently upgraded your version of Ruby, then the easiest way to install both is to simply install Compass using the following command:

```
gem install compass
```

Again, you can check everything is working by running the following command:

```
sass -v && compass -v
```

This will run each command one after the other.

Node and NPM

Node is somewhat more straightforward to install and update. I'm running 4.2.1; however, 5.0.0 is the most up-to-date release.

You will need NodeJS to follow along with Chapter 6, *Gulp – Automating Tasks for a Faster Workflow*, and Chapter 7, *Sourcemaps – Editing and Saving in the Browser.*
You can install/update NodeJS by simply downloading and installing Node from `https://nodejs.org/en/download/`.

Also, running the installers with Node already installed will simply update Node, so there is actually no need to uninstall Node first.

To check your version of Node, you can open the command line and type (I'm sure you can guess it by now…) the following command:

```
node -v
```

HTML5

Like most languages or tools in the web development industry, Sass requires knowing a few other things first. When I say HTML5 I do of course mean CSS3 as well. JavaScript is also often grouped in with the HTML5 family; however, for what we'll be covering, you'll only need to be proficient with HTML5 and CSS3.

HTML

The following markup and elements should all be familiar:

```
<!DOCTYPE html>
<html lang="en">
<head>
    <meta charset="UTF-8">
    <title>Mastering Sass: Example</title>
</head>
<body>
    <header>
        <h1>Mastering Sass</h1>
    </header>
    <nav>
        <ul>
            <li><a href="#">Home</a></li>
            <li><a href="#">About</a></li>
            <li><a href="#">Blog</a></li>
            <li><a href="#">Contact</a></li>
        </ul>
    </nav>
    <main>
        <section>
            <article>
                <header><h2>Post No 2</h2></header>
                <div><p>Some more text</p></div>
                <footer><time>2015-11-12 13:00</time></footer>
            </article>
            <article>
                <header><h2>Post No 1</h2></header>
                <div><p>Some text</p></div>
                <footer><time>2015-11-12 12:00</time></footer>
            </article>
        </section>
        <aside>
            <h3>Sidebar</h3>
            <p>Sidebar Text</p>
```

```
            </aside>
        </main>
        <footer>
            <p>&copy; 2015 Mastering Sass</p>
        </footer>
    </body>
    </html>
```

CSS

With regard to CSS3, I'll be covering most of what we'll need to know, but a good idea of the properties that still require browser prefixes is always extremely useful, especially when using Compass.

We won't be doing much (if anything) with animations or transforms, but we might use some transition effects.

You should understand how to use pseudo-elements and selectors comfortably. Pseudo-elements are `::before` and `::after`, while the selectors include `:first-child`, `:last-child`, and `::nth-child(n)`. I always put the double colon (`::`) before the pseudo-elements. They will work with a single colon (IE8 will work with a single colon), but technically they should have two. The idea is that pseudo-elements typically are to do with content, while pseudo-selectors are referencing a specific HTML element or elements, such as first or last paragraphs, or the third list item in an unordered list. You can read more about it in the CSS Tricks almanac: `https://css-tricks.com/almanac/selectors/a/after-and-before/`.

Finally, I'll be using the data attribute for layout styles in later chapters. So, understanding the following will be necessary (including what the symbols ^, *, and ~ do):

```
[data-layout~="grid"] .portfolio-image {
    width: 100%;
    height: auto;
}
```

Pseudo-selectors and pseudo-elements allow a great amount of control over your CSS, and also allows much more semantic markup.

Programming

I love programming! Did I mention that? Any day that goes by that I don't get to write some proper code or work on a problem that makes me scratch my head for at least 30 seconds is a sad day for me.

You don't have to be that extreme about it. However, whether it's Sass, JavaScript, PHP, ASP.NET, Ruby, or Python, it's important that you understand what we'll call the *fundamentals of programming*. To keep on the topic of Sass, as long as you can write a function and a mixin and use `if/else` statements, then you understand enough to follow along with what I'll cover.

The command line

For brevity, I'm only going to call it the *command line* from now on. So, regardless of your OS (Windows, Linux, or Mac), whether you use the terminal, Powershell, Cygwin, Babun, or plain old `cmd.exe`, when I say command line, you know what I mean.

If you don't know what I mean, then you'll need to brush up your command-line skills. I won't be using any software to compile or watch files and folders. We'll be using Sass and Compass mainly from the command line. I'll also be creating directories and files occasionally from the command line, and navigating around our project within the command line. We'll also be using Gulp from the command line a lot in later chapters.

When I'm working the command line, I prefer not to have to jump in and out of it to create folders and files. It's faster to just leave the mouse alone for as long as possible and keep typing. With practice, I'm sure you'll agree (hopefully, you already do).

So I'll quickly mention a few commands I often use so you'll know what I'm doing when you see them.

Windows and Unix users

To change into a directory (assuming you are in the documents folder, which contains a folder called `my-projects`), use the following command:

```
cd ./my-projects
```

Or simply use the following command:

```
cd my-projects
```

To create a directory, use the following command:

```
mkdir mastering-sass
```

 It's important to note that the Unix terminal is case sensitive, while Windows cmd is not.

We could also have combined those commands on one line using the and operator, &&, which I used earlier in this chapter:

```
cd my-projects && mkdir mastering-sass
```

You should now have a folder structure like this:

```
documents
    |-- my-projects
            |-- mastering-sass
```

To move up one directory (or out of the current directory into the parent directory), use the following command:

```
cd ..
```

Or you can use this command:

```
cd ../
```

To move up two directories, use this command:

```
cd ../../
```

 Another great way to quickly cd into a folder is to type cd followed by a space and then simply drag the folder you want to change into onto your command line. The full path will be instantly pasted into your command line so you only need to hit Enter. This works on Unix and Windows. Hooray!

Windows

We will discuss some useful command-line tips in this section.

The quickest way to open the cmd.exe command line in Windows from XP upwards is as follows:

1. Press the WinKey + *R*, which will open the **Run...** dialog.
2. Then simply type cmd and hit *Enter*.

The second tip that can be used is as follows.

Have you ever been in a folder and wanted to just open up the command line to be in that folder, without needing to copy the path, and right-click on the command line and go to **Edit | Paste**...ugh! It's actually really simple.

Hold down the Shift key and right-click in the window. Now the context popup will have an extra option, **Open command window here**.

You could even just hold down Shift, right-click, and then press W if that's still too much.

Why is this hidden by default? I wish I knew.

On the flip side, I bet there's been times you've been in the command line and wanted to simply open the **File Explorer** window in the current directory. To do that, simply type explorer and hit Enter.

To view files and folders in the current directory, use the following command:

```
dir
```

To create a file in the current directory, use this command:

```
notepad index.html
```

This will create a file if that file doesn't already exist, or it will open existing files in Notepad. When creating a file, you will have to click **Yes** to allow Notepad to create a file and then **Save** from within Notepad. It's not as nice as the Unix touch command or nano, but it's there if you need to create a file quickly. It's still quicker than opening another program, saving finding the right folder, and typing the name and perhaps having to choose an extension.

Unix (Mac and Linux)

To list files and folders in the current directory, use this command:

```
ls
```

To list all files and folders, including hidden files and folders (such as `.htaccess`, `.git`, `.DS_Store`), use this command:

```
ls -a
```

List files and folders with metadata such as file owner, timestamps, and file permissions using the following command:

```
ls -l
```

You can even combine them to show you everything, including hidden files and all meta data, as follows:

```
ls -la
```

To create a file, use this command:

```
touch index.html
```

To edit an existing file, use this command:

```
nano index.html
```

You know your command line

You made it! Nice! So those are the things I do most from within the command line. Moving around, looking at things, and creating folders and files. So if you can also do all of those things comfortably, you'll do just fine.

Summary

So, we should now be pretty much on the same page regarding what we need installed and what concepts we'll need to get the most from the next few chapters. The good thing is that by doing the installations and setup at this early stage, we can focus on Sass and Compass and all the fun stuff from now on.

In the next chapter, we'll get started with writing some Sass. That is, of course, why we're all here. We'll take a look at the Sass documentation and how to filter through it all to get to the most important and useful features in the order you'll most likely need them.

2

Sass – The Road to Better CSS

In this chapter, we will cover:

- Setting up a simple project based strongly on typography.
- We'll look at using Sass from the command line and the various options we can pass to take control of our output.
- We'll then set up our project's configuration variables using `!default` to allow easy overriding in future. These variables will control all of our functions and mixins and will allow the end user to have full control of our Sass library, without needing to touch mixins or functions.
- We'll look at writing a small but flexible library of functions and mixins that will deal with setting up a base typography style for our default body, text, and headings. This will be based around the optimal reading line length of 60-80 characters while keeping our font sizes and line heights uniform even when we change font families.
- We'll write functions and a mixin to handle the output of our headings and keep the best font sizes and line heights for each heading for sans and serif.
- We'll then look at using lists and nested lists to reduce repetition in our mixins. We'll look at tackling one problem with two different loops and the pros and cons of both approaches.
- Finally, we'll go back over all of our functions and add some much needed error handling by using `@error` and `@warn`.

A bit of sassy reminiscing

As I mentioned I started Sass some time ago. I even remember that illustration of the girl with the telephone. Remember her? I always imagined she was having a sassy debate with her friend about the latest web design trends and telling her friend to stop using IDs in her CSS.

Anyways, I can also remember it was actually pretty difficult to learn Sass. The only thing that got me to persevere was I could use as little as I wanted in the beginning, so I had that safety net of plain old CSS. So when I started out I really only used Sass for the variables, imports and the nesting. Even with that, it made my life so much better!

The version was Classy Cassidy(3.0.18), and even though Sass hadn't been offering the .scss syntax for long at that point, it was really starting to make waves, due to the fact you could just write css and use as little or as much of Sass as you wanted. When it's put like that to someone you'd wonder why it wasn't a feature in the first place.

Back then you actually didn't even install Sass, you installed Haml. Sass just sort of came with it, like a cool sibling. The whole Haml situation confused me. I wasn't quite sure if I had to use it use Sass, or what the heck Haml was in the first place. Also, back then I was still pretty green to programming and definitely to the command line. The fact that the documentation was geared towards Unix completely threw me off. I wasn't even sure if I could get Sass set up on Windows properly.

I also made the mistake of thinking the Sass reference was written in a strict order. So I spent hours trying to wrap my head around the Sass::Plugin options, thinking I needed to set those up first somewhere to get things going. I didn't really know any better.

So I want to help you avoid the mistakes I made along my journey through Sass, and make sure you're getting the best out Sass. Not just the advanced features, but also the simple ones that you may have missed. You have Sass all set up and ready to go so you probably want to set up a project and start writing some **Syntactically Awesome Style Sheets (Sass)**.

Setting up our project

You're probably eager to start writing some Sass, so let's jump right in. I'm going to create my project in my root (c:/) directory, but you can place your project wherever is easiest for you. I'll call it **mastering-sass** and inside I'll create the following files and folders in that folder: *sass* and *index.html* and within the *sass* folder create a file: *style.scss*.

Open your *index.html* file in your editor of choice and add the following markup:

```
<!-- mastering-sass/index.html -->
<!DOCTYPE html>
<html lang="en">
  <head>
    <meta charset="UTF-8">
    <title>Mastering Sass: Chapter 2</title>
    <link href="css/style.css" rel="stylesheet">
  </head>
  <body>
    <div>
      <h1>Heading 1</h1>
      <h2>Heading 2</h2>
      <h3>Heading 3</h3>
      <h4>Heading 4</h4>
      <h5>Heading 5</h5>
      <h6>Heading 6</h6>
      <p>This is a normal paragraph of text with <em>emphasised</em>,
<strong>strong</strong> text and, of course, a <a href="#">link.</a></p>
      <p> <img src="http://placehold.it/300x200" alt="Image from
Placehold.it" style="float:left;"> !!!ENTER SOME LOREM IPSUM OR SOMETHING
HERE!!!</p>
      <p><img src="http://placehold.it/800x600" alt="Image from
Placehold.it" style="float:right;"> !!!ENTER SOME LOREM IPSUM OR SOMETHING
HERE!!!</p>
      <ul>
        <li>List Item 1</li>
        <li>List Item 2</li>
        <li>List Item 3</li>
        <li>List Item 4</li>
      </ul>
    </div>
  </body>
</html>
```

Believe it or not, this simple page has pretty much all the elements you need to make a fully functional HTML website (as it was originally intended). Not counting the stuff in the <head> or the <body> tag, there's roughly 15 elements present in almost every webpage since the dawn of web time (circa.1991), and you're looking at them.

From these elements you can make navigation, break things into sections (with more divs of course) and get pretty much any message across to a reader that text and images will allow.

Sass

You noticed the link to the stylesheet located at *css/style.css*. You also surely noticed we never created that. Let's open up our command line and change directory to our *mastering-sass* folder.

Now in your command line simply run the following command:

```
sass --watch sass:css
```

This command will tell `sass` to compile all `sass` files in the `sass` directory into `css` files in the `css` directory. If the folder or the files don't exist `sass` creates them. Once it's finished it will watch the `sass` directory for any changes and automatically compile them to the `css` directory. The command line should look something like the following screenshot:

```
C:\WINDOWS\system32\cmd.exe - sass --watch sass:css

c:\mastering-sass>sass --watch sass:css
>>> Sass is watching for changes. Press Ctrl-C to stop.
   directory css
      write css/style.css
      write css/style.css.map
```

If you're wondering what the `style.css.map` file is all about, don't worry, we'll cover that in Chapter 7, *Sourcemaps – Editing and Saving in the Browser*.

So now open *style.scss* and we'll begin writing some Sass to style our typography. In *style.scss* let's set our box model and remove the padding and margins first:

```
// mastering-sass/ch02/scss/style.css
*, *::before, *::after {
  -moz-box-sizing: border-box;
  -webkit-box-sizing: border-box;
  box-sizing:border-box;
}

html {
  font-family: serif;
  font-size: 100%;
  -webkit-font-smoothing: antialiased;
}

html, body {
  padding:0;
  margin:0;
}
```

Next, we'll use our `div` to center everything and give it a reasonable width for reading text. It's said that between 55 to 75 characters per line is optimal for reading so let's set our divs `max-width`, because we still want it to be able shrink down for smaller screens (right now we're not worrying about mobile-first or anything like that):

```
// path: mastering-sass/scss/style.scss
body > div { // We only want to get the "wrapper" div
  max-width: 38rem; // approx 600px
  margin: 0 auto;
}
```

There's method to my madness. In fact, that first line actually has 65 characters exactly, and the image is `600px` wide. Between the end of that sentence and the images is *optimal line length*, depending on the font. For me, serif looks too small at 1rem (or em). Sans-serif works much better at the default size of 1rem (16px). So let's set the font family on our paragraphs to sans-serif and set up our line heights and margins:

```
// mastering-sass/ch02/scss/style.scss
p {
  font-family: sans-serif;
  font-size: 1rem;
  line-height: 1.5rem;
  margin-bottom: 1.5rem;
}
```

C'mon, where's the Sass already?!

Ok! Ok! We're finally ready to writing some Sass. We actually have two perfect reasons to start using Sass here.

We have some repeated values: both line height and margin bottom are 1.5rem.

Couldn't we write a mixin to deal with the issues of serif being too small at 1rem while sans-serif is just about right?

So let's create our variables at the top of our *style.scss* which we'll use to correct these common issues:

```
// mastering-sass/ch02/scss/style.scss
$base-font-family-sans: sans-serif; // 1.
$base-font-family-serif: serif; // 2.
$base-font-family-code: monospace; // 2.

$base-font-size: 1rem;
$base-line-height: 1.5;

$base-font-family: $base-font-family-code;
```

Then let's replace the values in our paragraph rule:

```
// mastering-sass/ch02/scss/style.scss
p {
  font-family: $base-font-family-sans;
  font-size: $base-font-size;
  line-height: $base-line-height;
  margin-bottom: $base-line-height + rem;
}
```

Now we can actually write a mixin that will check our current font-family and adjust all of our values accordingly, so we always have the best line length and spacing for our current font.

Let's create a separate folder inside our *sass* folder, called `helpers`, and inside that we'll create a file called *_mixins.scss*.

Inside that file create the following `mixin`:

```
// mastering-sass/ch02/scss/helpers/_mixins.scss
@mixin base-font-family-sizing() {
  // 1.
  // Check what $base-font-family we are using...
  // If $base-font-family-serif we need to multiply
```

```
    // our $base-font-size by 1.25 and increase
    // our $base-line-height accordingly

    // 2.
    // Otherwise, a font-family we haven't set
    // specific values for has been set so we
    // should leave the browser defaults in place.
}
```

Don't forget to include it at the beginning of our *style.scss* file following our variables also:

```
// mastering-sass/ch02/scss/style.scss
$base-font-family-sans: sans-serif; // 1.
$base-font-family-serif: serif; // 2.
$base-font-family-code: monospace; // 2.

$base-font-size: 1rem;
$base-line-height: 1.5;

$base-font-family: $base-font-family-code;

@import "helpers/mixins";
```

So I've explained the steps on how we need to tackle this problem in the comments. So let's write a quick if/elseif/else and output some content to see if our logic is correct before adding anything more complex:

```
// mastering-sass/ch02/scss/helpers/_mixins.scss
@mixin base-font-family-sizing($current-font-family: $base-font-family)
{
    @if $current-font-family == $base-font-family-serif { // 1
        content: 'Serif';
    } @else { // 2. If $base-font-family-code you should see...
        content: 'Not serif';
    }
}
```

Now, place our mixin inside our paragraph rule, like so:

```
// mastering-sass/ch02/scss/style.scss
p {
    font-family: sans-serif;
    font-size: $base-font-size;
    line-height: $base-line-height;
    margin-bottom: $base-line-height + rem; // Add our rem unit to make it
1.5rem

    @include base-font-family-sizing();
```

```
}
```

Seeing as $base-font-family is actually set to $base-font-family-code, you should see the following in your *style.css*:

```scss
// mastering-sass/ch02/scss/style.scss
p {
  font-family: sans-serif;
  font-size: 1rem;
  line-height: 1.5;
  margin-bottom: 1.5rem;
  content: 'Not serif'; }
```

Now, replace

```scss
$base-font-family: $base-font-family-code
```

with

```scss
$base-font-family: $base-font-family-serif
```

and you should see the following:

```scss
// mastering-sass/ch02/scss/style.scss
p {
  font-family: sans-serif;
  font-size: 1rem;
  line-height: 1.5;
  margin-bottom: 1.5rem;
  content: 'Serif'; }
```

For good measure, also check $base-font-family-sans. Do you get content: 'Not Serif'?

Great! It works! Now we can start adding the stuff we actually want into the @if/@elseif/@else blocks.

So, modify the font-family-sizing mixin as follows:

```scss
// mastering-sass/ch02/scss/helpers/_mixins.scss
@mixin base-font-family-sizing($current-font-family: $base-font-family)
{
    font-family: $current-font-family;
    line-height: $base-line-height;
    margin-bottom: $base-font-size * $base-line-height;

    @if $current-font-family == $base-font-family-serif {
        font-size: $base-font-size * 1.15;
```

```
    } @else {
        font-size: $base-font-size;
    }
}
```

Multiplying or adding a value with units such as *1rem * 1.5* will result in 1.5rem…the units are kept.

So that's a mixin that uses just a few of the basic features of Sass. Variables and mixins are pretty much what everyone utilizes in the beginning, not to mention nesting. Getting predictable results from your if statements can be tricky if you don't write them in a way that you can be sure they're working at every step of the process. It's easy to accidentally check for a false value when you meant true and throw an entire system into mayhem.

The key to coding anything, no matter how simple the problem seems, is to get feedback straight away from your code so you know the minute anything is wrong. Check the values you're getting back as early as possible. Otherwise, if you go too far without checking your results to see something isn't right, it can be near impossible to figure out what actually went wrong, and when it went wrong.

Using the CSS `content` property is a handy way of checking values so Sass won't through compilation errors due to incorrect types and values. There are other ways to debug your Sass, and we'll look at that method soon. However, output values to the content property can be useful while figuring mixins or functions out.

So now you have a simple mixin that will keep your line lengths in check between the main two font families, sans and serif. You only need to change the `$base-font-family` variable and everywhere this mixin is used it will update correctly. No more *small text in a box* scenarios.

Command line options in Sass

So before we get to our heading styles, let's look at some of the command line options that can be passed along with our Sass command. We saw the `--watch` option. This tells Sass to watch the *sass* file or an entire folder changes, and then automatically compiles CSS whenever we save any changes to our Sass files.

Watching files and directories

We also told Sass to watch an entire directory and compile to a separate directory. Therefore, any file we created or updated in our `sass` directory, whether it was a `.scss` or `.sass` file, would be compiled to a CSS file of the same name in the `css` folder.

> You can even use files with the indented Sass syntax and files written in the SCSS syntax in one project. So if you haven't started using the indented Sasssyntax simply because you don't fancy writing all of your mixins again, or you don't want to have to convert all your files, well you don't have to. Simply include any `.scss` files partials in a `.sass` (or vice versa) and everything will work just fine!

I highly recommend trying the indented Sass syntax. Once you've embraced it you won't go back.

> In practice I use the indented Sass syntax for work and personal projects; however, for demonstration purposes I'll be using the more commonly seen SCSS syntax for the remainder of this book.

Compile files and folders

There are times when you only need to make a very minute change to a Sass project, therefore you may wish to compile those updates, but not watch your files or folders for further changes. You can achieve this with the `--update` option:

```
sass -update sass/style.scss:css/style.css
```

The preceding code will compile any changes we've made to *style.scss* in the *sass* folder, into the *style.css* file in our CSS folder. However, if there are no changes detected, Sass is smart enough not to compile.

Force Sass to compile

If you want Sass to compile, even if it doesn't detect changes you can add the `--force` option, like so:

```
sass --force --update sass/style.scss:css/style.css
```

As you can see, the order doesn't really matter. You can place all of the options at the right, after the command, or all at the very end. What I tend to do is figure out what reads the most like what I want to achieve and that helps me remember it. Sass force update *style.scss* to *style.css*.

CSS output style

The next thing you might want to do is control how the CSS is compiled. By default, the CSS generated is in the *nested* format, which keeps the indentation of the original Sass file and places the closing bracket on the same last line of the rule. For example:

```
.navbar{
    font-size: 1rem;
    list-style:none;
    padding: 0;
    margin: 0; }
    .navbar > .menu-item {
        display: inline-block;
        padding: 1.25rem;
        margin-right: 1rem; }
```

I generally prefer to either have completely uncompressed CSS or completely compressed. For uncompressed CSS pass the value expanded to the style option, or if you want minified CSS, set it to compressed. To set your output style use the --style option, like so:

```
Sass --force --update sass/style.scss:css/style.css --style=expanded
```

Sourcemaps

You may also want to compile without sourcemaps once your project is ready to be deployed or uploaded to a git repository (although a .gitignore file is more suitable for this). To achieve this you can pass the --sourcemap=none option:

```
sass --force --update sass/style.scss:css/style.css --style=compressed
--sourcemap=none
```

You can press the up arrow to cycle through your previously entered commands so you don't have to keep typing them over and over.

For all the available option you can visit the Sass documentation at `http://sass-lang.com /documentation/file.SASS_REFERENCE.html#options`.

On the right heading!

So now you should have full control of Sass from the command line. Let's move onto another typography challenge, headings, and sizing them correctly for best results to match the work we did with our body text.

By default, the font-size of headings in most modern browsers is as follows:

- h1 is 2em
- h2 is 1.5em
- h3 is 1.17em
- h4 is 1em
- h5 is 0.83em
- h6 is 0.67em

So you can probably tell that doesn't look quite right. So continuing from our last example where we simply multiplied our font size by a ratio of 1:15 to get what worked best, we need to do something similar. Now that will work fine on our h4, which is 1em (or rem, which is what we are using); however, all the other headings work on a different ratio to each other. Now, I've worked them out already. The good thing is we know how to get our starting value for our h2 regardless of our base font-size. It's always exactly double that. Then we can use the following to calculate the rest of the headings:

- h1 / 1.3333 = h2
- h2 / 1.2821 = h3
- h3 / 1.17 = h4
- h4 / 1.2048 = h5
- h5 / 1.2388 = h6

This is the perfect time to use some functions. While mixins looks and feel pretty much like functions, they do have some stark differences in their core functionality. Mainly, mixins return, or rather they *output* CSS. Functions however, only return a single value, and they **MUST** return a value.

So let's create a file for our functions in our helpers directory called `_functions.scss`. Before we can tackle the problem of our headings, we need to be able to abstract out the

$base-font-size into a function that will dynamically generate it based on the $base-font-family. We'll then be able to use it to improve our previous mixin, but also to include that functionality in other future mixins.

So, inside our functions file let's keep our descriptive naming convention and call our function base-font-size-calc:

```
// mastering-sass/ch02/scss/helpers/_functions.scss
@function base-font-size-calc($current-font-family: $base-font-family) {
  // 1.
  // Calculate the $base-font-size based on
  // what the current $base-font-famliy is...
}
```

We've actually already solved this problem in a way. Remember in our base-font-sizing mixin we had font-size: $base-font-size * 1.15? That's basically what we're doing here. Simply abstracting that functionality out into a function. However, we can actually simplify our if statement in our function:

```
//mastering-sass/scss/helpers/_functions.scss
@function base-font-size-calc($current-font-family: $base-font-family) {
  @if $current-font-family == $base-font-family-serif {
    // If the family is serif we need to increase the font size...
    @return $base-font-size * 1.15;
  } @else {
    // ...otherwise we can leave it at the default
    @return $base-font-size;
  }
}
```

So now we can include our functions just above our mixin include (seeing as our mixins will be using it), and below our variables (seeing as pretty much everything depends on our variables):

```
// mastering-sass/ch02/scss/style.scss
$base-font-family-sans: sans-serif;
$base-font-family-serif: serif;
$base-font-family-code: monospace;

$base-font-size: 1rem;
$base-line-height: 1.5;

$base-font-family: $base-font-family-serif;

@import "helpers/functions";
@import "helpers/mixins";
```

We can now update our `base-font-family-sizing` mixin like so:

```scss
// mastering-sass/ch02/scss/helpers/_mixins.scss
@mixin base-font-family-sizing($current-font-family: $base-font-family)
{
    font-size: base-font-sizes-calc();
        font-family: $current-font-family;
    line-height: $base-line-height;
    margin-bottom: $base-font-size * $base-line-height;
}
```

With that one function we've completely removed the logic from our mixin. Our mixin now does what it's meant to do, output CSS, while our function handles the logic, or the *functionality* if you will. This keeps everything **DRY (Don't Repeat Yourself)** and means our mixin and function each have a single responsibility.

A better If

No, that's not the name for a psychological thriller novel. So what do I mean by "a better `if`" I hear you ask? Well, we can actually shorten our function even further. Right now it's about 5-6 lines depending on how you write your if statements. I bet we can get it down to 1 line! That's right, I'm talking about a ternary `if` statement.

Now, while it's true that Sass doesn't have a traditional ternary operator, like Ruby, PHP or JavaScript do…it does have a function which does what we need. So let's take a look at that now. In our `base-font-sizes-calc` function we can actually rewrite it like this:

```scss
//mastering-sass/scss/helpers/_functions.scss
    @function base-font-size-calc($current-font-family: $base-font-family)
{
        @return if($current-font-family == $base-font-family-serif, $base-font-size * 1.15, $base-font-size);
    }
```

How cool is that! If that doesn't make you feel good, nothing will. So let's break down exactly how the `if()` function works. The function takes three arguments. The first is called the expression. It's the condition which must evaluate to either `true` or `false`. The second argument is what is returned if the expression passes, and the third argument is returned otherwise:

```scss
$name: "Luke";
content: if($name == "Luke", "Your name is Luke", "Your name is not Luke");
```

The preceding code would obviously result in the following:

```
content: "Your name is Luke";
```

Anything else would result in, you guessed it, the following:

```
content: "Your name is not Luke";
```

So, once you've tested everything still works and changing the variable `$base-font-family` still gives the expected results, we can move onto our next function, calculating each of our header sizes correctly.

Our heading sizes mixin

So let's jump back into our *_functions.scss* file and start our `base-headings-sizes-calc` function. Remember back at the start of this section I mentioned the two most important things we know to get us started with this function?

- We know our `h4` should always be the same font-size as our paragraph font-size
- We know our `h1` is exactly double our `h4`

```
// mastering-sass/ch02/scss/helpers/_functions.scss
@function base-heading-sizes-calc() {
    $h4-font-size: base-font-size-calc();
    $h1-font-size: $h4-font-size * 2;
    @return $h1-font-size;
}
```

So, this is a good point to make sure we're getting the right values returned. To be exact, when:

```
$base-font-family: $base-font-family-sans; // Results in h1 {font-size:
2rem}
```

and...

```
$base-font-family: $base-font-family-serif; // Results in h1 {font-size:
2.3rem}
```

...then we can safely move on. We're sure our function is giving us what we expect, so let's start calculating the other headings font-sizes.

We already know the formula:

- h1 / 1.3333 = h2

- h2 / 1.2821 = h3
- h3 / 1.17 = h4
- h4 / 1.2048 = h5
- h5 / 1.2388 = h6

Also, now we have our h1, so we can simply implement this formula using variables like so:

```
// mastering-sass/ch02/scss/helpers/_functions.scss
@function base-heading-sizes-calc() {
    $h4-font-size: base-font-size-calc();
    $h1-font-size: $h4-font-size * 2;
    $h2-font-size: $h1-font-size / 1.3333;
    $h3-font-size: $h2-font-size / 1.2821;
    $h5-font-size: $h4-font-size / 1.2048;
    $h6-font-size: $h5-font-size / 1.2388;

    @return $h1-font-size;
}
```

Again, I would advise checking your values against a good old-fashioned calculator, but I'll leave that up to you this time.

Our next problem is how do we get the right values out when we need them? For instance, we need to get the $h3-font-size when we're in our h3 CSS rule and the $h2-font-size when we're in our h2 CSS rule. To do this we'll need to be able to tell our function when we want a specific value. So we simply add a variable with a number to represent the heading we want:

```
// mastering-sass/ch02/scss/helpers/_functions.scss
@function base-heading-sizes-calc($heading: 2) {
    $h4-font-size: base-font-size-calc();
    $h1-font-size: $h4-font-size * 2;
    $h2-font-size: $h1-font-size / 1.3333;
    $h3-font-size: $h2-font-size / 1.2821;
    $h5-font-size: $h4-font-size / 1.2048;
    $h6-font-size: $h5-font-size / 1.2388;

    @return $h1-font-size;
}
```

So I've added a variable called $heading and given a default value of 2, seeing as (in my opinion) h2 is going to be the most used heading overall. That or h3.

Now, we could start writing an obscene amount of @if @elseif to check our variable and return the correct variable, but a list would be much cleaner. We'll make a list containing the six heading sizes in order from `$h1-font-size` to `$h6-font-size`:

```
// mastering-sass/ch02/scss/helpers/_functions.scss
@function base-heading-sizes-calc($heading: 2) {
    $h4-font-size: base-font-size-calc();
    $h1-font-size: $h4-font-size * 2;
    $h2-font-size: $h1-font-size / 1.3333;
    $h3-font-size: $h2-font-size / 1.2821;
    $h5-font-size: $h4-font-size / 1.2048;
    $h6-font-size: $h5-font-size / 1.2388;

    $headings: ($h1-font-size, $h2-font-size, $h3-font-size, $h4-font-size,
$h5-font-size, $h6-font-size);


    @return $h1-font-size;
}
```

Our final task is getting the correct item from our `$headings` list. We can do this with the Sass function `nth()`. The `nth()` functions takes two parameters, first the list, which in our case is `$headings`, and second, the index, or position of the item in the list we want to retrieve.

To accomplish this, we simply update our function to return nth (`$headings`, `$heading`):

```
// mastering-sass/ch02/scss/helpers/_functions.scss
@function base-heading-sizes-calc($heading: 2) {
    $h4-font-size: base-font-size-calc();
    $h1-font-size: $h4-font-size * 2;
    $h2-font-size: $h1-font-size / 1.3333;
    $h3-font-size: $h2-font-size / 1.2821;
    $h5-font-size: $h4-font-size / 1.2048;
    $h6-font-size: $h5-font-size / 1.2388;

    $headings: ($h1-font-size, $h2-font-size, $h3-font-size, $h4-font-size,
$h5-font-size, $h6-font-size);
    @return nth($headings, $heading);
}
```

Three things you should know about lists

Here are three important things you should know about lists:

- Sass list indexes DO NOT start at zero
- You can separate the items in a list with spaces instead of commas

- You can even leave out parentheses

Let's dive deep in the preceding mentioned points.

Sass list indexes do not start at zero. Some of you who've dealt with arrays in most languages will be expecting to get a value of `$h3-font-size` with the preceding code. However, Sass lists are not 0 based. Their first index is, in fact 1, meaning we can use the number that makes sense (to people who don't do a lot of programming) and not be required to subtract 1 from our heading variable first.

You can separate the items in a list with spaces instead of commas. This is means we could have written our list like this instead:

```
$headings: ($h1-font-size $h2-font-size $h3-font-size $h4-font-size, $h5-
font-size $h6-font-size);
```

One thing to be very careful of when using space separated lists, is using strings. If you don't quote your strings, Sass will interpret each word as an item in the list:

```
$sentence: (This is a sentence obviously);
```

Instead of one item, `This is a sentence obviously`, we would instead have 5 strings:

```
content: nth($sentence, 4); // Would be the string: content: sentence
```

Worse, if you put the grammatically correct comma in that sentence…

```
$sentence: (This is a sentence, obviously);
```

You would in fact make two separate lists and checking for the 4th item would cause an error.

For this reason, you should *always quote your strings!* I would argue you should quote your strings even when you don't expect to be dealing with lists. The fact is, you can't be certain your functions or mixins will not be passed through another function or mixin which uses lists. Therefore, the safest bet is to *always quote your strings.*

Let's get even weirder. If you thought leaving out commas was strange, how about then leaving out the parentheses. That's right, you can leave out commas and parentheses! This is similar in a way to CSS shorthand:

```
padding: 10px 0 5px 5px;
```

For this reason, I'm ok with leaving out commas and parentheses, and *as long as you quote your strings* Sass will do a good job of figuring everything out. I would advise you simply be consistent. I'm used to using parentheses and commas in other languages so I continue to do so in Sass. Not because I don't like the idea of less typing, simply because when I go back to PHP or JavaScript I won't all of a sudden forget to write commas in my arrays.

Heading line heights

Next, we need to take control of the line height of our headings. They too look disproportionate when we switch between the font families. The good thing with this, however, is we've already done the groundwork. Our `base-heading-sizes-calc()` function will allow us to easily solve this problem. However, again we need to figure out the appropriate formula.

One way of setting the line height would be to simply use the font size of the next heading. For example, when we're using our sans font family:

```
h1 {font-size: 2rems;}
h2 {font-size: 1.5rem;}
h3 {font-size: 1.17rem;}
// ...and so on
```

Well, it just so works out that line heights based on the next headings `font-size` look about right.

```
h1 {
    font-size: 2rems;
    line-height: 1.5rem;
}

h2 {
    font-size: 1.5rem;
    line-height: 1.17rem
}

h3 {
    font-size: 1.17rem;
    line-height: 1rem;
}
// ...and so on
```

Therefore, we can almost copy our `base-heading-sizes-calc()` function again to get our line heights with only two small differences:

```
// mastering-sass/ch02/scss/helpers/_functions.scss
@function base-heading-line-height($heading: 2) {
    $h1-line-height: base-heading-sizes-calc(2); // We start at 2 instead
of 1
```

```
    $h2-line-height: base-heading-sizes-calc(3);
    $h3-line-height: base-heading-sizes-calc(4);
    $h4-line-height: base-heading-sizes-calc(5);
    $h5-line-height: base-heading-sizes-calc(6);
    $h6-line-height: (base-heading-sizes-calc(6) / $h1-line-height);

    $line-heights: ($h1-line-height, $h2-line-height, $h3-line-height, $h4-
line-height, $h5-line-height, $h6-line-height);

    @return nth($line-heights, $heading);
}
```

The first difference is straightforward enough. We simply start at 2 instead of 1, because we want to use the font size of the next heading down as the line height for the larger headings.

The second difference arises when we get to the h6 line-height. Obviously, we don't have a h7 font-size to use, so what should we do? Well, it turns out dividing our h6 font-size by 1.5 (or our $h1-line-height) works out perfectly.

I considered using our global $base-line-height; however, what happens when you set that to 1.25? The line-height of the h6 grows slightly while everything else shrinks. For that reason, the $h1-line-height is the best solution.

So now we can update our style.scss as follows:

```
// mastering-sass/ch02/scss/style.scss
h1, h2, h3, h4, h5, h6 {
    font-family: $base-font-family;
}
h1 {
    font-size: base-heading-sizes-calc(1);
    line-height: base-heading-line-height(1);
}
h2 {
    font-size: base-heading-sizes-calc(2);
    line-height: base-heading-line-height(2);
}
h3 {
    font-size: base-heading-sizes-calc(3);
    line-height: base-heading-line-height(3);
}
// ...and so on
```

Test the differences between sans and serif by switching your $base-font-family and double check everything looks right in the browser.

But wait, there's more...

There is another scenario we need to account for now. What happens when you want to use a different font family for the headings that the paragraphs? It's fairly common to see headings in serif and the body text in sans, or vice-versa. So we'll need to add this capability to our current mixins and functions.

Initially, this might sound like a tricky feature to include. However, due to the fact we've made each of our functions to handle a single problem well, we only need to make a few very small changes. If we take a look at our very first function, we'll notice we've already added in the ability to specify which `font-family` we want to use, it simply defaults to the current `$base-font-family`.

So let's create a similar global variable for our headings called `$base-headings-font-family`:

```
// mastering-sass/ch02/scss/style.scss
$base-font-family: $base-font-family-sans;
$base-headings-font-family: $base-font-family-serif;
```

Once we've done that we can simply go back into our functions and add our second parameter to each function, which will be passed through to each call of `base-font-size-calc()` inside those functions:

```
// mastering-sass/ch02/scss/helpers/_function.scss
@function base-heading-sizes-calc($heading: 2, $font-family: $base-headings-font-family) {
    $h4-font-size: base-font-size-calc($font-family);
    $h1-font-size: $h4-font-size * 2;
    $h2-font-size: $h1-font-size / 1.3333;
    $h3-font-size: $h2-font-size / 1.2821;
    $h5-font-size: $h4-font-size / 1.2048;
    $h6-font-size: $h5-font-size / 1.2388;
    $headings: $h1-font-size, $h2-font-size, $h3-font-size, $h4-font-size,
$h5 font-size, $h6-font-size;
    @return nth($headings, $heading);
}

@function base-heading-line-height($heading: 2, $font-family: $base-headings-font-family) {
    $h1-line-height: base-heading-sizes-calc(2, $font-family);
    $h2-line-height: base-heading-sizes-calc(3, $font-family);
    $h3-line-height: base-heading-sizes-calc(4, $font-family);
    $h4-line-height: base-heading-sizes-calc(5, $font-family);
    $h5-line-height: base-heading-sizes-calc(6, $font-family);
    $h6-line-height: base-heading-sizes-calc(6, $font-family) /
```

```
$h1-line-height;
$line-heights: $h1-line-height, $h2-line-height,
$h3-line-height, $h4-line-height, $h5-line-height,
$h6-line-height;
@return nth($line-heights, $heading);
}
```

Then we simply update our headings in *style.scss* to use our new `$base-headings-font-family`:

```
//mastering-sass/scss/style.scss
h1, h2, h3, h4, h5, h6 {
    font-family: $base-headings-font-family;
}
```

What's great about this is due to the fact we've set the default value of `$font-family` in our functions to already use `$base-headings-font-family` we don't even need to make any changes to the places where we've used those two functions. You can imagine what a relief this would be on a large project which is already live. This is the benefit of having many smaller functions, each responsible for solving one problem completely, instead of fewer functions trying to do everything.

Allowing for different font families for each heading

The only issue really now is if we want to use serif for our h1 and sans for h2, h3 and so on. Grouping them all together like we've done simply won't do if we want to allow for even more configuration. Really we should be adding the font family to each heading so we can set each one individually. However, simply adding the font family to each heading would be error prone. There's nothing stopping someone from doing this by accident:

```
h2 {
    font-family: $base-font-family;
    font-size: base-heading-sizes-calc(2);
    line-height: base-heading-line-height(2);
}
```

It would be quite easy for an end user not to realize the default heading sizes and line heights are actually being set for `$base-headings-font-family` and therefore need to be set accordingly to match the font family.

So we need to encapsulate these three properties together to prevent mistakes. We can do this quite easily with a small mixin that takes in two parameters, much like our functions in the previous examples. In our mixins file add the following:

```scss
// mastering-sass/ch02/scss/helpers/_mixins.scss
@mixin base-headings-font-family-sizing($current-font-family: $base-
headings-font-family, $heading: 2) {
    font-family: $current-font-family;
    font-size: base-heading-sizes-calc($heading, $current-font-family);
    line-height: base-heading-line-height($heading, $current-font-family);
}
```

Now we can update each of our headings to use this mixin instead:

```scss
// mastering-sass/ch02/scss/style.scss
h1 {
    @include base-headings-font-family-sizing($base-headings-font-family,
1);
}

h2 {
    @include base-headings-font-family-sizing($base-headings-font-family,
2);
}
// ...and so on
```

You'll notice I put the number second for our mixin, whereas in all of our functions it comes first. I actually wouldn't recommend doing this, seeing as it can be counter intuitive for someone who is used to the order things are in our functions. However, I wanted to point out that `sass` mixins and functions can take in arguments in any order, as long as you specify the original parameters names. The following will work just fine:

```scss
// mastering-sass/ch02/scss/style.scss
h3 {
    @include base-headings-font-family-sizing($heading: 2, $current-font-
family: $base-font-family-code);
}
```

It can be useful if you remember the names of what you need to put in but not the exact order. Now, that I've mentioned that, I'm actually going to update my mixin and headings so the heading number comes first and the font family second:

```scss
// mastering-sass/ch02/scss/helpers/_mixins.scss
@mixin base-headings-font-family-sizing($heading: 2, $current-font-family:
$base-headings-font-family) {
    font-family: $current-font-family;
    font-size: base-heading-sizes-calc($heading, $current-font-family);
    line-height: base-heading-line-height($heading, $current-font-family);
}
```

Don't forget to update everywhere you've called the mixin as well.

Remove repetition

We can now place all of our headings into a mixin to clean up our *style.scss* file even more. We could simply copy each rule and drop it into a mixin; however, I think this is a good chance to look at loops.

We will need to keep all of the functionality we've added so far, including the ability to choose separate font families for each heading. This will be the trickiest feature to include. We'll use nested lists to achieve this. There is a better data type called maps, for this purpose, but I'm saving those for later. I want us to get familiar with lists before moving onto maps.

So the best way to start is to actually take all of our headings from *style.scss* and put them into a mixin as is, and then call that mixin from our *style.scss*. This will just mean we can work entirely in our mixin and see the changes (or lack thereof) in our browser. So our mixin will look this:

```
// mastering-sass/ch02/scss/helpers/_mixins.scss
@mixin base-headings {
    h1 {
        @include base-headings-font-family-sizing(1, $base-headings-font-
family);
    }

    h2 {
        @include base-headings-font-family-sizing(2, $base-headings-font-
family);
    }

    h3 {
        @include base-headings-font-family-sizing(3, $base-headings-font-
family);
    }
    // ... h4, h5, h6
}
```

Then, back in our *style.scss* file we can replace where we had our headings with the following:

```
// mastering-sass/ch02/scss/style.scss
@include base-headings;
```

So, the first loop we'll look at is called a `for` loop. It looks like the following:

```
// mastering-sass/ch02/scss/helpers/_mixins.scss
@mixin base-headings {
  @for $i from 1 to 6 {
    h#{$i} {
      @include base-headings-font-family-sizing($i, $base-headings-font-
family);
    }
  }
}
```

The `for` loops simply start at the first number, which we set to one, and places it inside the variable `$i`. It the runs the code inside the brackets. After it's done that it adds 1 to our variable `$i` and runs again. So the second iteration, or loop would use `$i: 2` and so on to the second number we set, at which point it stops.

Now, this is where it's important to know what you're actually trying to do. In the above example we said "I want to loop from 1 to 6". This means it will loop 1, 2, 3, 4, and 5 but not 6 itself. Essential the word to means "up to 6, but not 6 itself". So our mixin would only run 5 times, giving us `h1`, `h2`, `h3`, `h4`, and `h5`...but no `h6`.

You could say `@for $i from 1 to 7` but there is in fact, a better way. Instead of using the keyword "to" we say "through", like this:

```
// mastering-sass/ch02/scss/helpers/_mixins.scss
@mixin base-headings {
  @for $i from 1 through 6 {
    h#{$i} {
      @include base-headings-font-family-sizing($i, $base-headings-
font-family);
    }
  }
}
```

This solves the problem of repetition; however, we can't choose which font family to use for each individual iteration. To do this we need another variable that can also be looped through and allows for configuring each headings font family, individually, allowing for any configuration. Before the arrival of maps in lists this was done with lists.

One way would simply create a list of font families in order from 1 to 6, which would match `h1` to `h6`. To do this, we would write our list with our other variables, after the `$base-headings-font-family` variable:

```
// mastering-sass/ch02/scss/style.scss
$base-headings: ($base-headings-font-family, $base-font-family, $base-
headings-font-family, $base-headings-font-family, $base-headings-font-
family, $base-headings-font-family)
```

Then we can use the `nth()` function in Sass to access these by their position in the list, using our `$i` counter variable:

```
// mastering-sass/ch02/scss/helpers/_mixins.scss
@mixin base-headings {
    @for $i from 1 through 6 {
        h#{$i} {
            @include base-headings-font-family-sizing($i, nth($base-
headings, $i));
        }
    }
}
```

While this works, it requires each item in `$base-headings` has to be in that order. It would be better if we could indicate which font family is for which heading. To accomplish this, we can use nested lists:

```
$base-headings: (
    (h1, $base-headings-font-family),
    (h2, $base-font-family),
    (h3, $base-headings-font-family),
    (h4, $base-headings-font-family),
    (h5, $base-headings-font-family),
    (h6, $base-headings-font-family)
);
```

We can then use an `@each` loop, which allows us to assign as many variables as we need to access the items in our lists. However, we still need a counter to be used in our `base-headings-font-family-sizing` mixin:

```
// mastering-sass/ch02/scss/helpers/_mixins.scss
@mixin base-headings {
    $i: 1;
    @each $heading, $family in $base-headings {
        #{$heading} {
            @include base-headings-font-family-sizing($i, $family);
        }
        $i: $i + 1;
    }
}
```

So we instantiate our counter variable `$i` outside of our `each` loop. We can then add 1 to it on each successful loop by using `$i + 1` and reassigning `$i` the new value `$i: $i + 1`.

Currently Sass doesn't have incremental (++) or decremental operators (−−) so we need to use the $i: $i + 1 previously mentioned.

So there are our mixins for creating our configurable base typography styles. Even though it works, it's not yet ready to be released for use by other designer or developers.

Error handling and type validation

There are a few simple things to keep in mind when writing any function or mixin which takes input from an external source. In our case, the external source is our configuration variables at the start of our *style.scss* file; however, this could also be other functions, other mixins inside mixins, and so forth. The aim is to prepare for times when things go wrong. Good code is pessimistic.

Usually you would do this as you write your functions and mixins the first time, so you don't need to revisit them later; however, I've left it to the end to keep the original functions and mixins from getting too complicated.

So let's start with our functions. We'll begin by sanitizing user input. That means checking the values passed in, making sure they are of the right type or format, and if not we will either convert them to the right format or providing an appropriate level of error message to the user that says where and why there was a problem.

Data types in Sass

If we look at the `base-font-sizes-calc()` function, we know it takes in a font family and then calculates the correct value to return. However, what if someone passed in a number? It's reasonable to assume something called `base-font-sizes-calc()` deals with numbers, right? So we need to make sure we are only getting a string, and if not we need to tell the user this function needs a string which is the font-family and not a number.

Sass has 7 main data types (8 if you count `arg` list):

- `string [unquoted, "quoted string", 'single quoted string']`
- `number [1, 0.5, 1rem, 5px, 2em]`
- `bool [true, false]`
- `null [null]`

- `list [(1, 2, 3, 4), ("one" "two" "three")]`
- `map [(h1: 2rem, h2: 1.5rem, h3: 1.17rem)]`
- `color [#bada55, red, hsl(10, 30%, 50%), rgb(255, 160, 80)]`

The way you check for a specific type is with the Sass function `type-of()`. So now we can update our function to perform this check with a simple `if else` statement:

```scss
// mastering-sass/ch02/scss/helpers/_functions.scss
@function base-font-size-calc($current-font-family: $base-font-family) {
    @if type-of($current-font-family) != string {
        @error "The base-font-size-calc()
        function takes a string as it's parameter,
        #{type-of($current-font-family)} type was given.";
    } @else {
        @return if($current-font-family == $base-font-family-serif, $base-
font-size * 1.15, $base-font-size);
    }
}
```

We can quickly make sure our error is showing by creating a simple CSS rule and entering the wrong data type into our function:

```scss
// mastering-sass/ch02/scss/style.scss
.test-error {
    content: base-font-size-calc(1);
}
```

This will output the following message to the command line:

```
The base-font-size-calc() function takes a string as it's parameter,
number type was given.
```

You can enter other data types and it will simply replace `number` in our message with the data type. This is due to the interpolated call to `#{type-of($current-font-family)}`, which allows for a more dynamic and helpful error message.

Let's look at different data types in detail.

@error

In the preceding example we used `@error` to product our message. Due to the fact functions a required to return a value, `@error` is the only one of the three error directives `@error`, `@warn`, and `@debug` which actually returns. However, this is the only reason I chose `@error` here.

@error is the highest priority level error message we have at our disposal. It stops everything once it's called and to the command line. This can't be turned off (@warn can be turned off at runtime with the --quiet option in Sass) and is ideal for any situation where an error cannot be overlooked or worked around. Adding a number instead of a font family is such an occurrence.

We'll mostly be dealing with @error for now, however let's take a look at the differences between all three error directives right now. As you've seen, @error stops Sass from compiling and displays the error in the command line. @warn and @debug do not stop Sass compiling, but they do display messages. I think of them as red, orange, and yellow level errors. @error is red, @warn is orange, and @debug is yellow.

@debug

@debug is the least severe. In fact, I wouldn't even call it an error directive. As the name implies it's mainly for debugging your functions and mixin during the process of development. It's should not be used in the finished *production-ready* Sass. It should be used much how we used the content property in our .test-error rule discussed previously. So let's write a rule with @debug to see the difference. We'll call our CSS the rule .test-debug and output base- font-size-calc($base-headings-font-family):

```
// mastering-sass/ch02/scss/style.scss
.test-debug {
    @debug base-font-size-calc($base-headings-font-family);
}
```

In the command line you should see something like this:

```
>>> Change detected to: scss/style.scss
/style.scss:40 DEBUG: 1.15rem
    write css/style.css
    write css/style.css.map
```

So it gives us the filename /style.scss, the line on which @debug was called, :40, and the value: DEBUG: 1.15. Sass will then continue to compile our css files as normal. However, what happens if we put a number in base-font-size-calc() like the previous example? Let's give it a go:

```
// mastering-sass/ch02/scss/style.scss
.test-debug {
    @debug base-font-size-calc(1);
}
```

Now in the command line you'll see the error with no debug info:

```
>>> Change detected to: scss/style.scss
        error scss/helpers/_functions.scss (Line 4: base-font-size-calc()
takes a string as it's parameter. number given.)
```

This is because @error will always win. If you call something that results in an error being output, the error will simply prevent everything else from happening and therefore will be the only thing output to the command line.

@warn

@warn is useful if you want to show a message to a user in the command line without stopping Sass from compiling. However, @warn is useful in final production-ready Sass. @warn is useful when a function or mixin is being deprecated and therefore will still work for a time, but perhaps the user should be notified to use another function or mixin instead.

So let's assume one day another library comes out that also has a mixin called base-headings() and we realize it's madness not to be name spacing our mixins and functions. So we are going to deprecate our base-headings() mixin for a mixin called mastering-sass-base-headings(). To do this we would use the @warn directive to alert those using our mixins that in a future release they will have to start using the new mixin, but in the meantime their code will still work:

```scss
// mastering-sass/scss/helpers/_mixins.scss
@mixin base-headings {
    @warn "Please use @include mastering-sass-base-headings() instead of
@include base-headings(). @mixin base-headings() will be deprecated in
version 2.";
    $i: 1;
  @each $heading, $family in $base-headings {
    #{$heading} {
      @include base-headings-font-family-sizing($i, $family);
    }
    $i: $i + 1;
  }
}
```

Then we would obviously need to copy our base-headings mixin and call it mastering-sass-base-headings so it can be used as well in the transition period, and of course when we remove the availability of the base-headings mixin.

Now that we've looked at each of the error directives let's get back to adding our error checking to our functions and mixins. Our next function is `base-heading-sizes-calc`. This function actually requires a few checks to be robust enough to be release into the wild web. We need to make sure the first parameter is a number and the second is a string. We then need to provide a user friendly error if a number greater than 6 is entered for our headings. First let's do our type checking and test that works:

```
// mastering-sass/ch02/scss/helpers/_functions.scss
@function base-heading-sizes-calc($heading: 2, $font-family: $base-
headings-font-family) {
    @if type-of($heading) != number {
        @error "The first parameter of base-heading-sizes-calc()
        must be a number, #{type-of($heading)} was given.";
    } @else if type-of($font-family) != string {
        @error "The second parameter base-heading-sizes-calc() must
        be a string, #{type-of($font-family)} was given.";
    } @else {
        $h4-font-size: base-font-size-calc($font-family);
        $h1-font-size: $h4-font-size * 2;
        $h2-font-size: $h1-font-size / 1.3333;
        $h3-font-size: $h2-font-size / 1.2821;
        $h5-font-size: $h4-font-size / 1.2048;
        $h6-font-size: $h5-font-size / 1.2388;
        $headings: $h1-font-size, $h2-font-size, $h3-font-size, $h4-font-
size, $h5-font-size, $h6-font-size;

        @return nth($headings, $heading);
    }
}
```

Now let's do a quick test to ensure it's working correctly:

```
// mastering-sass/ch02/scss/style.scss
.test-data-types {
    content: base-heading-sizes-calc("", 2);
}
```

This will give the following error in the command line:

```
error scss/helpers/_functions.scss (Line 11: The first parameter of
base-heading-sizes-calc() must be a number, string was given.)
```

Again, this is because we can only get one error and then everything after that is prevented from running. So change the first parameter to a number and you should get the following error:

```
error scss/helpers/_functions.scss (Line 13: The second parameter of
base-heading-sizes-calc() must be a string, number was given.)
```

Everything works, so we can move onto checking our number is from between 1 and 6 and not -1 or 0 or 7 or anything else which would could cause unexpected issues down the line. So once both variables have passed the data type, checks we'll end up inside the `@else` block of our conditional. Therefore, we need to write our check inside our `@else` statement, in a way that displays an error if the number given is outside of 1 and 6, otherwise our function runs the calculations as intended:

```scss
// mastering-sass/ch02/scss/helpers/_functions.scss
@function base-heading-sizes-calc($heading: 2, $font-family: $base-
headings-font-family) {
    @if type-of($heading) != number {
        @error "The first parameter of base-heading-sizes-calc() must be a
number, #{type-of($heading)} was given.";
    } @else if type-of($font-family) != string {
        @error "The second parameter of base-heading-sizes-calc() must be a
string, #{type-of($font-family)} was given.";
    } @else {
        @if $heading < 1 or $heading > 6 {
            @error "Second parameter of base-heading-sizes-calc()
            must be between 1 and 6, #{$heading} was given.";
        }
        $h4-font-size: base-font-size-calc($font-family);
        $h1-font-size: $h4-font-size * 2;
        $h2-font-size: $h1-font-size / 1.3333;
        $h3-font-size: $h2-font-size / 1.2821;
        $h5-font-size: $h4-font-size / 1.2048;
        $h6-font-size: $h5-font-size / 1.2388;
        $headings: $h1-font-size, $h2-font-size, $h3-font-size, $h4-font-
size, $h5-font-size, $h6-font-size;

        @return nth($headings, $heading);
    }
}
```

Now we test our error works correctly (you know what I mean):

```scss
.test-data-types {
    content: base-heading-sizes-calc(0, $base-headings-font-family);
}
```

This should output the error message:

```
error sass/helpers/_functions.sass (Line 16: Second parameter
of baseheading-sizes-calc() must be between 1 and 6, 0 was
given.)
```

You'll notice we didn't wrap the rest of our code in an `@else` block. This is because if the number is outside of 1 and 6 the error will trigger and stop the remainder of our function from running anyways, and if the number is between 1 and 6 the `if` statement will simply be ignored and our calculations will run as usual. So for brevity we can leave the `@else` out in these situations. The same would be true if we were returning a value. Once a function returns nothing else inside that function will run, similar to an error.

From here I think you how to check for errors. Basically, ask yourself the following:

- What happens if a user puts in the wrong data type?
- What happens if they enter a number which is outside of the intended range?
- Is this something I can account for without breaking the intending functionality?

Bonus round

I'm going to leave it up to you to go through the remaining functions and mixins and add useful error messages for any errors that may arise. However, for bonus points you could also add some smarts to the `base-heading-sizes-calc` function. For example, I think we could safely assume if the value was less than 0 we could automatically set it to 1, and if it was greater than 6 we could set it to 6 and a warning should be displayed to the user instead of an error.

Summary

We've covered a broad range of Sass features in this chapter. From using variables to allow for easy configuration of our Sass functions and mixins, to error handling and debugging information for times when things go wrong. We've also seen how lists and loops can be extremely useful in reducing repetition when dealing with incrementing values and lists.

In the next chapter we'll take a look at Compass. Compass is known for its great library of mixins and functions which not only help in writing CSS3 for cross-browser compatibility but also for dealing with color, images, sprites and typography. It's also very good at getting a project set up quickly and easily from the command line.

3
Compass – Navigating with Compass

In the previous chapter, we saw how using Sass can solve problems that would have been almost impossible with plain CSS. Possible or not, it would certainly have been unfeasible to attempt what we covered in the last chapter with vanilla CSS. In this chapter we'll look at one of the most well-known frameworks built with Sass, known simply as Compass.

Compass was created at a time when HTML5/CSS3 was still in its early stages of adoption, not only by the major browsers, but also by web designers and developers. This is commonly called the **experimental implementation phase**. This is where we get vendor prefixes from.

When I first began using Compass, it was mainly for its ability to automatically compile all of the necessary vendor prefixes and even those painfully verbose filters (also known as polyfills) in certain CSS3 properties. To me it was just a mixin library which made setting up and maintaining Sass projects much easier. I tried the Blueprint grid and the sprite generator, but mainly I was interested in creating a project quickly, watching for changes, and using the mixins for vendor prefixes. If you are currently using Compass only for vendor prefixing, then this is the chapter for you.

In this chapter we'll look at creating a project from scratch using Compass. We'll look at the default configuration of Compass and the folders and files it creates by default. We'll also learn how to take control of the default options through the command line, including the directories Compass creates by default.

Once our project is created, we'll look at setting up a vertical rhythm for a typography based webpage, such as a blog post or news article. We'll look at the reason Compass prefers to use the reset methodology over the normalize method. From there we'll set up our vertical rhythm and use the built-in baseline grid to make sure our text is staying within our grid. We'll also see how Compass can be used to give elements other than text heights based upon the vertical rhythm we've defined.

We'll take a look at using SassMeister or CodePen for times when you don't want to create a full Sass or Compass project. Perhaps you simply want to test out a framework, or try an idea or feature out really quickly, and setting up files and directories would either take too long, or simply not be worthwhile. We'll look at SassMeister and CodePen's similarities and parities and why we might choose one over the other in certain circumstances.

Finally, we'll create a few simple experiments to try out some of the mixins and functions Compass offers for dealing with CSS3 properties such as columns, transforms, and animations. We'll also see how Compass offers mixins to overcome some common and not so common design challenges. These include horizontal and unstyled lists, styling links, and tag clouds.

Setting up a Compass project

One of the biggest time savers Compass offers when you begin using it is when setting up a Sass project. While Sass saves time with the `watch` command, we still need to create the overall project folder and the directory for our Sass files and Sass files themselves. "That's unacceptable!" I hear you cry. "Manually create our own files and folders?! The nerve!" Thankfully, Compass can ease our pitiful plight with a single command from the command line.

Open your command line and `cd` into the *mastering-sass* folder. Within this folder you should have the `ch02` folder with the code from the last chapter. What we want to do now is create a new folder called `ch03`. However, we also want to create a `scss` folder inside that, inside which we'll create our `scss` files, which will then need to be compiled into `.css` files in our `css` folder. That sounds like a bunch of stuff preventing me from doing some actually important (and dare I say fun) work.

Let's take a look at a faster and better way. In your command line, type the following:

```
compass help
```

No, this isn't the faster and better way, but it will show us how to get there. The `compass help` command will show the commands Compass can run, and one of them is `compass create`.

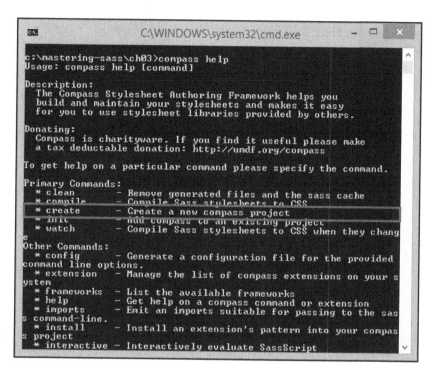

The description for `create` says it will `Create a new compass project`. That's the command we're looking for. So in the command line we'll type the following command:

```
compass create ch03
```

This will create our *ch03* folder and also automatically create our *sass* folder, a `stylesheets` folder for our CSS, and some files to get us started. This is a good start; however, I'm not too happy with the default structure. I much prefer to have my CSS, images, and JavaScript folders together in a folder called `assets`, and I'd like to rename `stylesheets` to `css`, because I much prefer the shortest possible names for my folders. Furthermore, I'd like my `sass` to be in a separate folder *outside* of the *assets* folder, so when I deploy to production I can easily leave the *sass* files and folders behind.

You'll notice Compass also created a file called *config.rb* directly inside our *ch03* folder. If you open this file in your text editor you should see the following:

```
// mastering-sass/ch03/config.rb
require 'compass/import-once/activate'
# Require any additional compass plugins here.

# Set this to the root of your project when deployed:
http_path = "/"
css_dir = "stylesheets"
sass_dir = "sass"
images_dir = "images"
javascripts_dir = "javascripts"
```

There are more options in the *config.rb* file that are commented out, but for now these are the only options that we are interested in. As you can see, `stylesheets` and `sass` are the directories that Compass created for us inside of the project folder *ch03*.

The way I see most people configure their Compass projects in the beginning is to simply run the `create` command as we have and then open this file and change everything and then rename their folders and move things around. I don't know about you but the thought of that makes me cringe. What's the point in letting Compass create the folder for you at all, then?

So let's try and learn a little bit more about the Compass `create` command to see if we can configure it to do what we want. Back in the command line, type the following:

```
compass help create
```

This will bring up the specific help documentation for the `create` command in our command line.

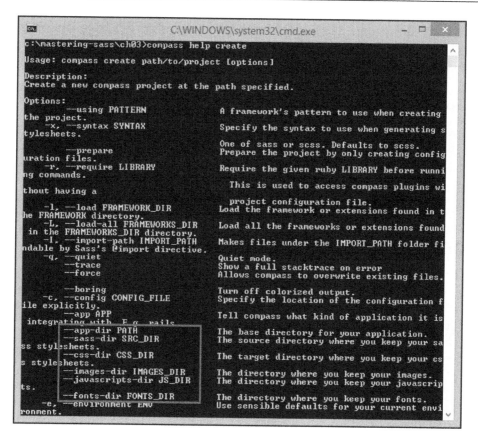

We can see there are options for the directories here. So we can tell Compass exactly where we want our folders and what we want to call them.

> Keep in mind that your *config.rb* file will always be created within the root of your project and all folders should be defined to be relative to that location. In our case, `ch03` is the project root, and *config.rb* will be created directly inside the *ch03* folder.
>
> We can also specify what syntax we prefer from the start, such as the original indented `sass` syntax. We can specify if we want line comments and what output style we want our CSS to be in. For now, we'll focus on our folder structure. We can set the other option from within the *config.rb* file. It's really just the folder structure that needs to be done exactly as we want it from the start (and setting the indented Sass syntax as way if you want to use that).

First, we need to delete the ch03 folder completely. You can do this from Explorer/Finder or from the command line. I'll leave that up to you. Once that's done, we'll make sure we are in the *mastering-sass* folder in the command line and we'll type the following command:

```
compass create ch03 --sass-dir=scss --css-dir=assets/css --javascripts-
dir=assets/js --images-dir=assets/img --fonts-dir=assets/css/fonts
```

Now, if we look inside our ch03, folder we'll see the correct folders have been created. If you open the config.rb again in your text editor, you'll see the options have also been created here matching the command-line options we specified. Now we're ready to start exploring what Compass is really made of.

Typography with Compass

In the last chapter we looked at how we could use Sass to help us implement a way of changing our entire typography style based on which font family we wanted to use. It may not be something that is necessary or useful in the majority of projects, but it allowed us to look at using Sass to solve a particular problem.

Compass, on the other hand, is designed to give us the tools and design patterns we need to overcome many of the common problems that we face on most of our web designs. Compass offers helpers that can be employed to tackle unique problems. Compass includes functions to help solve complex math problems, or accessibility issues with its color contrast and text functions. However, Compass also helps us solve complex design challenges such as setting a base typography grid and maintaining vertical rhythm throughout a design.

What is vertical rhythm?

Essentially, vertical rhythm is the alignment of your text and other horizontal elements on your page. Its determining factors are font size, line height, margin, and padding. If you've ever had a floated image that your text was wrapping around and wondered why there was too much space below the image…that's bad vertical rhythm.

You should always use font size, line height, margin, and padding to give your elements height. If you are using the height property for anything more than images and SVG elements, you will run into problems. Your content should always dictate its containing elements' height, never the other way around.

To see vertical rhythm in action, we'll need some HTML to work with. Luckily for us, we already have some from the last chapter. Copy the *index.html* file from the *ch02* folder into the *ch03* folder and open it in your text editor.

Next, we need some styles. Right now, our HTML is linking to *css/style.css*, which doesn't exist. So we'll need to update it to use our current stylesheet, which Compass created for us, located at *assets/css/screen.css*:

```
<link href="assets/css/screen.css" rel="stylesheet">
```

Now, open *index.html* in your browser. You'll notice one thing immediately, all of our headings are the same size as the body text. This is due to the fact that Compass, by default, imports a `reset` stylesheet that actually removes much of the default styling to give a uniform experience on all browsers.

In truth, I generally find the `reset.css` method to be overly aggressive. I much prefer the `normalize.css` method, which simply reduces the differences between browsers to an acceptable average state across all major browsers. A middle ground, if you will. `normalize.css` leaves the default headings sizes intact and doesn't remove padding/margin from forms, lists, and so on.

However, to attain vertical rhythm, it's a good idea to remove all unwanted paddings, margins, line heights, and yes, even font sizes. So, our *screen.scss* file should look something like this:

```
// mastering-sass/ch03/scss/screen.scss
@import "compass/reset";
```

Next, we'll copy two of our variables from our *style.scss* file from *ch02* into our *screen.scss* file, at the very top of the file:

```
// mastering-sass/ch03/scss/screen.scss
$base-font-size: 1rem; $base-line-height: 1.5;

@import "compass/reset";
```

I always structure my main Sass file like this:

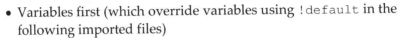

- Variables first (which override variables using !default in the following imported files)
- Required libraries and frameworks next (such as Compass, Bourbon, Susy, and so on)
- Finally, partials, which contain helpers, mixins and the styles

Eventually, I end up with one main file that acts as configuration (variables) and dependencies (importing libraries and frameworks) and partials (my Sassfiles). We'll work towards this structure as we progress.

Next, we'll need to import the Compass typography helpers just below the reset. We'll also add the rule for our container div to give at a suitable max-width of 38rem and center it horizontally:

```
// mastering-sass/ch03/scss/screen.scss
@import "compass/reset";
@import "compass/typography";

/* CUSTOM STYLES */
body > div {
    max-width: 38rem;
    margin: 0 auto;
}
```

The compass/typography import will give us access to the vertical rhythm mixins that Compass uses to establish and manage the vertical rhythm of our page. Next, we'll include the mixin that will establish our baseline grid, upon which everything else will be built. Include the establish-baseline mixin just below our imports in screen.scss, with a comment so we can easily locate it in our CSS:

```
// mastering-sass/ch03/scss/screen.scss
@import "compass/reset";
@import "compass/typography";

/* Establish Baseline */@include establish-baseline;

/* CUSTOM STYLES */
body > div {
    max-width: 38rem;
    margin: 0 auto;
}
```

Next, we'll start watching our project for changes using the `compass watch` command. The `compass watch` command must run from the directory where the *config.rb* file is located, *mastering-sass/ch03*. You don't need to specify the directories or files; this is all handled by the *config.rb* file that we set up when we created our *ch03* folder.

From the command line we simply run the following:

```
compass watch
```

Now, in the command line, you should see warnings and errors! You'll see four warnings all ending with "must resolve to a value in pixel units", or some similar messages, and then an error along the lines of "`6.25%*rem/px` isn't a valid CSS value".

This is because Compass requires pixel values for the `$base-font-size` and `$base-line-height`, and we are using `rems` and `ems` (`line-height`: 1.5 is the same as 1.5 em). To fix this, we need to update our variables:

```
//mastering-sass/ch03/scss/screen.scss
$base-font-size: 16px;$base-line-height: $base-font-size * 1.5; // 16px *
1.5 = 24px
```

Now our CSS should compile, and inside our *screen.css* you can find the comment with the content created by the establish-baseline mixin:

```
// mastering-sass/ch02/assets/css/screen.css
/* Establish Baseline */
/* line 106, ../../../../Ruby22-x64/lib/ruby/gems/2.2.0/gems/compass-
core-1.0.3/stylesheets/compass/typography/_vertical_rhythm.scss */
html {
  font-size: 100%;
  line-height: 1.5em;
}
```

As you can see, it takes care of setting our root `font-size` and `line-height`.

The next thing we need is a way to really **see** what we're doing. Right now, we're kind of working blind. We need some guidelines...or more appropriately, a grid. Luckily, for us Compass has just the thing.

Compass comes with an entire set of mixins and functions to help us display both column grids and baseline grids. You just include the mixin in the element where you want to display a grid. We need the grid for our entire page, so we'll place it in our HTML rule. You could also place it in the `body` rule.

Compass grids are generally imported with the layout module using `@import "compass/layout";` however, when using the typography module, the grid helpers are imported automatically as dependencies.

```
//mastering-sass/ch03/scss/screen.scss
html {
    @include baseline-grid-background;
}
```

Now when you refresh the page in the browser, you'll see our baseline grid. Right now, our main image is actually breaking our vertical rhythm ever so slightly. You'll notice the headings (even though they're all too small) and the first line all sit in the very center of the line. Then all the lines after the image are sitting nearer the top of the lines.

Vertical rhythm for images

Compass allows us to adjust elements margins and padding while keeping with our overall vertical rhythm. If we plan to leave this image where it is, we'll need reduce its height to *stay within the lines*. So we need to examine the height of our images and reduce them to within our line height. Let's first put the height and width attributes on our image and a class called `vertical-rhythm`.

In our *index.html* file, we'll also need to update the image:

```
// mastering-sass/ch03/index.html
<p>
<img src="http://placehold.it/600x300" alt="Image from Placehold.it"
height="300" width="600" class="vertical-rhythm">
Lorem ipsum dolar sit amet...
```

 It's a good idea to add height and width attributes to all of your images anyways. It helps with page performance, SEO, and accessibility.

We could be lazy and just do this for desktop, but that's not realistic. In the real world, we're going to need to make this responsive.

In our *screen.scss* file, place the following rule:

```
// mastering-sass/ch03/scss/screen.scss
.vertical-rhythm[height="300"][width="600"] {
    height: rhythm(6);
```

```
    width: auto; // important to maintain the aspect ratio
    display: block; // Make sure text starts on its own line
}
```

If you're not too familiar with using attribute selectors, what we're saying is "for each element with a class of `vertical-rhythm` and a height attribute equaling `300` and width attribute equaling `600` add these styles."

The function we're using tells Compass we want this elements height to be 6 *lines* of vertical rhythm height, basically our `line-height * 6`.

A few things you need to know

The first thing you'll need to know is that you could potentially have a media query every 50 – 100px to properly set heights for every few lines of our vertical rhythm. We're going to increase our rhythm by 2 at increments of around every 100px. Therefore, our next breakpoint will be around 420px. We'll write that media query in a moment.

The next thing you need to know is using CSS (even with Compass and Sass) to give images a vertical rhythm, while very possible, is quite a challenge and very time consuming on large, complex websites. Each image (or any element for that matter) of different aspect ratios (height/width) will require individual attention. This is really important, and also the reason why I wouldn't recommend using CSS to give images height for vertical rhythm. There's simply too many possibilities, and too much time needed to handle it for each image on each screen size and all the possible aspect ratios.

Also, what happens when you have a `column-based` grid layout? Your image will need to stay within a column with padding and on numerous screen sizes. To do this with CSS will result in numerous media queries that would depend entirely on your HTML structure to work. This is a bad idea for many reasons. It leads to very tightly coupled markup and styles, or a lot of presentational classes. We'll cover why both of those are bad in later chapters, but for now just know it's not really a realistic idea beyond very simple designs.

For that reason, setting vertical rhythm on images is the perfect candidate for some JavaScript to handle the calculations in a way that doesn't require any additional CSS or classes.

 I've actually written a small jQuery plugin called Rhythmic that does exactly that. You can find it at `https://GitHub.com/lukewatts/rhythmic`.

Lastly, these problems aren't only with images. You'll find other elements will often break your vertical rhythm, such as videos, embedded content, and advertisements.

Basically, vertical rhythm is hard, even with tools such as Compass to ease the way. With all that said, let's continue getting this page looking right. I'll leave it up to you to decide if you think vertical rhythm is something you want to use yourself.

Breakpoints and media queries

I can already feel many readers cringe at the thought of writing media queries for every 100px. A breakpoint for 420px, 520px, and 620px?! Many of you will have a very strict set of numbers you associate with breakpoints and media queries. Generally, these are 320px, 768px, 960px, 1024px, 1140px, 1280px, and any combination of these.

I was the same for a long time. I strived to fit my content into the *most common device sizes* or popular framework conventions. This include device orientation such as portrait and landscape. However, more often than not we shouldn't aim to fit the device. The device shouldn't be our prime concern, the content should. In this case we're not worried about how our image looks at 768px. We're worried about when we need it to grow to fit our content and our vertical rhythm the best. That just happens to be about 420px. So our next rule in `screen.scss` will be as follows:

```
// mastering-sass/ch03/scss/screen.scss
.vertical-rhythm[height="300"][width="600"] {
    height: rhythm(6);
    width: auto;
    display: block;
    @media (min-width: 420px) {
        height: rhythm(8);
        width: auto;
        display: block;
    }
}
```

Now, we've used `width: auto` and `display: block` once already, and they're going to be required for all of our `vertical-rhythm` classes, so let's move it in its own rule so we don't need to keep repeating it.

Just above our first `vertical-rhythm` rule, add the following:

```
// mastering-sass/ch03/scss/screen.scss
.vertical-rhythm {
    display: block;
    width: auto;
```

```
}

.vertical-rhythm[height="300"][width="600"] {
    height: rhythm(6);

    @media (min-width: 420px) {
        height: rhythm(8);
    }
}
```

For brevity's sake, I'm going to add the rest of our media queries together here. That way we can move on to the other image and also giving our headings correct sizes:

```
// mastering-sass/ch03/scss/screen.scss
.vertical-rhythm[height="300"][width="600"] {
    height: rhythm(6);

    @media (min-width: 420px) {
        height: rhythm(8);
    }

    @media (min-width: 520px) {
        height: rhythm(10);
    }

    @media (min-width: 620px) {
        height: rhythm(12);
    }
}
```

I think I can safely assume you understand the process for the next image. This also clarifies why we need to use our height and width attributes to target images correctly. Inside *index.html*, add the height and width attributes to the second image and add the class of vertical-rhythm:

```
// mastering-sass/ch03/index.html
<p>
<img src="http://placehold.it/300x200" alt="Image from Placehold.it"
style="float:left;" height="300" width="200" class="vertical-rhythm">
Lorem ipsum dolar sit amet...
```

Fortunately, our images maximum width is 300, so we don't need to add any media queries. This one rule will do:

```
// mastering-sass/ch03/scss/screen.scss
.vertical-rhythm[height="200"][width="300"] {
    height: rhythm(8);
}
```

Aspect ratio

This is where the aspect ratio and the dimensions of the image are important. For an image with an original width of 300px and height of 200px, our new height will be `rhythm(8)`, or 12em. However, an image of 300px width and 500px height requires its own calculations. This means to write CSS that deals with all possible image proportions is simply not realistic. So I want to stress that you should look at a JavaScript alternative instead of using CSS for vertical rhythm on elements such as images, video, and embedded material.

Sizing our headings

Let's move on to adjusting our headings font sizes, and then we'll move away from vertical rhythm. To adjust our heading sizes, we'll need to let Compass know we want to adjust their size in relation to the vertical rhythm we've defined. For this, we use the `adjust-font-size-to` mixin.

We'll also want to use the default heading sizes from the last chapter. However, this time we'll be multiplying them by our `$base-font-size` variable in order to get the pixel value. Remember, Compass uses pixels in all of its vertical rhythm mixins. So let's create a list with our heading sizes so we can loop through it to create our headings:

```
// mastering-sass/ch03/scss/screen.scss
$base-heading-sizes: (2, 1.5, 1.17, 1, 0.83, 0.67);
```

Now we can loop through each of items in this list and create all of our headings by multiplying the values by our `$base-font-size`, which will give us the pixel values for each heading:

```
// mastering-sass/ch03/scss/screen.scss
@for $i from 1 through 6 {
    h#{$i} {
        @include adjust-font-size-to($base-font-size * nth($base-heading-sizes, $i));
    }
}
```

If we take a look at our *style.css* file, we can see the generated CSS looks like this:

```
// mastering-sass/ch03/assets/css/screen.css
h1 {
  font-size: 2em;
  line-height: 1.5em;
}
```

```
h2 {
  font-size: 1.5em;
  line-height: 2em;
}

h3 {
  font-size: 1.17em;
  line-height: 1.28205em;
}

h4 {
  font-size: 1em;
  line-height: 1.5em;
}

h5 {
  font-size: 0.83em;
  line-height: 1.80723em;
}

h6 {
  font-size: 0.67em;
  line-height: 2.23881em;
}
```

Check *index.html* in the browser, and everything should still line up nicely with our grid. The last thing is to give our paragraphs a trailing margin to separate them from the next paragraph. Once again, Compass has a mixin for this. In fact, depending on your preferences, Compass allows you to add a margin or padding to the top or the bottom of elements, allowing you total flexibility. I like to have the margin at the end of my paragraphs, so I'll use the `trailer` mixin. If you want a margin before an element, you should use the `leader` mixin:

```
// mastering-sass/ch03/scss/screen.scss
p {
  // This tells Compass we want one line to be added after our paragraphs
  @include trailer(1);
}
```

In the next part, we'll move from our local files to and try out some online code environments that allow for writing Sass and Compass without worrying about files.

CodePen or SassMeister

I'm a big fan of CodePen. Ever since I first discovered it I've used it for testing ideas, trying out new frameworks, finding inspiration, and for tutorials. If you're not familiar with CodePen, it's like social media for web developers. You create something and other users can view it, like it, comment on it, follow you, and even fork your pen and work on it themselves. You can find CodePen at `https://CodePen.io`.

SassMeister is great for…Sass! SassMeister, unlike CodePen, it is designed solely for Sass and libraries built on Sass. In fact, if you open up the **Control Panel** and scroll down through the `Extensions` available, you'll see how many libraries SassMeister can use by default. SassMeister also allows you to try out the most up-to-date versions of Ruby and LibSass.

 LibSass is a library that allows the porting of Sass to other environments/languages, such as JavaScript, Python, Go, Scala, and Perl, to name a few. However, there are some features of Ruby Sass that are not currently present in LibSass.

Both CodePen and SassMeister can use Compass. To do so, you simply need to import it at the top of your project. Both also allow writing HTML using Jade, Haml, Markdown, and other templating languages.

Both sites also allow logging in with your GitHub account. However, unlike SassMeister, CodePen allows you to save and name your pens, and give them descriptions and tags. SassMeister, when logged in through GitHub, lets you save your work to Gists.

SassMeister also allows converting SCSS to Sass (and vice versa) by simply switching to syntax in the Control Panel. CodePen does not currently do this. Also, because SassMeister is all about Sass, I'll be using SassMeister for these examples. You can, of course, use CodePen if you prefer. You can find SassMeister at `http://www.SassMeister.com/`.

Getting setup

If you are signed up with GitHub, I recommend logging in through SassMeister so you can save your work to a Gist. Next, open the control panel and make sure **Ruby 3.4.x** is selected in the Compiler drop-down menu. Then select which Syntax you prefer.

I'll be showing the examples in the SCSS format; however, because it is so easy to convert SCSS to Sass and back in SassMeister, I would say use whichever syntax you prefer. Again, the original Sass syntax will allow you to work much faster, seeing as there is far less typing involved. Finally, select Compass from the extensions and it will import the entire Compass library:

```
@import "compass";
```

CSS3, Compass, and Vendor prefixes

Compass became popular when CSS3 properties were still not largely supported by browsers. By this, I mean browsers such as Firefox, Chrome, Internet Explorer, and Opera (before they selflessly switched to Webkit) required *vendor prefixes*. It wasn't uncommon to see something like this in many places of a stylesheet:

```
.element-with-rounded-corners {
    -webkit-border-radius: 5px;
     -khtml-border-radius: 5px;
       -moz-border-radius: 5px;
        -ms-border-radius: 5px;
         -o-border-radius: 5px;
            border-radius: 5px;
}
```

Of course, this is a wild exaggeration (I think). However, I can remember writing some CSS for the more *experimental* CSS3 properties which weren't far off this. The point is, Compass arrived and saved us from the inevitable carpal tunnel syndrome these CSS rules were bound to give many of us. Instead of writing the preceding code, we only had to write the following:

```
.element-with-rounded-corners {
    @include border-radius(5px);
}
```

Then Compass would generate the necessary vendor prefixes. It was a revelation. Once I started using it I refused to writing plain CSS with vendor prefixes from then on. However, it also meant people simply stopped keeping up to date with which browsers were actually supporting fully, myself included. After all, vendor prefixes are only a temporary step, while browser implementations and the official W3C spec *sync up*. Eventually, modern browsers simply drop the prefix as the property or feature becomes fully supported. It does take time, but it does happen. And in the case of many of the Compass CSS3 mixins, it has already happened.

Background-clip, background-origin, border-radius, box-shadow, box-sizing, gradients, opacity, text-shadow, and transition are all fully supported in modern browsers as of 2016. Even Flex (otherwise Flexbox) is fully supported in everything but IE11 and lower.

> Flex is supported in IE10 and IE11; however, a few bugs mean I wouldn't recommend using Flex for a website without fallback for IE11 or below.

That leaves animation (keyframes, animation-duration, animation-timing-function, animation-delay, and so on), CSS Regions, columns, and transforms that still require prefixes for modern browsers, such as Firefox, Chrome, Opera, iOS, or Safari. And out of those, transforms, animations, and occasionally columns are the only ones I've ever used, most likely in that order.

CSS regions

CSS regions were/are a really cool idea; however, they seem to be taking forever to gain support in browsers, even partial support. The reason for this may be due to the fact they're a bit complicated compared to other CSS concepts, they have performance issues, and they are deemed by many to break semantics.

The reason is that CSS regions allowed content to flow between numerous elements. You could tell a block of text that you wanted it to flow from one element into another element under certain conditions. This could even be to flow into or around a CSS shape.

> CSS shapes by themselves are a separate feature that is in the *candidate recommendation* phase, which means it's likely they will be implemented in browsers. Fingers crossed.

This meant CSS regions would allow the creation of complex magazine-like layouts with text. However, many saw this as an entirely presentational feature that caused many heated debates and articles about why they were bad. So, for those reasons, I feel they're not worth covering here.

Columns

Columns are similar in that they allow text to flow between multiple columns. However, the fundamental difference is they do not use multiple elements to do this. Instead, one element is styled to *look* like multiple columns, and the text simply flows naturally between these columns. Confused? Let's take a look at columns in SassMeister.

First, in the HTML panel, create an article element with a class of `newspaper-article`. Inside, place five paragraphs with some text (`Lorem ipsum` or whatever text you want):

```
<article class="newspaper-article">
  <p>Lorem ipsum dolor sit amet ... </p>
  <p>Nam ut auctor odio, a consectetur arcu ... </p>
  <p>In convallis dui eu euismod tempus ... </p>
  <p>Quisque et nibh at est ... </p>
</article>
```

Now we want our text to be in four columns. So the mixin for that is simply `column-count($number-of-colums)`. So, in your SCSS panel, let's place this mixin inside our `newspaper-article` rule:

```
.newspaper-article {
    @include column-count(4);
}
```

In the CSS panel, you can see we now have our vendor prefixes for Chrome/Opera/Safari (`-webkit-`) and Firefox (`-moz-`), as well as the default:

```
.newspaper-article {
    -moz-column-count: 4;
    -webkit-column-count: 4;
    column-count: 4;
}
```

Looks good right? Pretty straightforward too. However, we do have a problem. Open your Web Developer Tools in your browser and, using your Responsive Design Mode (Firefox) or Device Mode (Chrome), change the screen width to 320px. Then click on **Result** to view our design. You'll see we still have four really narrow columns. Not good.

So we need a way to make sure the columns never get below 320px wide. You might think we need media queries here, but that's where columns really make things easy. Instead of needing numerous media queries that explicitly say how many columns we want at each size, we can simply give our columns a minimum width, or more accurately an optimal width. To do this, we'll use `column-width($width-of-column)`. A good width in this case is 15em, but for different numbers of columns and different container widths you'll need to experiment with the `column-width` value to get the best results:

```
.newspaper-article {
    @include column-count(4);
    @include column-width(15em);
}
```

Now, if you view the result again in your browser at 320px, you'll see the text is full width. Now slowly drag the width out and you'll see that somewhere about 510 – 515px you'll have two columns. This is because around 513px or so, there is enough room for two columns of 15em width. If you keep increasing your screen width at about 768px you'll have three columns. Keep going, and eventually you'll have three columns again. So columns are inherently responsive when they have a width. Pretty sweet.

That's not all we can do with columns. We can also increase the gap between columns if we want. To do that, we can use the `column-gap` mixin. Let's say we want a gap of 2em:

```
.newspaper-article {
    text-align: justify;
    @include column-count(4);
    @include column-width(15em);
    @include column-gap(2em);
}
```

I've also justified the text to better show the space between each column. Finally, we can a rule, or line between our columns. This is the same as a border. It takes a width, style, and a color. For this we use the `column-rule` mixin. Let's add a light grey solid 1px line between our columns:

```
.newspaper-article {
    text-align: justify;
    @include column-count(4);
    @include column-width(15em);
    @include column-gap(2em);
    @include column-rule(1px solid darken(#fff, 20%));
}
```

Those are the main options with columns. It's not complicated by any means. Each property is named in a way that makes sense. There is one more property you can use, however…the shorthand, which is just "columns". Columns allows you to define the width and number of columns in the same property. One thing to note is this is one parameter. So this will work:

```
@include columns(4 15em);
```

But this will not:

```
@include columns(4, 15em);
```

This is to allow the values to be in any order.

There are further properties, such as `column-span` and `column-break`; however, support is poor for these, so I wouldn't recommend using them.

Transforms

I find transform mixins to be the most useful CSS3 mixins in Compass, not only because of the vendor prefixing, but because they allow simplifying the properties into their individual functions. For example, transform allows you to rotate, scale, translate (or move), skew, and even add perspective to an element. The only problem with this is they are all used in the transform property. Take, for example, a simple rotate of 45 degrees clockwise, with an origin in the top left. To achieve this with the necessary vendor prefixes, you would need to write the following:

```
-moz-transform: rotate(45deg);
-ms-transform: rotate(45deg);
-webkit-transform: rotate(45deg);
transform: rotate(45deg);
-moz-transform-origin: top left;
-ms-transform-origin: top left;
-webkit-transform-origin: top left;
transform-origin: top left;
```

However, with Compass we can simply write the following:

```
@include rotate;
@include transform-origin(top, left);
```

This would output the above transform with our vendor prefixes. You'll notice also we didn't specify 45 degrees in our rotate mixin. This is because Compass has variables which have the defaults already set for each transform properties value. For example, the default angle for rotations is as follows:

```
$default-rotate: 45deg;
```

If we knew we wanted our transform origin to always be top left, we could set our `$origin-x` and `$origin-y` configuration variables:

```
$default-origin-x: top;
$default-origin-y: left
```

So let's create a simple element which we can perform some transforms on. We'll make a `div` with a class of `transform-me` that contains the text `Transform Me!`. The text won't be in a paragraph tag or anything else:

```
<div class="transform-me">
    Transform me!
</div>
```

Next, we'll want some way to see the size and the edge of our element. We'll also center the text just to appease the designer in us all:

```
.transform-me {
    border: 2px solid red;
    width: 10em;
    line-height: 10em;
    text-align: center;
}
```

Now let's add the rotate we had in the previous example:

```
.transform-me {
    border: 2px solid red;
    width: 10em;
    line-height: 10em;
    text-align: center;
    @include rotate;
    @include transform-origin(top, left);
}
```

Let's replace the `transform-origin` mixin with a translate with a value of 100px. This will move the element to the right by 100px, from the center of the element, seeing as we have reset the transform origin to its default of center:

```
.transform-me {
    border: 2px solid red;
    width: 10em;
    line-height: 10em;
    text-align: center;
    @include rotate;
    @include translate(100px);
}
```

We can see our element has moved to the right by 100px; however, our `rotate` is no longer taking effect. This is because when using these mixins, we can only use one. This makes sense. If we look at the CSS we'll see there are two `transform` properties, so it makes complete sense that only the last one will be used:

```
.transform-me {
    border: 2px solid red;
    width: 10em;
    line-height: 10em;
    text-align: center;
    -moz-transform: rotate(45deg);
    -ms-transform: rotate(45deg);
    -webkit-transform: rotate(45deg);
```

```
    transform: rotate(45deg);
    -moz-transform: translate(100px, 1em);
    -ms-transform: translate(100px, 1em);
    -webkit-transform: translate(100px, 1em);
    transform: translate(100px, 1em);
}
```

To use multiple transforms, we would need to use the `transform` mixin. Let's rotate our element and move it to the right 100px and 100px down:

```
.transform-me {
    border: 2px solid red;
    width: 10em;
    line-height: 10em;
    text-align: center;
    @include transform(rotate(45deg) translate(100px, 100px));
}
```

There's one thing to be aware of when using multiple transforms…order matters! To many of you, myself included, the result of our transform doesn't look right. I expected it to be further to the right and higher up.

What has happened here is we've rotated our element by 45 degrees first, which also means we've rotated the element's *x* (left to right) and *y* (top to bottom) axis. This means when the translate happens, instead of moving to the right and down, it moves 100px towards the bottom right and then 100px back towards the bottom left corner.

You can see the difference if you place `translate` before `rotate`:

```
.transform-me {
    border: 2px solid red;
    width: 10em;
    line-height: 10em;
    text-align: center;
    @include transform(translate(100px, 100px) rotate(45deg));
}
```

Animations

Onto animations. Animations are a lot of fun, but the best animations are subtle and well thought out. Snow White and the Seven Dwarves didn't just happen overnight. It was storyboarded and characters were designed and the story was conceived, all before any frames were created. The only reason I'm mentioning this is so you don't run off and start animating everything under the sun without giving it some thought first.

With that said, here's the idea I came up with for the simple animation we're going to do. I thought it would be cool to do a new Compass logo that has an animation to make it pop. The name Compass makes me think of someone out in the woods or exploring. They might have a Compass in one hand and maybe a flashlight in the other. So I thought it would be cool if we made the logo look as though someone had flashed a light briefly across it as if looking for something.

So there's the story. All good animations have a solid story and a purpose. So the next step is the preparation and the design of everything before we're ready to do our animation. First, let's reset everything so we can start on clean canvas, so to speak. You can find a **Reset** button at the bottom of the **Cloud** menu, where you normally **Save**, **Update**, or **View** your Gist. Once that's done, you'll need to import Compass once again. Let's simply import the CSS3 mixins, seeing as that is all we'll be using in this example:

```
@import "compass/css3";
```

Once that's done, let's give ourselves some text to work with. Create a h1 with the text COMPASS, all uppercase. The final result will look better in all caps.

Let's pretend we've been tasked with redesigning the Compass website and Chris Eppstein and the rest of the gang at Compass want the new look to sort of have that flat look with the angled drop shadows, which was all the rage in 2015...but with a difference. The Compass website has had that skeuomorphic look to it, with bevelled/grooved lines and wells for as long as anyone can remember, and now it's time for a change. The gray and red are still really nice colors, so we've all agreed it's best to keep them.

So let's put those colors in some variables above our @import so we can use them later:

```
$compass-grey: #2f2f2f;
$compass-red: #fb292d;
@import "compass/css3";
```

Now we'll need to add a background-color to the body element, center, our h1 on the page, and add some text-shadow to it. Also, let's make the text the same color as our background so our text is only defined by the text-shadow. This will give it that flat, retro style:

```
@import "compass/css3";

body {
    background-color: $compass-grey;
}

h1 {
    font-family: sans-serif;
```

```
    font-size: 5em;
    color: $compass-grey;
    text-align: center;
    text-shadow: 5px 2px 0px $compass-red;
}
```

If you ask me, that looks groovy. Let's start working on our animation. We'll need to animate our text shadow so it moves from its current position, which is 5px right along the *x* axis and 2px down on the *y* axis, around in a circle for a brief moment like a light was shone across it.

We're going to be repeating `text-shadow` quite a bit; however, we know the blur is always going to be 0, and the color will always be `$compass-red`. So let's write a mixin so we only need to pass in the x and y values. We'll call our mixin `text-shadow-xy`, seeing as Compass has a mixin called `text-shadow`, so we can't use that:

> I recommend prefixing (or namespacing) your mixins and functions to avoid name clashes. However, we'll leave prefixes out of our names for now.

```
@mixin text-shadow-xy($x-and-y) {
    text-shadow: $x-and-y 0 $compass-red;
}
```

Now, let's replace where we've set our text shadow for our h1 with our mixin, to make sure it's working:

```
h1 {
    font-family: sans-serif;
    font-size: 5em;
    color: $compass-grey;
    text-align: center;
    @include text-shadow-xy(5px 2px);
}
```

Everything still works, so we're ready to move on to our animation. Animations in CSS are done in two parts. First, we create our animation, which will have the name of the animation and `keyframes` that let us say exactly what we want to happen at various points in the animation. So let's call the Compass mixin for `keyframes`. We'll give our animation the name `animate-text-shadow`:

```
@include keyframes(animate-text-shadow) {
    // Our frames will be defined here
}
```

To call this animation, we include the animation mixin with the name of our animation and how long we want it to run for, from start to finish. We place this in our h1:

```
h1 {
    font-family: sans-serif;
    font-size: 5em;
    color: $compass-grey;
    text-align: center;
    @include text-shadow-xy(5px 2px);
    @include animation(animate-text-shadow 5s);
}
```

Now we're ready to begin adding the frames. Frames are created by using percentages. For instance, 50% of the animation is at the halfway point. So let's add an animation at 50% that changes the text-shadow to -5px along the *x* axis, and 5px on the *y* axis, essentially changing its direction briefly:

```
@include keyframes(animate-text-shadow) {
    50% {
        @include text-shadow-xy(-5px 5px);
    }
}
```

 One thing about SassMeister is that sometimes, simply changing the Sass/SCSS won't update the result or the preview panel where you view the result. So after you make the previously mentioned change, the animation will run for the first time, but after that, changing the values might not always cause an update to the preview. To force it to update, you can simply add a space to the HTML…and then next time you want to update, simply delete the space again. CodePen, however, doesn't have this problem, so if you plan to work on a lot of animation-based projects, you may want to use CodePen instead.

We don't need to specify the 0% and 100% stages because by default, if the property you are animating is present before calling the animation, those values will be used as the start and end points.

Our animation looks okay, but I think we can do better. Let's make it look like the light goes over and back more than once. To do this we'll add a frame before and after 50%. I also think it will look better if the light is from below, meaning all of our *y* axis values will be negative. So we'll also need to change our 50% frames text-shadow values:

```
@include keyframes(animate-text-shadow) {
    15% {
        @include text-shadow-xy(-10px -5px);
```

```
    }
    50% {
      @include text-shadow-xy(-5px -5px);
    }
}
```

It's looking closer to what we want, but we now need an animation the other side of 50%. Let's make it 15% from the end, so 85%. We'll also make it move to the right, so we need a positive x axis value:

```
@include keyframes(animate-text-shadow) {
    15% {
      @include text-shadow-xy(-10px -5px);
    }
    50% {
      @include text-shadow-xy(-5px -5px);
    }
    85% {
      @include text-shadow-xy(10px -5px);
    }
}
```

And that's it. There's not a whole lot to that animation, but it makes everything stand out. Animation can be used to draw the users' eye or even maintain their attention at times when you simply can't avoid a delay. Loading animations are an example of this, but you can also see many great examples of animation used on forms to keep the user interested while you submit the information and give a response. It also gives instant feedback that something is happening.

Lists

Lists are used in web design for many things. From their obvious use in creating bulleted lists, to navigation, drop-down menus, tag clouds, grids, image galleries, and structuring lengthy forms. Apart from the trust `div`, lists are perhaps the most versatile of HTML elements we have at our disposal. For this reason, Compass has a few mixins to help reduce the repetition of dealing with lists. How many times have you created a list only to remove its styling or make its lists item display in a single line for a `navbar`, let's say? You probably do it each time from scratch, too. I know I've done these things hundreds of times by now.

First, let's reset our workspace in SassMeister and create a header with a `nav` element containing an unordered list to work with. We're going to first create a `nav` menu that works well on mobile devices. The list items and links should have enough space to tap, even with the thumb.

It's important to make mobile elements *thumbable*. Yes, I made that word up. If you think about a person using a mobile, it's often held in one hand with the thumb being the only digit in use. Personally, I'm partial to using my thumbs more than holding it in one hand and poking with my other hand (maybe because I'm a gamer):

```
<header class="main-header">
  <div class="branding">
    Compass Lists
  </div>
  <nav class="main-menu">
    <ul class="main-menu-list">
      <li class="main-menu-list-item active">
        <a href="#" class="main-meu-list-item-link">Home</a></li>
      <li class="main-menu-list-item">
        <a href="#" class="main-meu-list-item-link">Services</a>
      </li>
      <li class="main-menu-list-item">
        <a href="#" class="main-meu-list-item-link">News</a>
      </li>
      <li class="main-menu-list-item">
        <a href="#" class="main-meu-list-item-link">Contact</a>
      </li>
    </ul>
  </nav>
</header>
```

Now let's import Compass and begin styling our elements and creating the variables for our colors:

```
$bg-color: #26343f;
$bg-color-darker: darken($bg-color, 5%);

$link-color: darken(white, 20%);
$link-color-hover: #2a9181;
$link-color-active: #fb292d;

@import "compass";

body {
  padding: 0;
  margin: 0;
  font-family: sans-serif;
}

.main-header {
  background-color: $bg-color;
  }
```

```
.branding {
  padding: 0 1em;
  font-size: 1.5em;
  line-height: 3;
  text-transform: uppercase;
  color: white;
}

.main-menu-list {
  padding: 0;
  margin: 0;
}

.main-menu-list-item {
  line-height: 2.75;
  padding: 0 1em;
}

.main-menu-list-item-link {
  color: $link-color;
}
```

 Normally at this point I would create a mobile menu toggle button that will allow us to open and close our menu. However, I'm not going to do this for two reasons. Firstly, SassMeister doesn't allow importing external libraries such as jQuery, so writing plain JavaScript would be too much for this simple example. Second, this isn't a book about JavaScript, even though we'll probably be making a mobile nav toggle button later, locally.

The next thing I'd like to do is get rid of those bullets. Compass has a mixin called no-bullets that does this. We place it in our ul rule, which is main-menu-list:

```
.main-menu-list {
  padding: 0;
  margin: 0;
  @include no-bullets;
}
```

At this point, I'm noticing we've reset the padding and margin in a few elements to 0. Compass has a mixin called reset-box-model that actually resets border, padding, and margin to 0, so why don't we use that? However, I also want it to be in an extend that we can reuse in future if we need to. That will mean all of our reset elements will be in one place in our exported CSS. We can create a placeholder extend by using the % sign before our extend instead of a . or #.

Place our placeholder extends rule at the top of our SCSS below the `@import` rules:

```scss
%reset-box-model {
  @include reset-box-model;
}
```

We can then use this in place of any where we have:

```scss
padding: 0;
margin: 0;
```

With the extends, our SCSS should now look like this:

```scss
$bg-color: #26343f;
$bg-color-darker: darken($bg-color, 5%);

$link-color: darken(white, 20%);
$link-color-hover: #2a9181;
$link-color-active: #fb292d;

@import "compass";

%reset-box-model {
  @include reset-box-model;
}

body {
  @extend %reset-box-model;

  font-family: sans-serif;
}

.main-header {
  background-color: $bg-color;
}

.branding {
  padding: 0 1em
  font-size: 1.5em;
  line-height: 3;
  text-transform: uppercase;
  color: white;
}

.main-menu-list {
  @extend %reset-box-model;

  @include no-bullets;
```

```scss
}

.main-menu-list-item {
  line-height: 2.75;
  padding: 0 1em;
}

.main-menu-list-item-link {
  color: $link-color;
}
```

You can see now in the CSS that our body and `.main-menu-list` are together at the top of our stylesheet.

It's always a good idea to place extends at the very top of your stylesheet. This is because the resulting CSS is placed at the point where you write your extend. You will most probably need to be able to override these properties later, so it's generally a best practice to place extends first, before your general style rules.

The next thing we need to do is give our links color. We want the active link (as in the page we're currently) on to stand out. For this, we'll use `$link-color-active` and make the list items background `$bg-color-darker`. We'll also place each of these in their own extends, seeing as `color` and `background-color` are often the most repeated properties in any stylesheet.

So, just below our `%reset-box-model` extend, place all of the color extends:

```scss
%bg-color {
  background-color: $bg-color;
}

%bg-color-darker {
  background-color: $bg-color-darker;
}

%link-color {
  color: $link-color;
}

%link-color-hover {
  color: $link-color-hover;
}

%link-color-active {
  color: $link-color-active;
```

```
}
```

Don't try get too many things into an extend. The more an extend tries to include, the less you'll be able to use it. Much like a function, extends will be most useful when they solve one small problem well. It's best to be a master of one than a jack of all.

Now we need to use our extends in our `.main-menu-list-item.active` and `.main-menu-list-item.active > .main-menu-list-item-link` rules to get the desired look. We'll nest them within our `.main-menu-list-item` rule to save ourselves some typing, seeing as these can safely be assumed to depend on this structure for this particular style:

```
.main-menu-list-item {
   line-height: 2.75;
   padding: 0 1em;

&.active {
@extend %bg-color-darker;

  .main-menu-list-item-link {
  @extend %link-color-active;
  }
 }
 }
```

Next, I'd like to remove the underline from our menu links until they are hovered over. This won't affect touch devices, but for desktop machines it will work, and overall, it will look better.

Don't remove underlines from links completely. Either have them appear on `:hover` and `:focus` states or replace the underline with some other visual sign that these are links other than color alone. Color blindness (red/green color blindness) and monochromacy (total color blindness) affects between 8 and 10 percent of people, so using color alone to show an element is in different state is never a good idea.

Compass has a mixin for this called `hover-link`, which, when placed inside a links rule, removes the underline from the link but still uses the underline on the `:hover` and `:focus` states of that link. Use this mixin in the top level rule for `.main-menu-list-item-link`, not the nested one we just made:

```
.main-menu-list-item-link {
   @extend %link-color;
   @include hover-link;
```

```
}
```

The last thing we want to do for our menu is change it to a horizontal list when our screen is wide enough to allow it. For this, we'll need a media query at 768px. We'll nest our media query and use the Compass mixin `horizontal-list` in our `.main-menu` rule to create our horizontal list:

```scss
.main-menu-list {
  @extend %reset-box-model;

  @include no-bullets;

  @media (min-width: 768px) {
    @include horizontal-list;
  }
}
```

It couldn't be easier. However, we want the list to float to the right and also to have a bit more space between the list items. By default, the `horizontal-list` mixin has 4px padding between list items and it floats the `ul` left. We want about `1em` padding and for it to float right:

```scss
.main-menu-list {
  @extend %reset-box-model;

  @include no-bullets;

  @media (min-width: 768px) {
    @include horizontal-list(1em, right);
  }
}
```

Ah, that doesn't work as expected, does it. The problem with this mixin, in my opinion, is that it applies the float to the list items instead of the `ul`. This causes the order to get switched around. That's not what we want. So we have to remove the second parameter and instead use another mixin called `float-right` to float our `.main-menu` right but leave our list-items floating left:

```scss
.main-menu-list {
  @extend %reset-box-model;

  @include no-bullets;

  @media (min-width: 768px) {
    @include float-right;
    @include horizontal-list(1em);
  }
}
```

```
}
```

That's better, but now we can see that the padding has only been applied to the right side of the first list item, Home, and only to left side of the last list item, Contact. This problem unfortunately can't be fixed with Compass. Instead, we'll have to just apply our padding-left of 1em to li:first-child and padding-right of 1em to li:last-child. So we'll also need more nested media queries. So our entire .main-menu-list rule now looks like this:

```
.main-menu-list {
  @extend %reset-box-model;

  @include no-bullets;

  @media (min-width: 768px) {
    @include float-right;
    @include horizontal-list(1em);

    &:first-child {
      padding-left: 1em;
    }
    &:last-child {
      padding-right: 1em;
    }
  }
}
```

We then float our branding div, which has our site name of **Compass lists**, to the left to get everything inside our header:

```
.branding {
  padding: 0 1em;
  font-size: 1.5em;
  line-height: 3;
  text-transform: uppercase;
  color: white;

  @media (min-width: 768px) {
    @include float-left;
  }
}
```

Now, however, you'll notice we have another problem…our header looks to have no background-color. This is, in fact, due to the floats we've used on all of the elements within our .main-header element.

Floating is a hack

When you float elements, you essentially lift them out of the natural flow of the document. The original (and the only true) purpose of floats is to float images or elements inside a block of text to allow the text to float around it. So every time we float elements to get them slide into a row of columns, we're using a hack. This is why we need to use another hack known commonly as `clearfix`.

When you float all of an elements' child elements, the parent element (`.main-header` in this case) thinks it has nothing in it anymore, and its height collapses. This is the correct behavior for block-level elements. The simplest way to fix this is to apply `overflow: hidden` to the parent element (that is, the collapsed element).

Compass has a `clearfix` mixin that uses this method, so we'll include that in our `.main-header` rule. Again, we only require this on screens of `768px` and wider:

```
.main-header {
  background-color: $bg-color;

  @media (min-width: 768px) {
    @include clearfix;
  }
}
```

There you have it, our mobile-first navigation. Of course, it needs work. It needs more styling on both small and large screens, perhaps more breakpoints, and also some JavaScript/jQuery to allow toggling on mobile devices.

Tag clouds

Finally, we're going to take a look at the Compass mixin for creating tag clouds. Tag clouds are a popular feature of CMS, news and article-based websites, and blogs. Basically, a tag cloud is a list of categories or tags on a website. They are useful for showing what topics your content covers, and also which of those topics or terms is most popular, or most commonly used.

We're going to create a component called `tag-cloud-component`. Our tag cloud will contain the terms and topics covered in this chapter. So our HTML will a `div` with a class `tag-cloud-component`. Inside that we'll have an ordered list with a class `tag-cloud` and our tags will be alphabetical.

We're using an ordered list seeing as tag clouds are generally in an order, whether alphabetical or by popularity. Ours will be alphabetical; however, we'll display popularity with increases and decreases in font size:

```
<div class="tag-cloud-component">
  <ol class="tag-cloud">
    <li>Animation</li>
    <li>Breakpoints</li>
    <li>Clearfix</li>
    <li>Columns</li>
    <li>Compass</li>
    <li>Console</li>
    <li>CSS</li>
    <li>Float</li>
    <li>Functions</li>
    <li>Lists</li>
    <li>Media Queries</li>
    <li>Mixins</li>
    <li>Ruby</li>
    <li>Sass</li>
    <li>SCSS</li>
    <li>Transform</li>
    <li>Typography</li>
    <li>Variables</li>
    <li>Vertical Rhythm</li>
  </ol>
</div>
```

Next, we'll need to import Compass again. We'll also make sure our `$base-font-size` is set to 16px again:

```
$base-font-size: 16px;

@import "compass";
```

We want our `tag-cloud-component` to have a `max-width` of 20em:

```
.tag-cloud-component {
  max-width: 20em;
}
```

Now, to style our tag cloud, we want to remove the bullets (or numbers in this case) and make the ordered list an inline list. We'll use the `no-bullets` mixin and also the `inline-list` mixin. The `inline-list` mixin is not the same as the `horizontal-list` mixin we used to create our navigation menu in our previous example.

The `horizontal-list` mixin floats list items left, while preventing them from wrapping. The `inline-list` mixin creates one line, like a sentence, from our list using the `display: inline` property, hence the name:

```
.tag-cloud {
  @include no-bullets;
  @include inline-list;
}
```

Now we simply add our `tag-cloud` mixin and pass it our `$base-font-size`:

```
.tag-cloud {
  @include no-bullets;
  @include inline-list;
  @include tag-cloud($base-font-size);
}
```

We pass it our base font size because the `tag-cloud` mixin actually creates the rules for additional sizes to be applied to the list items within our tag cloud. This means we can size them by popularity. This is a common design pattern for tag clouds. If you look at the CSS generated you'll see we have `.xxs`, `.xs`, `.s`, `.l`, `.xl`, and `.xxl` classes we can now apply to our list items in our HTML. Let's go ahead and apply the class names to some of the list items in a random order to see the result:

```
<div class="tag-cloud-component">
  <ol class="tag-cloud">
    <li class="s">Animation</li>
    <li>Breakpoints</li>
    <li class="xs">Clearfix</li>
    <li class="xxs">Columns</li>
    <li class="xxl">Compass</li>
    <li class="l">Console</li>
    <li class="xl">CSS</li>
    <li class="xs">Float</li>
    <li class="l">Functions</li>
    <li>Lists</li>
    <li class="xl">Media Queries</li>
    <li class="l">Mixins</li>
    <li>Ruby</li>
    <li class="xxl">Sass</li>
    <li>SCSS</li>
    <li>Transform</li>
    <li class="xxl">Typography</li>
    <li class="xl">Variables</li>
    <li class="l">Vertical Rhythm</li>
  </ol>
</div>
```

That's it. A `tag-cloud` in only a few minutes.

Sticky footer, stretching, and sprites

I was torn between including the `sticky-footer` mixin and the mixins for stretching elements to fit their containing parent element. In the end I've decided not to include them, the reason being, they are all hacks to solve problems that have since been solved by Flexbox in much simpler and cleaner ways, especially the `sticky-footer` mixin, which even requires additional HTML to be included for it to work.

I'm not saying they're bad. Each of these mixins offers brilliant and useful solutions to these problems. However, Flexbox has completely removed the necessity for these mixins. For that reason I've decided not to cover the sticky footer or stretching mixins.

I also left out the spriting features in Compass from this chapter. Compass sprites are impressive. I can remember being blown away by them when I discovered Compass. However, for almost every situation you find you're creating sprites I would strongly recommend you look into SVG instead. That's not true for every situation, of course, but SVG is the future. It's accessible, responsive, SVG can be animated, and you can create SVG sprites. Where it makes sense to make an image sprite, it almost always makes more sense to use SVG instead.

Compass and the future

It's important to realize Compass began at a time when IE6 was still a concern for designers. You only need to look through the documentation and you'll see numerous IE6 and 7 hacks are still present in its codebase. While there still may be a small percentage actually using IE6 and 7, this shows that Compass is perhaps coming to the end of its usefulness.

In my opinion, the rapid adoption of Flexbox and SVG coupled with the decreasing need for vendor prefixing will reduce the need for Compass drastically in 2016-2017. This might seem sad to some people, but I think we should be happy. That means we no longer need as many hacks to make our designs. That means we're moving in the right direction as an industry.

Summary

In this chapter we looked at numerous features of the Compass framework. We looked at setting up a project using Compass and the benefits of knowing how to take full control of this process. We looked at the typography helpers for creating a vertical rhythm and discussed the challenges that Compass overcomes when creating a vertical rhythm in a design. We also looked at some online code editors that allow you to quickly and easily write Sass and Compass, such as SassMeister and CodePen, and we compared the two.

We also looked at the issue of vendor prefixes and how Compass helps eliminate having to write and maintain them on your projects. We also looked at using Compass to simplify creating an animation and also tag clouds, lists, and unstyled links. We also spoke about the possibility that Compass is nearing its "end of life" cycle. Perhaps that's for the best.

In the next chapter, we'll take a break from writing Sass and Compass and look at some of the theory and concepts you'll need to know to write better CSS. Better CSS knowledge will result in better Sass. We'll also take a look at some of the most popular methodologies of writing modular, maintainable, scalable CSS and you'll see how they all aim to overcome the same problems.

4
CSS and HTML – SMACSS, OOCSS and Semantics

In this chapter we'll talk about some CSS and HTML concepts which are vital to a good Sass workflow. While Sass exists to simplify writing CSS, it won't teach you the concepts that makes clean, scalable, reusable CSS. For that, you need to understand some basic concepts and methodologies such as BEM, OOCSS, SMACSS, and Atomic Design.

We'll look at some of the downsides of using CSS frameworks such as Bootstrap and Foundation. Frameworks such as these are not semantic and can often make your HTML and CSS bloated and rigid, making projects harder to maintain if the design changes.

We'll examine what makes HTML semantic and why this is something beneficial. Semantics will allow for cleaner markup, cleaner CSS, and easier maintainability and customization in both.

Next, we'll explore the benefits of using a naming convention in your HTML and CSS. We'll use the methodology of Block Element Modifier (**BEM**) to understand the benefits of using a naming convention. These include reusability and maintainability in our HTML and CSS.

We'll look at the most popular methodologies of writing reusable, scalable, modular CSS such as OOCSS, SMACSS, and Atomic Design. We'll work toward understanding the problems they aim to solve so we can take the best parts of each, rather than using each one as is. After we've done this we will be able to use the best parts of each for our own purposes.

We'll look at using the **Hue Saturation Lightness** (**HSL**) color model rather than hex codes or RGB. The benefit of using HSL is a more natural, intuitive way of using color in CSS. However, it does have a downside if you are using a program such as Adobe Photoshop or Sketch for designing concepts.

The good and the bad of CSS grids

I've heard it said that *CSS isn't hard*. I can't say I agree with that. Good CSS isn't hard...bad CSS will ruin your life! Whether it's your own badly written CSS or its badly written CSS you've inherited from someone else, we've all been there. We've all opened a CSS file to make a small change and had to use `!important` for some properties to get our change to work.

Sadly, there's a lot of bad CSS out there. It's becoming the case that if someone is creating anything more than a very small website, the first step is to go get a CDN link to Bootstrap or Foundation. That'll save loads of hassle, right? Not always. In fact, I'd say that's rarely the case.

With one word you can strike fear into the hearts of anyone who's overly reliant on a HTML/CSS framework such as Bootstrap or Foundation: redesign. To redesign a website that is strongly based on columns and rows means there can be no such thing as a redesign. A redesign for a website built heavily on a row/column-based grid will actually mean a rebuild. Redesign means changing your CSS. A rebuild means changing your HTML and then also your CSS.

I believe if your content requirements haven't changed then you should not need to change your HTML to do a redesign. In an ideal world we should all leave our HTML alone aside from adding new content and we should only change our CSS to inflict design and layout changes. Check out CSS Zen Gardens as a prime example of this principle: `http://www.css zengarden.com`.

To do this, we need to name our HTML classes to reflect our page elements and content, not what they look like or where they go. Take this example.

```
<div class="row">
    <div class="col-sm-12 col-md-6">
        <article class="post">
        ...
        </article>
    </div>
    <div class="col-sm-12 col-md-6">
        <article class="post">
        ...
        </article>
    </div>
</div>
```

We know from looking at this piece of markup exactly where these elements will be, from an aesthetic perspective. However, if I say to you now that I want three articles in a row instead, it means changing the classes as well as adding the necessary HTML.

First, we would need to change the classes that are on the div wrapping our article elements to col-md-3. Then we would need to add another div to wrap the article we want to add.

We could remove the need to add or change classes with this markup instead:

```
<div class="posts">
    <article class="post">
    ...
    </article>
    <article class="post">
    ...
    </article>
    <article class="post">
    ...
    </article>
</div>
```

I can add more articles with ease and simply change one property in CSS to have four in a row instead of three. This keeps our markup for content and our CSS for design and layout changes:

```
.posts {
    overflow: hidden;
}

.post {
    float: left;
    width: 25%;
    padding: 1em;
}
```

CSS frameworks can make certain simple things become unnecessarily complex. I would only recommend you watch out for times when the use of a grid system means unnecessary markup. If the thought of a redesign means deleting or adding HTML, then chances are your HTML is doing something it's not meant to be doing.

Semantics

Semantics simply refers to something's meaning. What does this symbolize? Take the copyright symbol. We know what that means when we see it. We also know the @ symbol means *at*. These are examples of good semantics. These symbols have a clear purpose and meaning. We can use them with confidence that people will instantly understand what we mean, or what we want to say when we use them.

Writing semantics HTML simply means our elements should be used for the purposes they were intended. Lists should contain groups of similar items and content, headings should explain the content they're placed before, paragraphs should contain text (and should not be used to separate elements simply because they have a margin), and tables should contain tabular data and not be used for layout purposes.

These are semantics. However, where the semantics argument has divided people is whether class names and IDs describe the content also, or is it alright to have class names such as `f-l p-10 w-1-4`?

I've seen frameworks with the preceding class names (or similar), such as Atomic CSS (`http ://acss.io`). To me, doing this would feel like a step above using inline styles: `style="float:left;padding:10px;width:25%"`. It makes sense when you know `p` means padding and `f` means float and everything after the dashes are your values; however, it turns your HTML into a real mess. This would be bad semantics.

One sign you may be writing unsemantic class names is the use of classes to style elements. Take this example:

```
<button class="button primary large">SEND</button>
<span class="error message large is-hidden">There was an error</span>
```

We can assume the error message is hidden because of the class of `is-hidden`. That's fine, it's telling us what the state is, and it's most likely necessary for JavaScript to hide or show it upon an error. We know it's an error message because of the class' `error message`. That's also not too bad, although `error-message` would be better. What if we use a class of `message` elsewhere? Would changing it mean an unwanted change to `error message`?

The real problem here is the use of `large` on both our button and our error message. Does this mean our button has large text, uppercase letters, and a lot of padding? Does that mean that's the same for the error message? We can't know without looking at the CSS. Sure, we can view the page in the browser, but semantics is about our markup being independent of design and layout.

The simplest test I can think of to determine if your HTML is semantic is just to imagine deleting your CSS files completely. Then look at your HTML and ask yourself if your class names still make sense? If not, then you've named your classes based upon your CSS and not your content.

A side effect of strongly semantic naming conventions would be less HTML. When you don't need to add divs just for rows, or columns, or clearfixing, you'll drastically reduce the amount of HTML you write.

Naming conventions

You've probably noticed some patterns in the class names I use and also the way I name variables and mixins and functions. Chances are you're not a fan of the long names I use. I get that. I do.

The first time I came across a strict naming convention for class names was something called BEM. **BEM** stands for **Block, Element, Modifier**. Chances are you've come across it. The naming convention for BEM looks like this:

```
.block__element--modifier {...}
```

The first time I came across BEM I stopped reading once I saw the rather verbose names it used. "Yuk!" I proclaimed and rapidly closed the tab. The thought of typing all those underscores and hyphens. No thank you.

However, I kept hearing about this BEM methodology and seeing it in tutorials and other people's code. Gradually, I realized the important part of BEM is not the exact naming convention it uses…it's the concepts. The problems it aims to solve and how it solves them. It can be broken down into one word, convention. A convention, not *the* convention.

So I kept *convention* in mind as I worked on future projects and after many variations I've settled on the naming convention I use today. I haven't given it a catchy name or anything like that, but if I had to I guess it would BEE… Essentially I name things by Block, Element, Element, Element, Element, and so on. I dropped the modifier part for one reason. Modifiers are to do with state. Modifier names would be *visible, hidden, disabled, checked*, and so on. The reason I don't like to tie those directly into a class name is because you can then simply have one class in one place in your style sheet and use JavaScript to add them dynamically when needed:

```
.is-hidden {
    display: none;
}
```

```
.is-visible {
    display: block;
}
```

Beyond that, I completely agree with the benefits of naming *components* or *modules* with the block or root element of that component first. It allows for possible reuse and compartmentalization. This means a *block* has no dependencies. The only dependencies with a BEM-like naming convention are planned and expected. Take the following HTML:

```
<div class="product">
    <img src="http://placehold.it/150x150" alt="Image of Product"
class="image">
    <div class="details">
    <h2 class="title"><a href="#" class="link">Product Name</a></h2>
        <div class="price">
            <span class="total">€55.00</span>
            <span class="sale"><del>€65.00</del></span>
        </div>
        <div class="description">
            <p>Lorem ipsum...</p>
        </div>
    </div>
</div>
```

We can see what's going on here easily enough when we look at the HTML. You can tell there's a container element called `product` and inside that there's an image that is possibly floated left or right, or not. It doesn't matter right now. There's `"details"`. So we can safely assume that's the details of the product, obviously, because it's inside our product. Then we have `"title"`, `"price"`, `"total"`, `"sale"`, and `"description"`.

These things all make perfect sense. They're in context. Show this to anyone who knows basic HTML and has seen an e-commerce website and they'll instantly form a picture in their head. This is semantic markup. What about the CSS (or SCSS)?

```
.product {
    padding: 1em;
}

.image {
    float: left;
    margin-right: 1em;
}

.title {
    margin-top: 0;
}
```

```
.link {
    text-decoration: none;
    color: inherit;
}

.sale {
    margin-left: 1em;
    opacity: 0.5;
}
```

Could you show someone this CSS and ask them what it's doing without looking at the HTML/ No. Definitely not. You can't even tell these are the same component. How do we fix this? We could nest everything couldn't we? Ok let's do that:

```
.product {
    padding: 1em;
    .image {
        float: left;
        margin-right: 1em;
    }

    .title {
        margin-top: 0;
        .link {
            text-decoration: none;
            color: inherit;
        }
    }

    .sale {
        margin-left: 1em;
        opacity: 0.5;
    }
}
```

That does indeed indicate the context. We can now tell our product block contains an image and it's floated left. We have a title that contains a link, and a sale element that is at half opacity, so we can assume it's of less importance to its surroundings. We can't tell what other elements are in this product block because they don't have styles, but that's fine.

So where's the problem? Well, notice in our "title" element we have color: inherit. So what would happen if somewhere above this in our SCSS someone adds these two rules?

```
$theme-primary-color: lighten(blue, 25%);

.title {
    color: $theme-primary-color;
```

```
}

h2 {
    color: black;
}
```

We're inheriting our color from the parent element, which is "title", but it's also a h2. H2 comes last so is the link now black, or is it light blue? Did we intend for it to inherit from outside of our "product" block?

This is the problem with simply nesting without a purposeful naming convention. With generic class names we do achieve semantic markup, but our CSS needs to be nested, to give it context. However, even with nesting, if our names are too generic we could end up with unexpected results from specificity and the cascade. These unexpected results are incredibly difficult to isolate and remedy at times.

So let's change our class names so they clearly tell us what block each element belongs to:

```
<div class="product">
    <img src="http://placehold.it/150x150" alt="Image of Product"
class="product-image">
    <div class="product-details">
    <h2 class="product-title"><a href="#" class="product-title-
link">Product Name</a></h2>
        <div class="product-price">
            <span class="product-total">€55.00</span>
            <span class="product-sale"><del>€65.00</del></span>
        </div>
        <div class="product-description">
            <p>Lorem ipsum...</p>
        </div>
    </div>
</div>
```

We can now write our SCSS without needing to nest anything:

```
$theme-primary-color: lighten(blue, 25%);

.title {
    color: $theme-primary-color;
    font-size: 6em;
}

h2 {
    color: black;
}
```

```
.product {
    padding: 1em;
}
.product-image {
    float: left;
    margin-right: 1em;
}

.product-title {
    margin-top: 0;
}
.product-title-link {
    text-decoration: none;
    color: inherit;
}

.product-sale {
    margin-left: 1em;
    opacity: 0.5;
}
```

There is, however, a lot of repetition in writing "product" over and over again. I agree. So we can make use of the parent selector and nesting to DRY everything up:

```
.product {
    padding: 1em;
    &-image {
        float: left;
        margin-right: 1em;
    }

    &-title {
        margin-top: 0;
        &-link {
            text-decoration: none;
            color: inherit;
        }
    }

    &-sale {
        margin-left: 1em;
        opacity: 0.5;
    }
}
```

That's our product block. Now we can reuse this, not only throughout our current website, but on future projects. It becomes reusable because its isolated from everything outside of it's "root" or containing element.

In this case it's product, but with this convention any block we create could be reused. This idea of reusability and isolation from surrounding elements is one of the key principles of another popular methodology called **OOCSS**.

OOCSS – Object-Oriented CSS

What is OOCSS? OOCSS is a methodology of writing modular, scalable CSS. It was pioneered by Nicole Sullivan (otherwise known as stubbornella) in 2008/2009. Much like BEM, OOCSS is built on a few straightforward concepts. First, separation of structure from skin, and second, separation of container from content.

Separation of structure from skin

This sounds more complicated than it actually is. The truth is, every web designer does this without even thinking. Let's just imagine I've asked you to create the header for a website about bananas. It will have a logo on the left and a search bar on the right, and following that, the navbar. Nothing new here, right?

You'll instinctively ask three important questions as you work out each component of this design feature. "What size is it, where does it go, and what does it look like?". For the header container you'll probably think, what width and height should this header be? So we'll make it 100% wide. As for the height, hopefully you understand by now that should always be determined by the content, not the container. So we've got a full width header now but nothing in it to give it height. Next you might turn your attention to the logo. Maybe it has its own container, maybe not. Either way the image or the container will have to float left because the search bar has to go all the way over on the right. The image's height will give you the header height. Don't forget to clearfix your header because of the floats.

Next, we build our search bar component. We will need to put it in its own div and set that to float: right. Perhaps give that div padding and margin to position it correctly. Next we make the input an inline block so the button is on the same line as the input (we could also achieve this by floating both the input and the button left). Then we move onto our nav. We would position it, get our list items in a row, and remove bullets and unwanted margins and padding.

Let's stop there. Up until this point we've been focused on layout and positioning. Layout is the size of an element, either from the height and width properties, or line height, font size, and padding. Positioning is done with floats, display, margins, and perhaps absolute or relative positioning.

The only part up until now that wasn't all about structure was removing the bullets from our nav. Essentially, that's to do with how it looks, which brings us to **skin**.

Skin would be our theme. What fonts should we use? What background color and text colors do we want? These are the questions we ask ourselves when we are creating the skin of a component or project. This, however, is where we often blur the lines. Even though we usually ask ourselves these questions at separate times when we conceive and plan our elements, and we all think of them as very different things, often we end up merging everything together when we actually apply them in our CSS.

How many of us wrote our CSS properties alphabetically for years? It was a common practice to write CSS like this:

```css
.christmas-box {
    background-color: red;
    border: 1px solid green;
    box-sizing: border-box;
    color: white;
    display: block;
    height: 100px;
    margin: 0 auto;
    padding: 20px;
    width: 100px;
}
```

However, that's not how we think. Writing CSS like this meant we thought of elements as a group of properties instead of logically grouping the properties themselves. To write our CSS rules as we think of them, that is, in the order we build them in our minds, we would write them more like this:

```css
.christmas-box {
    /* Dimensions */
    height: 100px;
    width: 100px;
    padding: 20px;

    /* Positioning */
    box-sizing: border-box;
    display: block;
    margin: 0 auto;

    /* Theme */
    background-color: red;
    border: 1px solid green;
    color: white;
}
```

For a time, I wrote my CSS like this. Of course I don't recommend it now, but when I started doing it this way I certainly found my designs were easier to debug. By that I mean, when something went wrong with an element, I realized I was only ever having problems with two things. Elements were either of the wrong size, or they were in the wrong place. Rarely do you have serious problems with colors and theme or skin. Usually something pops out of place for some reason, or has the wrong size. For me, writing CSS like this was a big step in the right direction.

So when I discovered OOCSS, I loosely understood the benefits of separation of structure from skin. However, I was still putting them all together in one rule. This leads to more repetition, which leads to larger CSS and more difficulty in maintaining larger projects where more than one person is regularly editing the CSS.

OOCSS, instead, is based on the idea of breaking those repeated patterns on each website into reusable components. This applies to elements such as the product component we made, but also to CSS properties themselves.

In any given project you can be sure that some of the most repeated properties in CSS are `float`, `margin`, `padding`, `color`, and `background-color`. If you don't believe me just go to any popular website and open up their main stylesheet and do find (Ctrl + F or Cmd + F) for the word `float`. Depending on the size of the website you'll usually find an average of about 50 – 60 occurrences of `float: left` alone.

OOCSS explains you can save hundreds or even thousands of lines of code in your CSS by abstracting these repeated patterns into their own reusable parts. Before OOCSS adopted Sass, this was achieved with the use of very small rules which had a single purpose.

```
.float-left {
    float: left;
}
.float-right {
    float: right;
}
.clearfix {
    overflow: hidden;
}
.bg-banana-yellow {
    background-color: hsl(52, 100%, 62%);
}
```

You would then use these rules in your HTML, much like you would `row` or `col-6` with a grid system. Let's stick with our banana website example from before:

```
<header class="header clearfix bg-banana-yellow">
    <div class="header-logo float-left">
```

```
        <img src="http://placehold.it/200x100" alt="Banana logo">
    </div>
    <div class="header-search float-right">
        <input type="text" class="header-search-input float-left">
        <input class="header-search-submit-button float-left" type="submit"
value="Search">
    </div>
</header>
```

This does lead to DRY CSS; however, we're back to our presentational names in our CSS. So the semantics die-hards were not convinced OOCSS was the answer.

When OOCSS moved to Sass it began to use extends, which allowed OOCSS to drop the need for additional classes in the HTML. Instead you could extend the `float-left` and `float-right` and whatever else from within your SCSS:

```
.float-left {
    float: left;
}

.float-right {
    float: right;
}

.clearfix {
    overflow: hidden;
}

.bg-banana-yellow {
    background-color: hsl(52, 100%, 62%);
}

.header {
    Width: 100%;
    @extend .clearfix;
    @extend .bg-banana-yellow;

    &-logo, &-search-input, &-search-button {
        @extend .float-left;
    }

    &-search {
        @extend .float-right;
    }
}
```

This still meant, however, that you had the rules for `float-left`, `float-right`, `clearfix`, and `bg-banana-yellow` in your CSS output:

```
.float-left, .header-logo, .header-search-input, .header-search-button {
  float: left;
}

.float-right, .header-search {
  float: right;
}

.clearfix, .header {
  overflow: hidden;
}

.bg-banana-yellow, .header {
  background-color: #ffe53d;
}

.header {
  Width: 100%;
}
```

That's not bad, but imagine more extend rules for background colors, colors, margins, and padding. Eventually your CSS file has presentational class names sprinkled throughout and rules at the beginning of CSS that aren't necessary. This is why Sass added placeholder extends. These are probably my favorite addition to Sass. If you know when to use extends instead of mixins you can remove hundreds of lines from your final CSS output.

Placeholder extends allow you to create an *extend-only* rule. This means if you are creating a rule which is only for the purpose of extending you don't need to generate a class in the final CSS. You can create a placeholder extend by using a % instead of a . when creating your extend. For example, `.float-left` would become `%float-left`.

Using placeholder extends, our SCSS would instead look like this:

```
%float-left {
    float: left;
}

%float-right {
    float: right;
}

%clearfix {
    overflow: hidden;
}
```

```scss
%bg-banana-yellow {
    background-color: hsl(52, 100%, 62%);
}

.header {
    width: 100%;
    @extend %clearfix;
    @extend %bg-banana-yellow;
    &-logo, &-search-input, &-search-button {
        @extend %float-left;
    }
    &-search {
        @extend %float-right;
    }
}
```

Our CSS would then be as follows:

```css
.header-logo, .header-search-input, .header-search-button {
  float: left;
}

.header-search {
  float: right;
}

.header {
  overflow: hidden;
}

.header {
  background-color: #ffe53d;
}

.header {
  width: 100%;
}
```

You'll notice we have three rules for `header` each with only one property. This is because our `clearfix` and `bg-banana-yellow` extends were only used once each. This is why it's important to always view your CSS output frequently. You should do a search in your text editor for each class name and property to find repetition and then decide where you can use or move repeated patterns and properties into their own `@extend` rules.

This is how I use OOCSS. Much like with BEM, I don't follow its naming conventions. Instead I prefer to try and achieve an understanding of its concepts and principles and then keep those in mind while developing my own projects.

Separating container from content

The name of this principle is perhaps a bit misleading. To me, content is the innermost elements of a page. Anything you can't remove without losing the message you are trying to get across, is the content. The text, the video, and the images. These are content. Everything else to me is container.

For that reason, I think this principle is better explained as separating container from component. The idea is that a component should not be influenced by where it is in your design. If you imagine a component in a grid system, whether it's an h1 (heading 1) or a complex component of numerous elements, it should mean the same thing and look the same in a full width column, as a quarter width column. This may sound like a very difficult concept to actually apply and achieve. However, I believe it can be simplified by following a couple of simple rules:

1. Firstly, a reusable component should have no set dimensions. If you place your component on its own in an empty page, it should simple take up the entire width of the page and its height should be determined only by its content. Additionally, if you place your component in an element of 50% width, your component should now be contained perfectly within that element.

    This is simply how HTML normally behaves. A h1 element will take up 100% width on a page, regardless of how many characters, so too will paragraphs and any other block level element. These are HTML's natural components. HTML is completely responsive without any CSS. If you put text on a page and expand and shrink the screen, the text wraps to fit.

2. The other rule for reuse is that our component should be isolated from everything outside of it. We covered this concept with our product element when we spoke of a naming convention. Our naming convention keeps our component's styles separate from outside elements and isolated from any changes therein.

With these two simple rules we can create complex but reusable components. However, separation of container from content does not just relate to components which contain other elements. It also relates to the simplest components.

Take an h3 element. OOCSS states that a standard h3 in a sidebar should look the same as an h3 in the footer, or the main body of the page. This is achieved by giving elements such as headings, their own classes, and avoid doing the following:

```
h3 {...}
.main-content h3 {...}
.sidebar h3 {...}
.footer h3 {...}
```

Instead, you should give any h3 its own class which would give it any special properties. This way you are not merely overriding the default h3 style with rules that are dependent upon where they are in a design. If you need your sidebar h3 to look a certain way, you should give it a class name that is semantic and descriptive of the content. This allows for reuse and keeps everything isolated and independent from where it is:

```
.sidebar-heading {...}
```

OOCSS also has its own **design patterns** in the form of common components we all seem to use in some form or another. However, I'm not going to cover them here, seeing as they use presentational classes, and I much prefer taking the ideas and putting them into practice on building my own components. We will build a few reusable components for our project in Chapter 8, *Building a Content-Rich Website Components*.

Atomic Design

Atomic Design is a methodology created by Brad Frost in 2013. Atomic Design recommends thinking of a design from its smallest components first, styling them, and then adding them together to make more complex design elements. It is called Atomic Design due to its analogy of combining the smallest parts (atoms) to create gradually more complex structures (molecules) and finally combining those to create larger, finished design components (organisms).

Essentially, I call this designing *inside-out*. It's how I prefer to begin my projects. I start with the text, heading tags, paragraph tags, form fields, inputs, labels, buttons, links, and so on. These are elements that cannot be broken down further. Then you can combine these to create molecules. For example, an input, a label, and submit button would be a natural molecule in web design. All of these elements naturally work together to perform a function. Lists, tables, and forms are all examples of molecules in Atomic Design.

Next, you would put together larger components from combinations of these molecules called organisms. An organism could be the header, footer, sidebar, galleries, sliders, and other combinations of elements in a design. This is as far as I take Atomic Design. The next structure is templates and then complete pages. Templates are explained as being the assortment of organisms into something which you can show the client. Perhaps a wireframe or prototype. From there you can begin to polish the design into finished pages which will become the finished deliverable.

SMACSS

Scalable Modular Architecture for CSS (SMACSS) was created by Jonathan Snook from methods he learned while working at Yahoo. SMACSS is different from other methodologies listed here. Instead of dealing with how you should write CSS or Sass, it recommends where you should write it. **Architecture** is the key word here. SMACSS works great with Sass because of the ability to use multiple files and import them into one main file. This file is often called a `manifest`.

SMACSS recommends breaking your Sass into the following topics: base, layout, modules, states, and theme.

Base

Base is where your base elements of HTML would go. These would be your `reset.css` styles or `normalize.css` styles, your base typography styling of h1 through h6, paragraphs, blockquotes, `cite`, `pre`, `code`, em, `strong`, `ul`, `ol`, `dl`, `dt`, `li`, `input`, `label`, `button`, anchor tags, and so on. There wouldn't be any classes or nested rules here.

Layout

Layout contains the overall layout of the larger elements on your page. Your grid, header, footer, sidebar, and so forth would be dimensioned and positioned within this file. The idea is that you could then drop your modules or components into these "containers" afterwards.

Modules

This is where I usually deviate from the SMACSS standard slightly. Only in the order, not the use. I prefer to create my modules or components before thinking of layout. Using **Atomic Design** and **OOCSS** as a starting point and applying those concepts to SMACSS, base would contain your atoms, then modules would be your molecules and OOCSS components. After that, layout would be your organisms. So modules would contain your reusable, isolated components which could be dropped into your layout.

State

State would contain your styles that are related to JavaScript or some state (obviously). I mentioned these in the section about naming conventions. For instance, state would be prefixed with the word `is` or `has`, such as, `is-open`, `is-closed`, `is-checked`, `is-unchecked`, `has-error`, and `is-valid`. Mostly these will be prefixed with `is-` however, sometimes `has-` will be more appropriate. The naming convention isn't important here. It could be `checked`, `valid`. The main thing is to be consistent. Choose a convention and stick with it.

A method I like is to use a data attribute for state. This way you keep your class names semantic, and you would add data attributes for state with an attribute `data-state="is-valid"`.

```
<div id="login-form" class="login-form">
    <div class="login-form-field">
        <label for="username" class="">Username</label>
        <input type="text" name="username" class="login-form-input" />
        <span id="login-form-message-username" class="login-form-message"
data-state="is-hidden">Error</span>
    </div>
    <div class="login-form-field">
        <label for="password" class="">Username</label>
        <input type="password" name="password" class="login-form-input" />
        <span id="login-form-message-password" class="login-form-message"
data-state="is-error">Error</span>
    </div>
    <div class="login-form-field">
        <input type="submit" value="Login" class="login-form-submit" />
        <span id="login-form-message-submit" class="login-form-message"
data-state="is-hidden"></span>
    </div>
</div>
```

Here, we have a `login` component which has IDs simply for JavaScript. You would use both JavaScript validation and server-side validation. The spans have IDs also to allow for easily accessing them with JavaScript. The idea is that if the username or password is incorrect, the `data-state="is-hidden"` would change to `data-state="is-error"` and either JavaScript or your server-side language would populate the empty span with the appropriate message. Perhaps your password was too short or simply incorrect. Then, your *state.scss* file might have styles like this:

```
[data-state="is-hidden"] {
    display: none;
}
[data-state="is-error"] {
    display: block;
    padding: 0.75em;
    background-color: transparentize(red, 0.25);
    border: 1px solid red;
    color: white;
}
```

This is how I prefer to do it. If you want to use classes or even BEM modifiers, then that's up to you. I simply think we can use data attributes to avoid overloading our class attributes and perhaps indicate intent better in both our HTML and CSS.

Theme

Theme is where all of your *look and feel* styles would go. Your specific colors, fonts, and custom font sizes and perhaps icons and background image-based styles would go here. This is really useful since you could then switch out theme files and have an entirely new color scheme.

Let's take our product component from before and add a theme (or a skin) to it. Let's make it stand out by having a subtle box shadow around it and make the overall text Verdana. The title will be uppercase and the link on the title will be a `hover-link` from Compass. We'll also add a View Product button which will go to the full product (at least in the real world scenario it would). We'll make the button red with white text:

```
<div class="product">
    <img src="http://placehold.it/150x150" alt="Image of Product"
class="product-image">
    <div class="product-details">
    <h2 class="product-title"><a href="#" class="product-title-
link">Product Name</a></h2>
        <div class="product-price">
            <span class="product-total">€55.00</span>
```

```
        <span class="product-sale"><del>€65.00</del></span>
    </div>
    <div class="product-description">
        <p>Lorem ipsum...</p>
    </div>
    <a href="#" class="product-button">View Product &rarr;</a>
</div>
</div>
```

So, first let's place our layout specific styles in our *_layout.scss* files, which would be imported into *screen.scss* after importing Compass:

```scss
// mastering-sass/ch04/scss/_layout.scss
.product {
    padding: 1em;
    overflow: hidden;
    &-image {
        float: left;
        margin-right: 1em;
    }

    &-title {
        margin-top: 0;
        &-link {
            text-decoration: none;
            color: inherit;
        }
    }

    &-sale {
        margin-left: 1em;
        opacity: 0.5;
    }
    &-button {
        padding: 0.25em 0.5em;
        float: right;
    }
}
```

In our *theme.scss* file we would have the *look and feel* styles for the component:

```scss
// mastering-sass/ch04/scss/_theme.scss
%theme-text-transform-uppercase {
    text-transform: uppercase;
}

%theme-color-crimson {
    color: crimson;
```

```
}

.product {
    box-shadow: 0px 0px 5px;
    font-family: Verdana, Arial, sans-serif;
    &-title {
        @extend %theme-text-transform-uppercase;
        a { // Because hover-link uses the parent selector we cant use &-
link here...oh well
            @include hover-link;
            @extend %theme-color-crimson;
        }
    }
    &-total {
        font-weight: bold;
    }
    &-sale {
        font-style: italic;
    }
    &-button {
        @extend %theme-text-transform-uppercase;

        text-decoration: none;
        color: white;
        background-color: crimson;
        border: 1px solid transparent;
    // placing a transparent border here prevents a "pop" from happening on
the hover state if box-sizing is not set to border box.
        &:hover {
            @extend %theme-color-crimson;

            background: transparent;
            border: 1px solid crimson;
        }
    }
}
```

That's all there is to it. The downside of breaking theme specific styles into their own files is that you will have the rules repeated. However, the benefits of knowing exactly where everything is, outweighs the drawbacks of some repetition. In fact, you'll be rather surprised how little of a design the actual theme is. Also, as long as you use extends and watch out for repeated patterns and properties, you can use extends to reduce repetition elsewhere.

Why aren't you using HSL?

What if I asked you "what is the hex code for yellow in CSS?" It's `#ff0`. Now I don't know if you knew that or not, but let's keep going. What is the hex code for purple? What is the hex code for green? What is the hex code for red? How many of those did you know off by heart? Probably not a whole lot, if any. When it comes to hex color codes, I know what black and white is and then things quickly move towards needing a color picker of some kind. Just FYI, purple is `#7f00ff`, green is `#0f0`, and red is `#f00`.

What if I said you can use the RGB model? With a bit of color theory, you could figure out all of those colors without needing anything else. Let's start with red. Well that's easy! RGB stands for Red, Green, Blue. We know 255 is 100% of that color, so red is RGB(255, 0, 0). Green would be RGB(0, 255, 0) and blue RGB(0, 0, 255).

So what is yellow? Ok, yellow is an equal mix of red and green. So 1 to 1 of red and green, therefore yellow is RGB(255, 255, 0). What about purple? Well purple is equal parts red and blue, so it would be RGB(255, 0, 255).

Those colors are easy enough with the RGB model and some basic color theory. They're one part color A and one part color B, or in other words 50% of each. What if you need to get orange? Well, that's one part red and one part yellow…but we don't have yellow in the RGB model. So we're left with 100% red and 50% green. Half of 255 is 127.5, but we can't use decimals in the RGB model. So we use RGB(255, 127, 0) or RGB(255, 128, 0). Same thing essentially.

What we are doing here is dealing with "hue". The color of something is its hue. And using the RGB model is okay for this purpose. However, in web design, or any design for that matter, we rarely use the true hues of a color for anything. Plain red, and yellow, and orange, and green are often too much. They overwhelm a design. They're distracting. So instead, once we know we want to use a blue, we'll augment that "true red". We might lighten it or darken it, or reduce its "richness" and make it more pastel-like.

A look at hue, saturation, and lightness

First thing you need to understand about HSL is how to get a pure, or true color. Quite simply, you set Saturation to 100% and Lightness to 50%. This is because 0% lightness is black and 100% lightness is white, regardless of what your hue or saturation is. 0% saturation, on the other hand, is monochrome, or grayscale. After all, grayscale is simply 100% **desaturation**.

Once your saturation is 100% and your lightness is 50% you only need to tweak the hue value to get all the true colors there are. The hue color wheel is different to the RGB model. Instead of a maximum of 255, the hue value in the HSL model starts at 0 degrees and ends at 360 degrees. 0 degrees and 360 degrees are the same thing. They are the same point on the wheel. 0 and 360 are both red.

Below is a table with the main colors you can achieve by mixing red, green, and blue, as we demonstrated before. It includes the HSL value, the name of the color, and the RGB value.

NAME	HSL	RGB
Red	HSL(0, 100%, 50%)	RGB(255, 0, 0)
Orange	HSL(30, 100%, 50%)	RGB(255, 127, 0)
Yellow	HSL(60, 100%, 50%)	RGB(255, 255, 0)
Yellow-green (lime)	HSL(90, 100%, 50%)	RGB(127, 255, 0)
Green	HSL(120, 100%, 50%)	RGB(0, 255, 0)
Cyan-green (aqua)	HSL(150, 100%, 50%)	RGB(0, 255, 127)
Cyan	HSL(180, 100%, 50%)	RGB(0, 255, 255)
Cyan-blue (dark cyan)	HSL(210, 100%, 50%)	RGB(0, 127, 255)
Blue	HSL(240, 100%, 50%)	RGB(0, 0, 255)
Purple	HSL(270, 100%, 50%)	RGB(127, 0, 255)
Magenta	HSL(300, 100%, 50%)	RGB(255, 0, 255)
Pink	HSL(330, 100%, 50%)	RGB(255, 0, 127)
Red	HSL(360, 100%, 50%)	RGB(255, 0, 0)

So that is one benefit of using HSL over RGB. With HSL you only need to change the hue value to move through all of the possible true color values. With RGB, you need to tweak two, or sometimes all three, to get every possible color from the color wheel.

The second value in HSL is saturation. When using saturation, there are two things you should keep in mind. First, the lower the saturation, the less vivid the colors are. This means at 0%, the color will be completely void of color, therefore monochrome. This doesn't mean it will be black, it simply means it will be a grey hue. The grey will be dependent on how much lightness is set. At 100% saturation you will have full color.

The second thing is something I only know from my hobby, digital painting. Black and dark colors have high saturation, while white and light colors have low saturation. This can be useful to know when trying to find a color that is deep or dark. You simply can't get those colors with low saturation.

It's a bit counter-intuitive. When you think of dark colors, you would think simply removing the saturation would give you the desired effect. However, adding black, or removing saturation from a color, will simply give you a dull color. So saturation has the opposite effect to lightness. Higher saturation will make deeper, richer colors.

The final value in HSL is lightness. Lightness is easy to understand. 0% light gives you pure black, regardless of hue or saturation. 100% lightness gives you pure white, regardless of hue or saturation. 50% lightness will give you pure color and allow for hue and saturation to take full effect on the true color. Once you move below 50% lightness you are essentially adding black into the color, while above 50% you are adding white into the color. When you use the lighten and darken functions in Sass you are increasing and decreasing the lightness value from the HSL model.

Don't use Photoshop to get HSL values

This caught me out a few times before I copped it. Photoshop has hex color values and also RGB. These are identical to CSS. However, the HSL model is not used in Photoshop. Photoshop uses the HSB (aka HSV) model. **HSB** stands for **Hue Saturation Brightness** (while **HSV** stands for **Hue Saturation Vibrancy**. These are used interchangeably).

HSB works differently than HSL. Brightness is not the same as lightness. Let's say we begin with a value of HSB (30, 80%, 80%). This would actually give you a value in HSL of HSL (30, 67%, 48%). As you increase the brightness to 90% you would have HSL (30, 79%, 54%). So you can see brightness acts almost like a mixture of saturation and lightness in the HSL color model.

For this reason, it's impossible to use the HSB colors for HSL. Only the hue value is the same in both at all times. Even if you tried to use the hue and saturation from the HSB model in HSL, they're not the same. Both models treat the relation between saturation and brightness/lightness completely differently.

Just to clarify, this is the same in all of the image editors I've tried, even ones that are for the Web. Photoshop, Illustrator, GIMP, and even Sketch, which everyone says is better for web design concepts than any of the others, use HSB. The only one I've used that uses HSL is Inkscape, which is good for creating SVGs. However, Inkscape, for some infuriating reason, has each value ranging from 0 to 255, the same as RGB, so it's pointless to try to use it for HSL in CSS.

So you've been warned. If you are using Photoshop (or any other program) for sampling colors you should stick to RGB, and hex colors. If you need a converter from HSB/HSV to HSL I recommend the Work with Color website: `http://www.workwithcolor.com/color-converter-1.htm`.

reset.css versus normalize.css

This has been a topic of debate for a long time now. Some popular frameworks and libraries favor `reset.css`, like Compass does, while others favor `normalize.css`, such as Twitter Bootstrap, ZURB Foundation, and HTML5 Boilerplate. I myself prefer `normalize.css`. As I mentioned in `Chapter 3`, *Compass – Navigating with Compass*, I simply find `reset.css` to be overly aggressive and (perhaps) lazy in its approach. However, `normalize.css` is not perfect either. Let me start by explaining the differences.

reset.css

`reset.css` was created by Eric Meyer in 2008. It removes all browser styles across the board. All margins, padding, and borders are set to 0. Font-sizes are set to 100% and line-heights are set to 1. Blockquote, pre, code, KBD, and table styles are also removed. This means everything looks exactly the same. Everything just looks like normal 16px text. From headings to sub, sup, blockquotes, and anything else are all the same size and you are expected to re-style everything to be as you want it. Depending on your needs this can be a good thing or a bad thing.

normalize.css

`normalize.css` was created by Jonathan Neal and Nicolas Gallagher in 2011. `normalize.css` differs from `reset.css`. Instead of removing or resetting all user agent styles it simply targets inconsistent browser styles and sets them to a common default among the majority of browsers. This way all browsers match each other's default styling as closely as possible out of the gate.

Normalize also offers some common hacks for known issues in all browsers from iOS, Android, Opera, Safari, Mozilla, Chrome, and IE. However, this is where `normalize.css` has come under criticism. Some of its hacks are for browsers which perhaps many users do not require, such as `IE8>` or old mobile browsers.

Normalize also has a lot of comments in the CSS. This is both a good thing and a bad thing depending on the situation. The comments are very useful when first getting associated with what `normalize.css` is doing for you. However, if you do not remove the comments, they can add a lot of bloat to your CSS. However, I would recommend every user looks through them and determines which styles you need or do not need. You should then remove rules you feel you do not need for each project.

sanitize.css

Another less known alternative to `reset.css` and `normalize.css` is `sanitize.css`. `sanitize.css` is a project created in 2012 by Jonathan Neal, co-creator of `normalize.css`. `sanitize.css` is a more modern approach to the same browser inconsistencies both `reset.css` and `normalize.css` aim to alleviate. The difference is, it focuses on only supporting modern browsers, to be specific; the last three major releases of that browser. So each time a new Edge is released and supported the oldest is dropped. Same with Chrome, Firefox, Safari, Opera, and so on.

Another difference between `sanitize.css` and `normalize.css` is that while `normalize.css` targets each element one by one where there are inconsistencies, `sanitize.css` targets the uppermost element requiring attention and then uses inherit values and the natural cascade to apply its styles. This is better for performance overall.

Make your own

For best performance and support for the browsers you want or need to support, you should perhaps consider making your own base stylesheet which handles any browser inconsistencies which you find problematic. I would recommend looking through each of the preceding methods and finding which best suits your needs and then modify it to best suit each project.

Summary

In this chapter, we've covered more theory than any of the previous chapters. We've looked at some of the most popular methodologies and practices for writing maintainable and reusable CSS, such as BEM, SMACSS, OOCSS, and Atomic Design. We've also looked at some of the downsides of using out-of-the-box CSS projects such as Bootstrap, Foundation, `reset.css`, and `normalize.css`.

Each of these projects we've looked at is designed to solve the same problems; however, each tackles them in a different manner. These problems include scalability, reusability, and maintainability among others. Regardless of whether you choose to employ any of these methodologies as is, you will encounter the problems each tries to solve in some form or another as you work on larger projects. Therefore, it is perhaps more useful to understand the methods of overcoming these problems instead of using opinionated, pre-build packages, which can often include parts you either don't need or don't understand.

CSS is a misleadingly complex subject. While its syntax is very simple, this also means it can be easy to give it less attention than it often needs, leading to large, unmanageable files on even medium sized websites. It's important to understand that writing **Don't Repeat Yourself (DRY)**, elegant Sass functions and mixins will not necessarily create DRY or elegant CSS. For that, you need to first learn to write good CSS and then apply that knowledge to your Sass for the best of both.

In the next chapter we'll look at some of the more advanced features of Sass. We'll look at lists some more and also maps, the content directive, and more.

5
Advanced Sass

In this chapter we'll look at some of the more advanced features of Sass. We'll take a comprehensive look at variables and in particular variable scope and using the `!default` and `!global` flags. We'll look at the problems which can arise when using local and global scope in mixins, functions, and selectors.

Then we'll look at creating a `mixin` which generates pure CSS arrows. To create this `mixin` we'll need to use extends and interpolation to dynamically use those extends from within our `mixin`. We'll also see how we can simplify checking for multiple values within an if statement using the index function.

We'll then create a mixin which will simplify writing media queries. We'll use the `@content` directive which allows us to pass additional properties, mixins, or extends to a mixin.

Lastly, we'll look at using maps. **Maps** will allow us to group similar variables into a key value set. We'll look at how to retrieve values and how we can simplify the process of retrieving deeply nested values from maps. We'll also look at additional functions for dealing with maps in Sass.

Variables

Variables in Sass are not an advanced topic. They're one of the first things we start using in Sass. However, there are a few things you should understand about variables in Sass which are different to other languages. These include the !default flag and also how Sass handles scope.

!default

When you work on any medium-to large-sized Sass project you will want to make your project configurable from one place. The easiest way to achieve this is with well-made mixins and functions and, of course, variables.

Working on large projects can leave you with dozens and dozens of variables ranging from colors to padding, margins, font families, and font sizes. These might be used throughout your project or they may only need a few files (or one file). Some of these variables might only be used in one or two mixins or functions; however, these mixins and functions will need those variables in order to work.

This is where the `!default` flag is extremely useful. While working on a project you will inevitably want to break your Sass into smaller, more manageable files. Take the SMACSS paradigm, for example. You would have at least six files:like *_base.scss*, *_layout.scss*, *_theme.scss*, *_state.scss*, *_components.scss*, (or *_modules.scss*) and a file which imports all of these: *_style.scss*.

If you were to create variables which configured each of these *topics*, it makes sense to create them in those files. That way when you are working on a color scheme in *_theme.scss* all of the variables related to color are right there. If you need more variables, you simply create more and implement them.

However, this is not practical for a finished project which will be used by the *public*. Let's say the project you've been working on is a framework such as Bootstrap or Foundation. You could have hundreds of files each containing variables doing different things. To configure the colors for a new color scheme, users would have to hunt down the appropriate variables in those files and change them there. Then another designer decides to make further changes and doesn't even realize such changes can be made with variables so they hard code it into the *_theme.scss* file. Soon this becomes unmanageable and ultimately makes using variables for configuration pointless.

That is where `!default` comes in. When developing you still want to create your variables where they are needed, but you can't expect end users to have to find them. So when you create your color variables in *_theme.scss* you assign it `!default`:

```
// _theme.scss
$primary-color: hsl(210, 50%, 50%) !default;

.product-button {
    background-color: $primary-color;
}
```

The !default flag is like saying "if this $primary-color hasn't already been defined, then set it to hsl(210, 50%, 50%), otherwise use the previous value". So, you can then create a file just for configurable variables to be used by anyone wanting to override colors or anything else. This would then be imported before any other partial files in your project:

```
// _config.scss
// Primary Color of your theme. This is the colors of buttons.
$primary-color: hsl(210, 50%, 50%);
```

In your *style.scss* file, you then import all of your files after your *_config.scss* file:

```
// style.scss
@import "config";
@import "theme";
```

You might be wondering what the point is. Why not just have a config file and copy all of your variables to that file as you work or once you're finished? Well, you could do this. I can remember doing this for a while until I learned about !default. In fact, there are even scripts which automate this exact process, such as **Octophant** from Zurb. It is used to automate the process of creating the Foundation settings file (even though they use !default, it still would make sense for them time to automate the task of making a setting file). You can find the files at https://github.com/zurb/octophant.

However, let's imagine you've finished your framework and now you start the task of moving all of your variables to a config file:

* This could lead to errors. You might not want every variable to be in the config file. A lot of variables often don't belong in a config file.
* Copying all these files is another step to do before you can release your project and the less you have to do the better.

Instead, I much prefer simply creating variables as I work and if I think a variable might be useful in a config file, I set it to !default and continue to work. This gives me the flexibility of either having a config file or not. I can make that choice at the end. !default allows for that flexibility.

Variable scope

Variable scope is something that is present in all programming languages and it is a topic which can trip up even the most experienced developers. Sass is no different. However, because Sass deals with CSS rules, its scoping nuances can be even trickier to grasp in some situations, as we'll see later in this section.

Local scope

In Sass there are mainly two scopes to be concerned with, `global` and `local`. When you define variables outside of functions or mixins at the root level of the document, you are defining them in the **global scope**. These variables can be accessed by mixins, functions, inside selectors, and in extends.

When you define a variable inside a function, mixin, or selector, it is **locally scoped** to that function, mixin, or selector. To demonstrate this, we'll need to create some markup and some Sass to work with. For this example, create three divs:

```
<div class="square1"></div>
<div class="square2"></div>
<div class="square3"></div>
```

Then, in our SCSS create a Sass variable at the top of our file:

```
$bg-color: red;
```

Each of our squares will share the same size and will float left, so we can create an extend for this called `%square`:

```
%square {
    width: 100px;
    height: 100px;
    float: left;
}
```

Next, we'll define each CSS rule for our squares (`square1`, `square2`, and `square3`). Each will extend our `%square` placeholder:

```
.square1 {
    @extend %square;
}
.square2 {
    @extend %square;
}
.square3 {
    @extend %square;
}
```

Next, we'll set each to have a background color:

```
.square1 {
    @extend %square;
    background-color: $bg-color
}
```

```
.square2 {
    @extend %square;
    background-color: $bg-color
}
.square3 {
    @extend %square;
    background-color: $bg-color
}
```

So far, there is nothing new here. We should now have a row of three red squares side-by-side. Now set `square2` to have a variable within it:

```
.square2 {
    $bg-color: blue;
    @extend %square;
    background-color: $bg-color
}
```

`square2` is now blue. However, the last square, `square3` is still red. This is because the variable inside `square2` is in the local scope of `square2` and therefore overrides the global variable `$bg-color`.

Now set `square3` to have a variable with a value of orange within it:

```
.square3 {
    $bg-color: orange;
    @extend %square;
    background-color: $bg-color
}
```

You can see how using local variables, that is, variables inside our CSS properties, can override global variables (variables at the top level of our Sass file or variables defined anywhere outside of CSS rules, mixins, or functions) for that CSS rule only. Everything after that CSS rule will still use the global variable value.

!global flag

However, in the preceding example let's say we wanted the color from `square2` to remain the global value used from that point onward? Let's remove the variables from `square2` and `square3`. You should have all red squares once again.

Now let's say we want our second and third squares to be blue. You might be tempted to do the following:

```
$bg-color: blue;
.square2 {
    @extend %square;
    background-color: $bg-color;
}

.square3 {
    @extend %square;
    background-color: $bg-color;
}
```

This is a perfectly valid option. However, we have an alternative, the !global flag. Cut and paste the variable you just created into square2 again. We should have red, blue, red once more:

```
.square2 {
    $bg-color: blue;
    @extend %square;
    background-color: $bg-color;
}
```

Now add !global after the variable in square and you should now have red, blue, blue:

```
.square2 {
    $bg-color: blue !global;
    @extend %square;
    background-color: $bg-color;
}
```

Isn't this fun!

What the !global flag does is tell Sass that we want this variable to be treated as a global scoped variable. That means it will be as if we had defined it outside of our selector, at the root level of our SCSS file.

Variable scope in functions

This behavior is the same for mixins and functions as well. However, using scoped variables in functions and mixins can lead to complicated code which can be very hard to maintain and debug.

Add a function just below our first variable at the top of our file. Call this function `bg-color`. It takes no parameters and simply returns `$bg-color`:

```
$bg-color: blue;

@function bg-color() {
    @return $bg-color;
}
```

Replace the `background-color` variable in `square2` with our function `bg-color()`. Nothing should change:

```
.square2 {
    $bg-color: blue !global;
    @extend %square;
    background-color: bg-color();
}
```

Now add a variable inside our `bg-color` function:

```
@function bg-color() {
    $bg-color: black;
    @return $bg-color;
}
```

`square2` should turn black. Now add the `!global` flag to the variable in our function. You should have `red`, `black`, `black`:

```
@function bg-color() {
    $bg-color: black !global;
    @return $bg-color;
}
```

This has instantly made our code a lot more complex. Even though we are getting the expected behavior and the same behavior as before, the way we are achieving it has become much more complicated. This is especially true for anyone looking through our code for the first time who is trying to figure out what is happening.

It's quite likely your functions and `config` variables will be in a separate file to these CSS rules. Imagine you have hundreds of squares and at some point a function is called which changes `$bg-color` to black. Looking at the code, it would be very easy to miss that `bg-color()` function.

For this reason, scope can be one of the hardest things for developers to debug in any language. There are no errors thrown so you can't quickly find a line number for where the problem is coming from. You're left manually reading through lines of code, which can take a very long time. Even then, it's very easy for someone not to realize a function or a mixin is the culprit.

The preceding example is bad enough, but it can get much *stranger!* Brace yourselves…we're about to head into Inception territory.

Before we continue, let's remove the `$bg-color: black` variable from our function so we have all red squares once more:

```
@function bg-color() {
    @return $bg-color;
}
```

Now make `square3` orange by adding a local variable:

```
.square3 {
    $bg-color: orange;
    @extend %square;
    background-color: $bg-color;
}
```

Then create two more squares in you HTML; `square4` and `square5`:

```
<div class="square4"></div>
<div class="square5"></div>
```

Now add `square4` and `square5` to our SCSS file and extend `%square` and add a property `background-color` which contains the `bg-color` function:

```
.square4 {
    @extend %square;
    background-color: bg-color();
}

.square5 {
    @extend %square;
    background-color: bg-color();
}
```

At this point, the full SCSS file should look like this:

```
$bg-color: red;

@function bg-color() {
```

```
    @return $bg-color;
}

%square {
    width: 100px;
    height: 100px;
    float: left;
}

.square1 {
    @extend %square;
    background-color: $bg-color;
}

.square2 {
    @extend %square;
    background-color: bg-color();
}

.square3 {
    $bg-color: orange;
    @extend %square;
    background-color: $bg-color;
}

.square4 {
    @extend %square;
    background-color: bg-color();
}

.square5 {
    @extend %square;
    background-color: bg-color();
}
```

You should have two red squares, an orange square, and two reds again.

Now, let's say you want `square4` to be `blue`. We could just do what we did for `square3` and add a variable inside the rule, right? Let's see:

```
.square4 {
    $bg-color: blue;
    @extend %square;
    background-color: bg-color();
}
```

Nothing happens. This is one of those situations, as I mentioned before, where it can seem like something is broken, however this is the correct behavior. Let's examine what is going on.

Our function `bg-color()` is using the `$bg-color` value defined in the **global scope**. However, the variable we have defined inside `square4` is in square4's **local scope** and has no effect on the global scope, and therefore has no effect on any functions or mixins which are using the global scope variable, regardless of where the functions or mixins are called. This is where relying on variables defined in the global or local scope can have limitations and can even lead to serious problems.

So what happens when we set our blue `$bg-color` variable in `square4` to override the global scope with the `!global` flag? I'm glad you asked:

```
.square4 {
    $bg-color: blue !global;
    @extend %square;
    background-color: bg-color();
}
```

As you might have expected, everything from that point is blue. However, that isn't what we were going for, was it? Originally, we only wanted `square4` to be `blue` and `square5` to remain `red`. Unfortunately, there is no clean way around this. We could use `!global` again somewhere to reset everything back to red, however what happens then when the original variable at the top of our file is changed to green? Everything would start off green, turn orange, then blue, and finally red! This is hard to debug and even harder to maintain. Imagine you were five weeks into a large complicated project and things like this started to pop up? It would not be good.

Still not confused? Ok. Let's get even weirder. Let's go one level deeper and see what happens when you have a dream, inside a dream, inside a…errr…I mean a function, inside a mixin, inside a CSS selector.

Deeply nested variable scope

So our `bg-color()` function was a completely academic example. You're never going to create a function whose purpose is to simply apply the value of a variable. So let's look at something a bit more practical. What if all of our squares had a number shown, but we weren't sure what the colors were going to be? This leads to a possible problem…what if the square is black? Well, the color of the number would need to be white. The same as if the square was white the text would need to be black. We then want a mixin to apply the `background-color` and `color` properties for us.

First things first, let's add the numbers to our squares in HTML:

```
<div class="square1">1</div>
<div class="square2">2</div>
<div class="square3">3</div>
<div class="square4">4</div>
<div class="square5">5</div>
```

Next we'll create global `$bg-color` variable in `hsl` (to allow us control of the lightness) at the top of our file like before. We'll set this color to a dark red. We'll also define a placeholder extend called `%square` which will position and set up each element we apply it to:

```
$bg-color: hsl(0, 100%, 25%);

%square {
    width: 100px;
    height: 100px;
    line-height: 100px;
    float: left;
    text-align: center;
}
```

With that done, we'll create a mixin called `colors`. It has no parameters and inside it sets our `background-color` property to our global `$bg-color` variable and the color is simply inherited from its parent:

```
@mixin colors() {
    background-color: $bg-color;
    color: inherit;
}
```

Now we need to check the lightness of the `$bg-color` variable and set our `color` property value accordingly. To do this we can use the lightness function available in Sass. This takes a color as a parameter and returns the lightness in a percentage value. So if we checked the lightness of white it would be 100% and black would return 0%. Let's create a function called `set-color()`:

```
@function set-color() {
    @if lightness($bg-color) > 50% {
        @return black;
    } @else {
        @return white;
    }
}
```

So, when the lightness of our color is higher than 50%, our text color is set to black and everything else would be dark so our text color would be white.

Now apply this to our color property in our colors mixin:

```
@mixin colors() {
    background-color: $bg-color;
    color: set-color();
}
```

Now add the mixin to square2, square4, and square5 to replace where we had background-color: $bg-color:

```
.square2 {
    @extend %square;
    @include colors;
}

...

.square4 {
    @extend %square;
    @include colors;
}

.square5 {
    @extend %square;
    @include colors;
}
```

Now we should have this:

This shows our mixin and function is working and correctly setting the best contrast color for our text, white on dark red. As you can see, the text in square1 remains black.

Here's where things get interesting. What happens if we, for some reason, we make our set-colors function change our global variable to red when the background is light?

To do this we'll set a $bg-color variable at the top of our file to hsl(0, 50%, 75%) and place another $bg-color variable with the !global flag inside the if statement, changing $bg-color to red:

```
$bg-color: hsl(0, 50%, 75%);

@function set-color() {
    @if lightness($bg-color) > 50% {
        $bg-color: red !global;
        @return black;
    } @else {

        @return white;
    }
}
```

So, square2 has the original global value of hsl(0, 50%, 75%) and then square4 and square5 have a background of red. Of course, square4 and square5 being red makes total sense, however why wasn't square2 also red instead of pink? The $bg-color: red !global is in our set-color function, which is called in square2 after all. Well, if you think about it, the original $bg-color: hsl(0, 50%, 75%) triggers our if statement. The statement evaluated that the lightness was 75% and once that had happened, everything inside of the if block runs, including setting the overriding $bg-color global value. No further checks are performed inside that if statement so even though the $bg-color was indeed set to red, the background-color property was set to hsl(0, 50%, 75%) and the color property was set to black. The next time the mixin was called however, the value was red and this triggered the @else block.

Again, this isn't something you should ever be doing in reality. However, if you understand these examples and why they work the way they do, then you fully understand variable scope in Sass, and indeed many other languages.

So, you should by now understand the limitations and possible problems of variable scope if not used correctly. Variable scope isn't something you can avoid but you can avoid misusing it. Basically, use !global with caution and if you do need to use it and things start to get weird, now you know the things to look out for.

Making arrows in Sass

We're going to create a mixin which will create pure CSS triangles for us with ease. We'll then be able to use these later in our design for numerous things from drop-down arrows to tooltips. However, first we need to look at how we create these triangles so we can understand exactly what we're doing.

Creating *arrows* or triangles in CSS isn't really a hack as much as a side effect of the expected CSS behavior used in an unexpected case. CSS triangles are done by creating an element with a border width of whatever height you want your triangle to be, then reducing the element's dimensions down to zero, so our border is the only height. Finally, we change the border color to transparent on three of the four sides, thus leaving a triangle.

I don't expect you to understand that so let's break it down and see it happening step by step. First, we want a black triangle pointing upwards, with a height of 20px. So let's first create an element of 20px height and width and give it a black border of 20px. So our SCSS will be as follows:

```
.triangle {
  width: 20px;
  height: 20px;
  border: 20px solid black;
}
```

Then we create our `div` with a class of triangle:

```
<div class="triangle"></div>
```

Our element should now look like a white square of 20px inside a 20px wide black line.

If you have a box-sizing set to `border-box` you'll instead see a 20px black square. Box-sizing by default adds border and padding onto the height and width, while setting it to `border-box` means the height and width stay as they are, and border and padding are applied to the inside of the element.

Next, we remove the `height` and `width` so we simply have a black square of 40px height and width:

```
.triangle {
  height: 0px;
  width: 0px;
  border: 20px solid black;
}
```

 This is just so you can see how we create an arrow step by step. Normally you would simply start with a height and width of 0.

Next, we simply set our `border-left-color` to transparent. Then we do the same for the `border-top-color` and finally the `border-right-color`, leaving us with a triangle of `20px` height and a width of `40px`:

```
.triangle {
  height: 0px;
  width: 0px;
  border: 20px solid black;
  border-left-color: transparent;
  border-top-color: transparent;
  border-right-color: transparent;
}
```

So now you know exactly what is going on when we create a CSS triangle, it's time to make a mixin to make this more reusable. Create four HTML elements with the following classes, `triangle-up`, `triangle-down`, `triangle-left`, and `triangle-right`:

```
<div class="triangle-up"></div>
<div class="triangle-down"></div>
<div class="triangle-left"></div>
<div class="triangle-right"></div>
```

In Sass, create a mixin called `arrow`, which creates a down arrow:

```
@mixin arrow {
  height: 0;
  width: 0;
  border: 20px solid black;
  border: {
    left-color: transparent;
    right-color: transparent;
    bottom-color: transparent;
  }
}
```

Next, create your rules for the `up`, `down`, `left`, and `right` arrows and apply the mixin to each:

```
.triangle {
    &-up {
        @include arrow;
    }
    &-down {
        @include arrow;
    }
    &-left {
        @include arrow;
    }

    &-right {
        @include arrow;
    }
}
```

Ignoring the fact all of our arrows are facing downwards, you'll notice our CSS has a lot of repetition. This is why it is important to always check how your CSS looks and not just assume, because your Sass is relatively clean and dry, that your CSS will automatically be.

It's incredibly useful to do a quick scan over CSS and look for repeated patterns which you can break out into either an extend, or, in some cases, you'll see how you can create better mixins. It works both ways.

So we can move height and width to its own extend, which we call %arrow-base, which we can use inside of our mixin now:

```
%arrow-base {
  height: 0;
  width: 0;
}
```

```
@mixin arrow {
  @extend %arrow-base;
  border: 20px solid black
  border: {
    left-color: transparent
    right-color: transparent
    bottom-color: transparent
  }
}
```

Looking at your CSS again you should see how much cleaner everything is. I reduced my CSS from 32 lines to 29. On large projects this could have removed dozens, if not hundreds, of lines of CSS output. So let's keep refactoring our Sass to get the most optimized CSS output possible.

We can see we are setting the `border-color` to transparent on the left and the right in every CSS rule also. However, this will only be the case if our arrow is pointing up or down.

Next we'll need to add the functionality for our mixin to call the appropriate extends. After all, a mixin that only creates down arrows isn't very impressive is it? So let's make it so our mixin takes a `$parameter` called `$direction` and we'll give it a default value of "up":

```
@mixin arrow($direction: "up") {
  ...
}
```

Next, in our mixin we want to *clean* our variable. This means we want to make sure what is passed in our code works as it should. We do this first by ensuring the value is a string. If it is anything other than a string, we give an error. That way if they pass a number, or color, or anything else, they will get useful feedback on why things don't work as they should:

```
@mixin arrow($direction: "up") {
  @if (type-of($direction) == 'string') {
    $direction: unquote($direction);
  } @else {
    @error "Value of $direction in arrow mixin must be a string. #{type-of($direction)} was given.";
  }

  @extend %arrow-base;
  ...
}
```

If it is a `string`, we still want to make sure it is lowercase and to also remove quotes so everywhere inside our mixin we can use `$direction` and know for sure it is what we expect. This helps eliminate any chance of odd behavior because of quotes or capitals. If someone enters "Up" or up it will work the same as "up" or uP or "UP". It won't matter:

```
@mixin arrow($direction: "up") {
    @if (type-of($direction) == 'string') {
        $direction: unquote(to-lower-case($direction));
    } @else {
        @error "Value of $direction in arrow mixin must be a string. #{type-
of($direction)} was given.";
    }

    @extend %arrow-base;
    . . .
}
```

Next, we'll need to be sure the `$direction` given is a valid direction. We don't want people entering *diagonal* or *sideways* or anything else. We'll create a list with our `$valid-directions` in it for use in our check. To do this, we'll be taking advantage of the `index` function in our `if` statements; however, first we need to define the valid options to check for:

```
@mixin arrow($direction: "up") {
    $valid-directions: (up, down, left, right);
    @if (type-of($direction) == 'string') {
        $direction: unquote(to-lower-case($direction));
    } @else {
        @error "Value of $direction in arrow mixin must be a string.
#{type-of($direction)} was given.";
    }
    . . .
}
```

So, if our arrow is up or down, we will have `border-left-color` and `border-right-color` set to be `transparent`. Likewise, if our arrow is left or right, we will have a `border-top-color` and `border-bottom-color` set to `transparent`. Let's create four extends; `%arrow-up`, `%arrow-down`, `%arrow-left`, and `%arrow-right`. Give `%arrow-up` and `%arrow-left` the correct properties:

```
%arrow-up {
    border: {
        left-color: transparent;
        right-color: transparent;
    }
}
```

```
%arrow-left {
    border: {
        top-color: transparent;
        bottom-color: transparent;
    }
}

%arrow-down {
  @extend %arrow-up;
}
%arrow-right {
    @extend %arrow-left;
}
```

Next is where our up, down, left, and right extends will come into play. However, first we want to be sure the direction passed into our mixin was a valid option. To do this, we can use the index() function in Sass:

```
@mixin arrow($direction: "up") {
  $valid-directions: (up, down, left, right);
  @if (type-of($direction) == 'string') {
    $direction: unquote($direction);
  } @else {
    @error "Value of $direction in arrow mixin must be a string. #{type-of($direction)} was given.";
  }

  @extend %arrow-base;

  @if index($valid-directions, $direction) {
    @extend %arrow-#{$direction};
  }
  @else {
    @error "$direction must be up, down, left, or right in arrow
    mixin. #{$direction} was given.";
  }
  ...
}
```

So let's take a look at how the index function works and why it's perfect for this situation. It takes two parameters; the first is the list and the second is a value to search for in that list. If the value is found in the list the position (or index) is returned, otherwise null is returned:

```
index((up, down, left, right), down) // Returns 2
index((up, down, left, right), diagonal) // Returns null
```

However, a side effect of this check is it passes or fails in `if` statement conditional. After all, null is what is called *falsey*, or false-like as far as `true`/`false` checks go. A number is a successful result so it is *truthy*.

So using the `index` function in this manner allows us to check if a value is in the list of values. It means we don't have to write this:

```
@if $direction == up or $direction == down or $direction == left or
$direction == right {
  // Do something
} @else {
  // Give error
}
```

Now that we understand what `index` is doing for us here, we can finally see the benefit of having an extend for each direction instead of simply horizontal or vertical. Let's finish our `if` statement:

```
@if index($valid-directions, $direction) {
  @extend %arrow-#{$direction};
} @else {
  @error "$direction must be up, down, left, or right in arrow mixin.
#{$direction} was given.";
}
```

Then lastly, we need to set the `border-color` left, right, top, or bottom. Now we can use the `$direction` value as is for `left` and `right`, however up and down will need to be converted to `top` and `bottom`. We'll use the `index` function again to check if the value is up or down and then the Sass `if` function to set it to `top` or `bottom`, accordingly. So our full mixin should now look like this:

```
@mixin arrow($direction: "up") {
  $valid-directions: (up, down, left, right);

  @if (type-of($direction) == 'string') {
    $direction: unquote($direction);
  } @else {
    @error "Value of $direction in arrow mixin must be a string. #{type-
of($direction)} was given.";
  }

  @extend %arrow-base;

  @if index($valid-directions, $direction) {
    @extend %arrow-#{$direction};
  } @else {
```

```
      @error "$direction must be up, down, left, or right in arrow mixin.
   #{$direction} was given.";
     }

   border: {
     width: 20px;
     style: solid;
     color: black;
   }

   @if index((up, down), $direction) {
     $direction: if($direction == up, top, bottom);
   }
   border-#{$direction}-color: transparent;
 }
```

Update each of our arrow mixin parameters:

```
.triangle {
   &-up {
       @include arrow(up);
   }

   &-down {
       @include arrow(down);
   }

   &-left {
       @include arrow(left);
   }

   &-right {
       @include arrow(right);
   }
}
```

Now, you'll notice our arrows are not working. Instead of arrows, we have some funky geometric artwork going on (which actually looks pretty cool too). If we look at the CSS, our extend is working correctly and our CSS is being created…so what is the problem?

Well, what's happened here is the perfect storm of Sass and CSS giving unwanted, although entirely expected, results. We have three factors to understand here:

- Placeholders are created and grouped together in your CSS wherever the extend was first created. It's a good practice to place them at the top so you can override some of those properties later in your CSS if you need to. It's good to have the option. That leads us to our next factor, which is the C in CSS.

- As you know, CSS stands for Cascading Style Sheets. This means stylesheets are interpreted by the browser from the top down. Meaning as the file is read, properties are added to what came before to create your styles. However, if a property is given a value again, the value lower down the file is applied and so on. The problem here is our placeholders are at the top, so properties later can override them. Which brings us to the third factor…the border property shorthand.
- The reason only the one side of each triangle is transparent and the other sizes are black is because our `border` property is overriding the `border-#{direction}-color` and setting them back to black.

Come back, !important, all is forgiven

The solution is to use the much vilified `!important`. Generally, I do everything in my power to avoid its use but this just so happens to be one of the few times it's completely necessary and in fact benefits our CSS rather than causing problems down the line.

The reason it's safe to use it here is because we'll never be using the *arrow-left/right* or *arrow-up/down* extends anywhere other than our arrow mixin, and without two transparent borders, it can't be an arrow. So `!important` is perfectly fine here. In fact, it feels darned good to see `!important` used properly for a change. Too often it gets used as a battering ram or a machete to beat and cut away at other people's CSS (and sometimes our own) instead of using it to make our CSS better, which this situation proves it can do.

So update our arrow placeholders to use `!important`:

```
%arrow-up {
  border: {
    left-color: transparent !important;
    right-color: transparent !important;
  }
}

%arrow-left {
  border: {
    top-color: transparent !important;
    bottom-color: transparent !important;
  }
}
```

We're nearly done with our arrow mixin. However, we will probably want to be able to change the color and the size. So let's quickly add a `$size` and `$color` parameter and replace the `border-width` value and `border-color` values in our mixin:

```
@mixin arrow($direction: "up", $size: 20px, $color: currentColor) {
  ...
  border: {
    width: $size;
    style: solid;
    color: $color;
  }
  ...
}
```

So we could leave our `arrow` mixin at that, however an `arrow` that can't be positioned isn't really much good to us. Of course, we can't possibly include all of the possible combinations of positioning properties inside our mixin. We could leave it up to the user to simply add any additional required properties outside the mixin, however it makes more sense to have them grouped with the mixin somehow. This will show they are part of the mixin's functionality and should be updated (possibly) if the mixin's parameters are updated or should be removed if the mixin is removed. This leads us on to our next feature, `@content`.

@content directive

To use `@content` in our arrow mixin is simple. We just add `@content` within our mixin in the spot we want the user's properties to be placed. This would most likely be at the very end of the mixin so the user can override some functionality of the mixin or extend the mixin with additional properties, mixins, extends, or any other valid CSS:

```
@mixin arrow(...) {
  ...

  @content
}
```

Then the user can simply place whatever they need to within curly braces and it will be placed into the mixin's output.

This is one use for the `@content` directive, however a more common use is when you want the content placed into the mixin to be wrapped by other rules or directives, such as a media query. Let's face it, writing out media queries can be a chore at the best of times. The syntax can be long and making even a minor mistake can cause odd layout problems that can be tricky to isolate and debug.

Using @content for media queries

So let's look at writing a mixin which abstracts away the unsightly media query syntax behind a simpler mixin. The first thing I like to do when writing a mixin is ask myself "what would be the nicest syntax to be able to use for this feature?" In other words, how would I like to write this when I'm using it?

For example, I don't like having to write this:

```
@media (min-width: 768px) {
    ...
}
```

I'd much prefer to decide what sizes I would like my project to adjust to and then write something as close to English as I can, so it makes sense to anyone reading over it. So, instead, my goal would be to write something like:

```
$small: 768px;
$medium: 1020px;
$large: 1280px;

@include media($small) {
    // Styles to take affect from small screen sizes upwards
}
```

Then I begin to work on how to achieve this and possibly make it better. The first target is getting this syntax to work. To know this particular mixin is working, we need some HTML and CSS first to visually signal that our changes are taking effect as and when they should.

We'll need three elements with some text in them. Our first will be an element which is best suited for mobile to medium screens. The next element will be best suited for medium to large screens, and the final element will be best suited for large screens and up. For this, we'll simply create the following HTML:

```
<div class="small">
    <p>Small screen device</p>
</div>
<div class="medium">
    <p>Medium screen device</p>
</div>
<div class="large">
    <p>Large screen device</p>
</div>
```

We then need to create some base styles to get everything to a good starting point:

```
// These styles simply remove unwanted browser defaults
```

```
// and set the box model
*, *::before, *::after {
  box-sizing: border-box;
  padding: 0;
  margin: 0;
}

// Here we simply make our elements stand out visually
.small, .medium, .large {
  padding: 2em;
  border: 2px solid red;
  margin: 0 auto;
}
```

As I said before, the aim here is to end up with this:

```
@include media($small) {...}
```

So let's first define our three breakpoints in variables:

```
$small: 480px;
$media: 768px;
$large: $980px
```

Now it's time to create our mixin. It will accept one parameter, called $size, which will be passed straight to our media queries inside:

```
@mixin media($size) {
  @media (min-width: $size) {
  @content;
  }
}
```

Next, we need to apply our new styles to the small element when the screen is at $small or above. We also need some styles to let us know our media queries are working. So when our screen is at the correct width or above, let's set our background color to black and our text color to white. It'll look tacky but it'll be clear if our mixin works or not:

```
.small {
  @include media($small) {
    background-color: black;
    color: white;
  }
}
```

So now if you resize your browser window or use your browser's dev responsive design tools, you'll see when we get to 768px and above our colors change. So our media query works.

Next, we'll add both medium and large media queries in the respective elements and change the colors again. Now, because we'll be reusing these two properties, this would seem like a good time to use an extend, right? Let's create a placeholder extend with our styles:

```
%breakpoint {
  background-color: black;
  color: white:
}
```

Now apply that to our small element instead of the `background-color` and `color` properties:

```
.small {
  @include media($small) {
    @extend %breakpoint;
    max-width: $small;
  }
}
```

At this point you'll get an error:

> **You may not @extend an outer selector from within @media. You may only @extend selectors within the same directive.**

What this is telling us is we can't use an extend created outside of the media inside the media query (or media directive). This is another kind of scope. We defined our placeholder in the `root` scope, but each `@media` directive is a unique scope. Basically, Sass just can't do it.

When you think about it, extending properties from the `root` scope inside media queries would rarely be that useful a feature anyways. Really, you shouldn't need to re-declare and duplicate properties from your general styles into your media queries all that often anyway. The whole point of media queries is to change or add properties, not reuse them.

You might instead think you can simply create the extend inside the media directive…but then some odd things can happen. Take this code, for example:

```
.small {
  @media (min-width: $small) {
    %color-red {color: red; }
    @extend %color-red;
  }
}
```

Not only is it completely pointless, but it has some unexpected CSS output. You get the following CSS:

```
@media (min-width: 480px) {
  .small .small {
    color: red;
  }
}
```

This is because we're nesting the media directive inside our class, as Sass allows us to do, but it compiles nested as well. Even if you place the small rule completely inside the media directive you'll get the same CSS. For this reason, I've never used extends when it comes to media queries. I don't even consider it a possibility.

However, we still don't want to write out those properties again and again. So we could write a mixin:

```
@mixin breakpoint {
  background-color: black;
  color: white;
}
```

However, we now need a way to know when one media query stops and the other begins. For this, we'll give our elements a max width so we can better see when each media query is taking effect.

Our small element will have a max-width which is equal to $small, .medium will have a max-width of $medium, and so on. We can add this to our breakpoint mixin so we can pass it in dynamically:

```
@mixin breakpoint($size) {
  max-width: $size;
  background-color: black;
  color: white;
}
```

Now we could place our media mixin inside this mixin and clean up our code even more. We'll also rename our breakpoint mixin to breakpoint:

```
@mixin breakpoint($size) {
  @include media($size) {
    max-width: $size;
    background-color: black;
    color: white;
  }
}
```

Then we can finish out our Sass and test everything works:

```
.small {@include breakpoint($small)}
.medium {@include breakpoint($medium)}
.large{@include breakpoint($large)}
```

Now, at full laptop/desktop screen size you should see a pyramid of black blocks with red borders and white text.

How could we make this better? Well, it would be nice if our variable names made more sense. `$small`, `$medium`, and `$large` don't say a whole lot about what their purpose is. If these were in a manifest file with 50-100 other variables it wouldn't be very clear what their purpose is.

But if we rename them `$breakpoint-small` and so on we would end up with this:

```
.small {@include breakpoint($breakpoint-small)}
.medium {@include breakpoint($breakpoint-medium)}
.large{@include breakpoint($breakpoint-large)}
```

That just won't do. I still want to be able to write `$small`, `$medium`, `$large`, or something similar.

We looked at lists before. Could we write a nested list like this instead:

```
$breakpoints: (
    (small 480px),
    (medium 768px),
    (large 980px)
);
```

That certainly fixes our variable naming problem, but now we would need to do some looping and checking for `small`, `medium`, `large` and whatever else we add with the index function. It would be a lot of trial and error to get this working in a way that is flexible. However, it would be nice to use `small`, `medium`, `large` instead of variables.

So if not lists, then what? Well, Sass 3.3 introduced a new data type called maps. Let's see if maps would solve our problem.

Maps

Maps in Sass are like **associative arrays** in PHP, dictionaries in Python, and hashes in Ruby. If you're familiar with any of these data types, then you'll understand what a map in Sass is.

Essentially, a map is a set of unordered key/value (or name/value) pairs. The key is a string that holds a value that can be any data type; a string, integer, Boolean, list, or even another map.

Maps look a lot like nested lists in Sass, however they use a descriptive name which actually holds the value. The value is (usually) the part we're really interested in, however the descriptive keys allow you to explain what that value is, or what its purpose is.

Take the following list, which we may have used for our media mixin previously (if we didn't have maps):

```
$breakpoints: (
  (small 480px),
  (medium 768px),
  (large 980px)
);
```

What we're doing here is technically abusing a list. Here, we're using the first index of each nested list (small, medium, large) to name the second index (480px, 768px, 980px).

One problem with this is, again, somewhat semantic. Lists should be kept for similar, or grouped values. small and 480px are not really similar. You could say they make up a group; the small breakpoint, but really small, is the name for 480px.

Another problem is that we don't need to retrieve small or medium or large for our media mixins, we would just write small or medium or large. We're using them just to explain what the value is.

Another problem is that retrieving the values is overly complicated for our needs. We would need to loop through each list and then get the nth index. So let's do it...just for fun!

We will need a function to retrieve the value based on the list and the string passed in. If the string exists it should return the appropriate value, if not, it will return false. Our function will be as follows:

```
@function list-get($list, $value) { // 1
  @each $item in $list { // 2
    @if $value == nth($item, 1) { // 3
      @return nth($item, 2); // 4. Success
    }
  }
  @return false; // 5. Fail
}
```

Ok. It wasn't that complicated to write a function to get our value:

1. First we take the list we want to use as our first parameter and then the name we want to search for to get the associated value.
2. Then our function loops through each $list and then checks each nested list for the $value in position 1 of that list.
3. The function checks for a matching string in position 1 of any of those lists.

4. If it finds a matching string it stops looping and returns the value which is in that list at index position 2. The important thing here to note is that on success it will stop and return and not execute any further code in the function.
5. If the loop finishes without finding a match we will exit the loop and return false instead. This would be the same as writing our function like this:

```
@function list-get($list, $value) { // 1
  @each $item in $list { // 2
    @if $value == nth($item, 1) { // 3
      @return nth($item, 2); // 4. Success
    } @else {
      @return false; // 5. Fail
    }
  }
}
```

It's essentially the same thing but just a tiny bit less code to write. If we use @debug now we can test it all works. Create a file called *list-get.scss* and inside that you should have the following:

```
$breakpoints: (
  (small 480px),
  (medium 768px),
  (large 980px)
);

@function list-get($list, $value) {
  @each $item in $list {
    @if $value == nth($item, 1) {
      @return nth($item, 2);
    }
  }
  @return false;
}

@debug list-get($breakpoints, small);
```

Then open the command line and run this command:

```
sass list-get.scss
```

You'll will get the output straight to the terminal without needing to compile to a file. This is called `stdout`:

```
list-get.scss:16 DEBUG: 480px
```

So we can see we got our value of `480px`. If we enter a name which doesn't exist, such as `desktop`, we'll get `false`:

```
@debug list-get($breakpoints, desktop);
```

The command line should look like this:

```
list-get.scss:16 DEBUG: false
```

So even though it's possible, hopefully by now you realize that using a list isn't the best way to go about this. Instead, we could (and certainly should) use a map.

Create a new file called *_map-get.scss* and inside it, our breakpoints map would look like this:

```
$breakpoints: (
  small: 480px,
  medium: 768px,
  large: 980px
);
```

That is much cleaner already. You define a map much like a list, using parentheses, however you don't need to wrap the contents in subsequent parentheses, you simply place a colon after the key (`small`, `medium`, `large`) and Sass then knows this is a map and not a list.

Now how do we retrieve the values we want from a map? Well, we use a function just like the one we wrote for getting our list value. Where our `list-get` function took a `list` and got a value, our function to get a value from a map is called `map-get`:

```
@debug map-get($breakpoints, small);
```

In the command line you should now see `480px` again:

```
map-get.scss:16 DEBUG: 480px
```

So now that we know how to use a basic map, we can refactor our previous active-breakpoint and media mixins to use our $breakpoints map:

```
@mixin media($size) {
  @media (min-width: map-get($breakpoints, $size)) {
    @content;
  }
}
```

All we've done here is replace $size with our map-get function. Next, we need to update the breakpoint mixin as well:

```
@mixin breakpoint($size) {
    @include media($size) {
        max-width: map-get($breakpoints, $size);
        background-color: black;
        color: white;
    }
}
```

Now we can use the names for our sizes, small, medium, and large, where we've called our breakpoint mixin:

```
.small {
    @include breakpoint(small);
}

.medium {
    @include breakpoint(medium);
}

.large {
    @include breakpoint(large);
}
```

So that's the standard way we can use maps to group similar variables together under one variable and use names to retrieve them. However, what if you have a map which contains multiple levels? How do we retrieve deeper values within a map? Take this map, for example:

```
$primary-theme: (
  font: (
    family: (
      serif: (Georgia, Times New Roman, serif),
      sans: (Verdana, Arial, sans-serif),
      code: (Monaco, Consolas, Courier New, monospace)
    ),
```

```
    size: (
       small: 0.75em,
       normal: 1em,
       large: 1.33em,
       x-large: 2em
    )
  ),
  color: (
    blue: (
      default: hsl(210, 50%, 50%),
      light: hsl(210, 50%, 75%),
      dark: hsl(210, 50%, 25%)
    )
  )
);
```

It's not unlikely that you may want to do something like this. That way you could simply replace this map to change the entire theme throughout your design. However, we have a map which is three levels deep and could possibly go even deeper than that, although three is about as deep as I would recommend.

So how do we get at the deepest value? Let's say we want to get font => family => sans. Well, first we need to retrieve the top level of the map; font:

```
@debug map-get($theme, font);
```

You'll see we get back the contents of font, which is itself a map. So to retrieve another key's contents, we need to wrap this map-get in another map-get. Our first map-get call is passed as the first parameter of this map-get and we then pass the key we want to retrieve as the second:

```
@debug map-get(map-get($primary-theme, font), family);
```

Now we have the contents of the family map, which contains serif, sans, and code. As you might have guessed, to get one of these we need to wrap everything in yet another map-get:

```
@debug map-get(map-get(map-get($primary-theme, font), family), serif);
```

Yeah…it's pretty awful. When I first realized this was the syntax for dealing with maps I wasn't too impressed. So I set about coming up with something simpler.

It's a common solution or pattern when dealing with complex arrays to loop over them as a way to drill down to the value you want without having to do much work. You do this by creating a new array on each iteration which contains the result of the last loop, thus iterating deeper and deeper into a multidimensional array. The same can be done for maps. You'll probably be surprised how simple it actually is.

So the syntax we are aiming for is as follows:

```
get($map, $first-level-key, $second-level-key, $third-level-key);
```

This function should then loop over $map and search for the key $first-level-key. It will create a new array which only contains the contents of $first-level-key. It then will loop again looking for the key $second-level-key and will replace our current array with the contents of $second-level-key. It will do this for as many keys as we pass in until we have the desired value. The loop exits and that value is returned:

```
@function get($map, $arglist: ()) {
    $m: $map; // 1.
    @each $item in $arglist { // 2.
        $m: map-get($m, $item);
    }
    @return $m;
}
@debug get($primary-theme, (font, family, serif));
```

The preceding code can be explained as follows:

1. Here, we are setting then reassigning the $map parameter passed in to a new variable, $m. This allows us to replace the map on each iteration, or loop.
2. Then we loop over the values passed into the list $arglist. Each result is passed to $item for use inside the loop.
3. For each item in $arglist we place that value in $m, replacing the previous map with a new map until the value is no longer a map. Then the loop exits and $m is returned. This will be the value of the last $arglist item.

This works well, however there is a feature in Sass which will allow us to remove the need for a list as our second parameter. That way we can remove the need for brackets. This feature is called arglist.

You create an arglist by placing three dots after a variable name:

```
@function get($map, $arglist...) {
    $m: $map;
    @each $item in $arglist {
```

```scss
      $m: map-get($m, $item);
    }
  @return $m;
}
@debug get($primary-theme, font, family, serif);
```

`arglist` allows any number of arguments to be passed in in its place; therefore, it's perfect for this situation. So that's how you get values from maps.

There are other functions which you can use for maps, such as `map-merge`, which joins two maps together, or can be used to add a key value pair to a map like so:

```scss
$map: (
  one: 1,
  two: 2
);
$map: map-merge($map, (three: 3));
@debug $map;
```

This would give us the following:

```
Line 6 DEBUG: (one: 1, two: 2, three: 3)
```

Then there's `map-remove`, which removes a key and its value. Placed immediately after our previous example, we can use it to remove the key/value pair we just merged:

```scss
$map: map-remove($map, three);
@debug $map;
```

This would give us the following:

```
Line 8 DEBUG: (one: 1, two: 2)
```

To get a list of all the keys in a map we can use `map-keys`:

```scss
@debug map-keys($map);
```

This results in the following:

```
Line 9 DEBUG: one, two
```

Alternatively, to get the values we can use map-values:

```scss
@debug map-values($map);
```

This returns the values only:

```
Line 10 DEBUG: 1, 2
```

Summary

We've covered quite a lot in this chapter. We started by talking about why you should use the `!default` flag when defining variables throughout large projects to allow you to create manifest files (or `config` files) to allow easy customization of your project. From there we moved on to looking at the many issues which can arise from using (or rather misusing) variable scope in selectors, functions, and mixins.

Then we created a mixin for creating CSS arrows. This mixin used extends to reduce repetition in our CSS and allow dynamically including those extends, depending on the direction passed in to the arrow mixin using variable interpolation.

From there we moved on to using the `@content` directive to allow us to add properties to a mixin. We created a set of mixins which took advantage of the `@content` directive to simplify the creation of media queries.

Finally, we looked at using maps to group our breakpoint values while using useful names to identify them, which we were able to use in our media and breakpoint mixins. We then looked at how we can loop over a map to simplify the process of retrieving deeply nested values. We also quickly looked at some examples of other functions in Sass for dealing with maps.

After all that, you'll probably need a break from Sass. I know I do. So in the next chapter, we'll start to look at improving your Sass workflow. To do this we'll look at a task runner called `GulpJS`, which automates compiling or watching Sass and Compass and can even boot up a Node server and auto refresh your browser when your HTML or CSS changes!

6
Gulp – Automating Tasks for a Faster Workflow

From this point onwards, almost everything we do will be for our actual project. We'll be creating the homepage for a busy, content-rich website. Content-rich like a blog, a news website, or a tutorials website. We'll write mixins and functions which will be used throughout our project. Some of these will simply be for small design elements and others will be for large components, or features such as media queries and a custom built grid system.

However, before we get to actually writing code for our project we're going to look at removing and automating the repetitive tasks. Think about how many times we've had to run `compass compile`, or the `sass --watch` commands. Then we need to switch to our browser and hit *F5* or click **Refresh** to see the changes. Then we jump to our editor and make some changes and repeat.

So, in this chapter we'll focus on setting up our project to use GulpJS to make our task easier and less repetitive from this point forward. We'll examine the technologies which Gulp is built on including NodeJS and npm. We'll take a quick look at how to use both Node and npm to run certain tasks, so we can see how Gulp makes everything much easier for us to configure and maintain.

We'll look at installing and configuring Gulp in our project. Gulp runs on numerous plugins, each with a specific purpose. We'll look at using the `gulp-ruby-sass` plugin as well as `gulp-sourcemaps`, and `browser-sync` to live reload our browser on changes to our files.

Setting up our project

First thing we need to do is create our project's folder structure from scratch. We'll follow the SMACSS style and group each part in its own folder, which will contain its partials. The main Sass file *style.scss* will import all of the other files. This file will act as our *table of contents* for where our files are and in what order they're loaded. We'll also maintain an actual table of contents, so we can easily see where each section is when looking at this file.

Creating our folder and files

We're going to use Compass to bootstrap our project structure. This will create our project folder, our *scss* folder, and our *css* folder, and generate some files for us too. Let's refresh our memories on how to do this by running `compass help create` (create being the command which will generate our project folder):

```
compass help create
```

Here we can see a list of the options we can use to create our project folder just the way we want it. We're going to specify the folders we want and the output style. Our project is going to be called `mastering-sass-swag`. Yep, that's right! Our website is going to be about Mastering Sass Developer goodies for all those hipster developers looking to get some nerdy fashion goods and stickers and coffee mugs and such. So technically an e-commerce website...but one that doesn't take itself too seriously. So, with that established, let's create our project:

```
compass create mastering-sass-swag --sass-dir=assets/scss --css-
dir=assets/css
```

Compass should now create our main project folder and inside our *config.rb* and an *assets* directory. Inside the *assets* directory should be an *scss* folder and a *css* folder:

```
mastering-sass-swag
   |-- assets
   |     |-- scss
   |     |     |-- ie.scss
   |     |     |-- print.scss
   |     |     |-- screen.scss
   |     |-- css
   |     |     |-- ie.css
   |     |     |-- print.css
   |     |     |-- screen.css
   |-- config.rb
```

Before we go any further, we have some cleanup to do. We're going to delete six of these files and rename one. From the command line `cd`, go into the `css` directory and delete everything in that folder first:

```
cd mastering-sass-swag/assets/css && rm ie.css && rm print.css && rm
screen.css
```

If you're on Windows, the preceding command will work by installing and using Git Bash, Cygwin or Babun. Babun is an awesome project for getting the Cygwin setup on Windows in one click. You'll then have access to every Unix command from Windows such as `touch`, `nano`, `vim`, `mv`, `rm`, `ls`, `ssh`, `sed`, and many more. I can't recommend it enough! `http://bab un.github.io`

> After installing Babun you can get all the Unix commands to work through CMD by appending `;C:\babun\.babun\cygwin\bin` to your global PATH variable.

Otherwise you can use the following command in CMD:

```
cd mastering-sass-swag/assets/css && del ie.css print.css screen.css
```

Next delete the `print.scss` and `ie.scss` (no need for `ie` specific styles any more and for brevity' sake we're not going to worry about printing either).

```
cd ../scss && rm ie.scss && rm print.scss
```

Then rename `screen.scss` to `style.scss` (this is mostly personal preference). The move command (`mv` in Unix and `ren` in Windows) can be used to rename files:

```
mv screen.scss style.scss
```

Why Gulp and not Grunt?

When I started out with task runners it was way back when **Grunt** first hit the scene and Gulp wasn't even a thing yet. Grunt has changed quite a bit since then and other tools like Yeoman have arrived on the scene as well as Gulp.

When I tried Grunt back then it was lost on me. I liked the idea of not having to refresh my browser and only having to run one command to do lots and lots of different things, but because I didn't understand how you did any of this before Grunt. I felt like the setup of Grunt, the Grunt CLI, and then all those brackets, were overly complex.

That was entirely because I had no experience with NodeJS before trying Grunt. When something went wrong (and things went wrong for me often) I had no concept of why it might be going wrong. I didn't have any comprehension of the technology behind Grunt. Most of the time it was a Node problem, or rather a problem with one of the many packages Grunt was using, and my system not installing things properly behind the scenes.

In the end I completely gave up on Grunt. To be honest, I've still never gotten it to work on any of my many computers since then and I've tried many, many times. Grunt and me just don't like each other. So when I discovered a new task runner was making big waves I was really excited to try it out.

Gulp won me over immediately. I preferred its syntax. Requiring everything in at the top of the files felt like PHP, so I just understood it. Then the syntax of writing your tasks in closures also reminded me of PHP, or just plain old JavaScript, which I was at least familiar with. In the beginning I thought that, aside from the syntax, Grunt, and Gulp were exactly the same in what they did. Now I know that's not the case. The results are the same, but the way each works is very different.

When I started learning **Gulp** I was determined not to make the same mistakes I made with Grunt. I was going to take my time and learn how to fix things if they went wrong. To be fair to Grunt things went wrong with Gulp just as often and in much the same manner. The only difference was for some reason, when Gulp broke I was more comfortable debugging the problem. I could console log things and strip it all back until I had isolated the problem.

Now I know there's Grunt users out there right now getting angry because you can do the exact same things in Grunt when stuff goes wrong. I'm not saying Gulp is better or has anything Grunt doesn't have. It's just to me Gulp is *easier*. For me Gulp is less intimidating. I don't know why Grunt intimidates me, perhaps it's because I tried it when I was a total noob and I've got a mental block now. Either way, for me, Gulp is my preference.

So, if you're a Grunt aficionado, then you'll be able to follow along with Grunt. After all, pretty much all the Gulp plugins I'll mention here were either inspired by Grunt plugins or the underlying Node packages. So with some research you should be able to get Grunt to do everything we're going to cover here. Or you could try out Gulp. I'll leave that up to you.

Node and npm

Before we look at Gulp I want to look at Node and npm first. Like I said, a lot of the problems I've encountered have actually been more easily solved once I understood, after understanding what Gulp is built on. So that means understanding how Node and npm can be used to run and automate tasks.

Let's set up our project for Node using `npm init`. From the root of our `mastering-sass-swag` run:

npm init

This will then ask you to fill in a series of fields which npm uses to generate the *package.json* file. Those fields and what you should type are as follows:

```
name: mastering-sass-swag
version: 1.0.0
description: Front-end for Mastering Sass Swag
entry point: index.js
test command:
git repository:
author: Your Name
license: ISC
```

When asked "Is this ok? (yes)", hit *Enter* to accept. If you made any mistakes, or you want to change something, you can always open up `package.json` and make your modifications there. In fact, open up `package.json` anyways. Notice right now there's an object called `scripts` and inside that you'll see:

```
// mastering-sass-swag/package.json
"test": "echo "Error: no test specified" && exit 1"
```

In the command line run:

npm test

You'll see the message `Error: no test specified`. This is a handy feature of npm which allows us to not only run commands, but give them a nice alias; like `"test"`. Let's use npm to run a few Sass commands. Modify scripts in your *package.json* file like so:

```
// mastering-sass-swag/package.json
"scripts": {
    "test": "echo "Error: no test specified" && exit 1",
    "sass:compile": "sass --update --compass
assets/scss/style.scss:assets/css/style.css",
    "sass:watch": "sass --watch --compass
assets/scss/style.scss:assets/css/style.css"
},
```

Now, you may be tempted to run the command `npm sass:compile`, however that won't work I'm afraid. npm has a few special commands which can be set up in the scripts section. `"test"` is one and `"start"` is another which is frequently used.

For any custom script aliases however, you need to add the keyword `run` before the alias of the script to run:

```
npm run sass:compile
```

It might take slightly longer to run than simply executing the command itself, but that's to be expected. However, using `npm` in this manner to run long command line operations can save you a lot of time typing. You could have commands for watching and compiling for development which would preserve line-comments and `sourcemaps` and compile to expanded `css`, and then you could have commands saved for compiling without comments or `sourcemaps`, with the compiled CSS fully compressed to a distribution folder.

You'll also notice in our scripts we're using Sass, and not Compass and we're simply using the `--compass` flag to include Compass. Unless you deleted the line `@importcompass/reset` you'll see *style.css* was indeed compiled with the reset styles, so we know Compass works. This is another reason we no longer need a *config.rb* file.

Let's modify our scripts so when we're developing we want to watch our Sass and compile to expanded output with line comments and `sourcemaps`, but when we're ready to compile for the final `dist` version, we compile our *style.scss* compressed to another folder called *dist/assets/css* and a file called *style.min.css*.

```
// mastering-sass-swag/package.json
"scripts": {
    "test": "echo "Error: no test specified" && exit 1",
    "sass:watch": "sass --watch --compass --style=expanded --line-comments
--line-numbers --sourcemap=auto
assets/scss/style.scss:assets/css/style.css",
    "sass:compile": "sass --update --compass --sourcemaps=none --
style=compressed --force assets/scss:assets/css"
},
```

Now we can use `npm run sass:watch` while we develop and then `npm run sass:compile` to create a minified version for a final build version. We'll get to that later in this chapter. For now though, let's move on from npm and look at doing all of this Node.js.

Node.js, node-sass, and fileWatch

Using `npm` to run shell commands is all well and good, but as you can imagine it has its limits. When you want to really complicate things, you'll need to start writing tasks in Node.js. To do this we'll need that *index.js* file we specified in our *package.json* entry point field.

Create a file called *index.js*. Next we'll need to download a package which compiles watches our Sass files. The package is `node-sass`. The `node-sass` is a Node "wrapper" of the `LibSass` port of Sass. This means we write code familiar to Node which then uses `LibSass` to actually compile and do whatever else we ask.

So first we'll run the command to download and install `node-sass` into our project:

```
npm install node-sass --save-dev
```

This tells `npm` to download/install the `node-sass` package from the `npm` registry. The `--save-dev` flag tells it to automatically add it to our *package.json* file for us as a development dependency. This means this package is only necessary while we develop our site, but wouldn't be necessary when we launch. To include packages as dependencies for production you would use the `--save` flag. However, all of this is really only necessary if you are making a Node app with Express or Ember or something that depends on certain packages to work on a Node server. This could also be if you are writing your own `npm` packages and it has dependencies. For our purposes however, `--save-dev` is all we need.

Now we'll need to include our package in `index.js` so we can access it. We do this with the `require` function:

```
// mastering-sass-swag/index.js
"use strict";
var sass = require("node-sass");
```

I'm using the `"use strict"` keyword to force JavaScript to be less forgiving of certain things. The main difference for me is this means we can't instantiate variables for the first time without having `var` before them. For Node applications, which can be very large and spread across multiple files, this is a good idea. You could also place it inside your functions instead of at the root of your files. This would mean your function would need to abide by these rules but code outside of it doesn't need to. This is useful if you're creating a plugin or module to work with other people's JavaScript.

For us to be able to use the `node-sass` package it needs to be able to watch files and write changes to files. This means dealing with the file system of your operating system. Node comes with many built in modules to simplify specific tasks. One of them is the `File System` module, however you'll more often see it called `fs`. Seeing as it is built-in there is no need to install it using npm, we can simply include it using `require`:

```
// mastering-sass-swag/index.js
"use strict";
var sass = require("node-sass");
var fs = require("fs");
```

With that done we should probably do a quick test to ensure our file has no syntax errors. Let's do a quick `console.log` below the rest of our code:

```
// mastering-sass-swag/index.js
"use strict";
var sass = require("node-sass");
var fs = require("fs");

console.log("OK");
```

To run our `node` app we simply run the following from the command line:

node index.js

If all went well, you should see `OK` in the command line. Otherwise you'll most likely get a `SyntaxError` indicating where exactly the problem is. Fix any errors you might have and run `node index.js` again. Once you see `OK` you're good to move on. You can remove the `console.log` also.

The first thing we're going to do is simply get `node-sass` to compile our Sass when we run node. To do this we will use the `node-sass` render function. This function takes a number of options before passing the data (which will be our SCSS files) to a function where we can manipulate it. From there, we could print it to the console for simple debugging or pass it in a "stream" to another module or we can simply render it to a file, which is what we'll be doing.

First we need to pass in our options. For our example we'll only really need the `file` option, meaning the SCSS file we want to compile. However, we'll also pass two additional options `outputStyle` and `sourceComments`:

```
// mastering-sass-swag/index.js
"use strict";
var sass = require("node-sass");
var fs = require("fs");

sass.render(
    {
        file: "assets/scss/style.scss",
        outputStyle: "expanded",
        sourceComments: true
    }
);
```

If you run this nothing, will happen. You won't get any errors, but it also won't do anything with our *style.scss* file. Of course this makes sense. We haven't told `node-sass` where we want to save the input to or how we want to handle errors or any of that. To do that we need to pass an anonymous function as the second parameter of the render function. This anonymous function also takes two parameters. The first is a variable for handling errors and the second is the data (or input) from our file *assets/scss/style.scss*.

Inside this function, we'll check for errors and if none are found we will compile our file using the file system `writeFile` function, once again checking for errors which may occur with this process:

```
// mastering-sass-swag/index.js
"use strict";
var sass = require("node-sass");
var fs = require("fs");

sass.render(
    {
        file: "assets/scss/style.scss",
        outputStyle: "expanded",
        sourceComments: true
    },
    (error, scssData) => {
        if (!error) {
        //If there are no errors reading the data write the scssData.css
data
            // to "assets/css/style.css" or else handle any errors thrown
            fs.writeFile("assets/css/style.css", scssData.css, (err) => {
                if (!error) {
                // Print a message to the console so we know everything
worked
                    console.log("Compiled!");
                } else {
                    // Print an error message to the console
                    console.log("There was an error writing to the css
                    file");
                }
            })
        } else {
            // Print an error message to the console
            console.log("There was an error reading the Sass data");
        }
    }
);
```

I'm using **arrow functions** from the ES2015 (aka ES6) spec. Arrow functions are used instead of nested anonymous functions to allow for a lexical `this`. Meaning if you use `this` inside your nested function, it will refer to the parent object. This is much the same way object-oriented languages work. We won't be using `this` but I like the terseness of arrow functions either way.

What we've done in the preceding steps is fairly straightforward. Node Sass has taken the data in from the file we specified in the options. It converts this to `css` but retains it as data in a buffer. This means we can manipulate it in any way we might need. We want to write it to a file so we use `writeFile` to do this. `writeFile` takes the destination file as the first parameter, the buffered data with the extension `css` and lastly a function to handle errors and output messages on success/failure.

It's important to note the second parameter is not in quotes and must have `.css` or else the `css` file will simply have `undefined` written to it.

Assuming you still have the *assets/scss/style.scss* and *assets/css/style.css* files from before, you can add the following code to them to ensure everything is working as it should. In the *style.scss* file, add a quick test:

```
// mastering-sass-swag/assets/css/style.scss
.test {
    content: "Test 01";
}
```

Now, in the command line run:

```
node index.js
```

You should see `Compiled!` in the console. Check your *style.css* file and it should have the preceding rule in it.

Watching for changes and writing to a file

The last thing we'll do before moving on to Gulp is to show how we can use `node` and `node-sass` to watch a `.scss` file for changes and automatically run the previous code then. It's actually really easy, because the `node` File System module comes with a built in file watcher, `fs.watch`. Watch takes a string (the file to watch) as its first parameter and a listener callback as its second argument. The listener callback takes two parameters also;

event and `filename`. Inside the listener callback we can check for a `change` event.

This will mean our watched file has changes and we can do something. Our full code is as follows:

```javascript
// mastering-sass-swag/index.js
"use strict";
var sass = require("node-sass");
var fs = require("fs");

console.log("Node Sass is watching for changes...");
fs.watch("assets/scss/style.scss", (event, filename) => {
    if (event === "change") {
        sass.render(
            {
                file: "assets/scss/style.scss",
                outputStyle: "expanded",
                sourceComments: true
            },
            (error, scssData) => {
                if (!error) {
                    // If there are no errors reading the data
                    fs.writeFile("assets/css/style.css", scssData.css,
(err)
                    => {
                        if (!error) {
                        // Print a message to the console so we know
                            everything worked
                            console.log("Compiled!");
                        } else {
                            // Print an error message to the console
                            console.log("There was an error writing to the
                            css file");
                        }
                    })
                } else {
                    // Print an error message to the console
                    console.log("There was an error reading the Sass
data");
                }
            }
        );
    }
});
```

Now run `node index.js` again and you should see our message `Node Sass is watching for changes....` Make some changes to `style.scss` and save them and they will be instantly saved to `style.css`. One thing you'll notice about `node-sass` is because it is built on `LibSass` it's incredibly fast.

The only downside to `LibSass` is it doesn't quite have all the features of Ruby Sass. This includes Compass. However, the better you get with Gulp and Sass the less you'll want to (or need to) use Compass.

Setting up Gulp

The first thing we need to do to use Gulp in our project is install it in our dev-dependencies. We do this using `npm` install:

```
npm install --save-dev gulp
```

Once gulp is installed, our next step is changing our *package.json* file so our `main` script is *gulpfile.js* instead of *index.js*:

```
// mastering-sass-swag/package.json
"main": "gulpfile.js",
```

We're going to delete our *config.rb* file. Surprised? We'll, we're not going to be running commands like `compass watch` or `compass compile` so we won't need the *config.rb* file. Instead we're going to do everything from this point on through Gulp. So keeping *config.rb* would just confuse things:

```
rm config.rb
```

We can also delete `index.js` at this point for the same reasons:

```
rm index.js
```

Next we need to create the *gulpfile.js* where we will add all of our Gulp tasks. Create a file *gulpfile.js* in the root of our project, and inside add the following:

```
// mastering-sass-swag/gulpfile.js
'use strict';
var gulp = require('gulp');

gulp.task('log', () => {
    console.log('Gulp is working!');
});
```

I like to create a task called `log` which I use to quickly check if things are working while I set everything up. To run this task, we simply type `gulp log` in the command line:

```
gulp log
```

You should see the following in the command line:

```
[17:18:20] Using gulpfile ~\mastering-sass-swag\gulpfile.js
[17:18:20] Starting 'log'...
Gulp is working!
[17:18:20] Finished 'log' after 254 µs
```

So we create a task by calling the `task` method. The first parameter is a `string`, which is the name of the task. That's what we type after `gulp` in the command line to run the task. Next is a callback within which we place our task code. You'll notice the code you place in here often follows a similar pattern.

First you define the `src`. This is where the task will look for files to run the task on. Next you'll chain a series of `pipes` to that. Each of these will run an operation on the `stream` before finally saving the output to a folder or file, specified with `dest`.

I've chosen to use `gulp-ruby-sass` here because it is more stable than the `gulp-sass` plugin at the time of writing this. The issue with `gulp-sass` is that it is a wrapper for `node-sass` which is itself a port of `LibSass`, which means when something doesn't work everyone tends to play *pass the parcel* and simply point at someone else and says it's their problem. So finding solutions takes longer, and even when a bug is finally submitted to the correct place it means `LibSass` has to fix the bug, then `node-sass` needs to update `LibSass`, then `gulp-sass` needs to update its version of `node-sass`. So...it's just too messy.
At the time of writing this, the `LibSass` implementation has numerous problems regarding incorrect line numbers and `sourcemaps` not generating correctly. Therefore, I'll stick with gulp plugins either using `ruby-sass` or `compass`. The `gulp-compass` works well also.

Let's install `gulp-ruby-sass` and see an example of all of this working with a simple `sass:compile` task. Install `gulp-ruby-sass` and save it as a `dev-dependency`:

```
npm install --save-dev gulp-ruby-sass
```

Once that's installed, add it to your `gulpfile`:

```
// mastering-sass-swag/gulpfile.js
'use strict';
var gulp = require('gulp');
var sass = require('gulp-ruby-sass');
```

Now let's create another task called `sass:compile`. This will recursively look in the `assets/scss` directory for `.scss` and `.sass` files. We do this using a `glob` pattern. You'll see these a lot in Gulp:

```
// mastering-sass-swag/gulpfile.js
gulp.task('sass:compile', () => {
    return sass('assets/scss/**/*.{scss,sass}');
});
```

The preceding glob tells Gulp we want to look in `assets/scss`. The `**/*` tells Gulp we want to search all directories inside here also. We'll need this if we have a folder for "partials". The last part `.{scss,sass}` tells Gulp we want to use `.scss` files and `.sass` files. This means we can use both `.scss` and `.sass` files in our project if we need to.

 There is no space between items inside braces in glob patterns. Meaning there is no space after the comma in `{scss,sass}`.

If we run this, we'll get no errors but we also won't compile any changes made to the files in `assets/scss`. This is because the task will run fine but we haven't told Gulp what we want to do with the data it has gathered from those files. Much like running `node-sass` it needs to know what to do and where to save the results. For that we need to pipe it to its destination in *assets/css*:

```
// mastering-sass-swag/gulpfile.js
gulp.task('sass:compile', () => {
    retrun sass('/assets/scss/**/*.{scss,sass}')
    .pipe(gulp.dest('assets/css'));
});
```

First let's delete everything in the *asset/css* directory so we know exactly what `gulp-ruby-sass` is doing now:

`rm assets/css/*`

This command will delete all the files in *assets/css*. Now we can run our task:

`gulp sass:compile`

You can see `gulp` create our *style.css* file, however it has no source comments and it also doesn't create a `sourcemap` (`style.css.map`). Before we address this, I want to create some variables to store our paths and glob patterns so we don't need to keep repeating them. I also want to use the Node path module so we can create absolute paths. This will help reduce errors to do with invalid file paths. First let's require in the path module:

```
// mastering-sass-swag/gulpfile.js
'use strict';
var path = require('path');
var gulp = require('gulp');
var sass = require('gulp-ruby-sass');
```

We can now create some variables to hold our paths and globs:

```
// mastering-sass-swag/gulpfile.js
var pathto = {
    "scss": path.join(__dirname, '/assets/scss'),
    "css" : path.join(__dirname, '/assets/css')
};

var glob = {
    "sass": path.join(pathto.scss, '/**/*.{scss,sass}')
}
```

Now let's use our `log` task to print out everything so we can see how `path.join` created absolute paths for us which are formatted correctly for your operating system. Meaning if you're on Windows it will use \ to separate directories and for Unix operating systems it will use / to separate directories:

```
// mastering-sass-swag/gulpfile.js
gulp.task('log', () => {
    console.log(pathto.scss);
    console.log(pathto.css);
    console.log(glob.sass);
});
```

Now if you run `gulp log` you'll see full paths printed to the console for each of the preceding statements. We can now replace the paths in our `sass:compile` task and check everything still works:

```
// mastering-sass-swag/gulpfile.js
gulp.task('sass:compile', () => {
    return sass(glob.sass)
    .pipe(gulp.dest(pathto.css));
});
```

Now it's time to pass some options to `gulp sass` so we can control how our CSS looks and whether we get line comments and `sourcemaps` and anything else we might want. We do this by passing options to `sass` as the second parameter:

```
// mastering-sass-swag/gulpfile.js
gulp.task('sass:compile', () => {
    return sass(glob.sass, {
        style: 'expanded',
        lineNumbers: true,
        sourcemap: true
    })
    .pipe(gulp.dest(pathto.css));
});
```

When you run `gulp sass:compile` again you'll notice the resulting `css` has line-numbers and also the output style is expanded, however we don't get any `sourcemaps`. This is because to generate the actual `sourcemap` file and save it correctly most `gulp` plugins (even JavaScript plugins) use a separate plugin dedicated to handling `sourcemaps`. This plugin is called `gulp-sourcemaps`. No surprises there. Let's install it:

npm install --save-dev gulp-sourcemaps

With that done, we can pipe our stream through the `gulp-sourcemap` functions to generate the correct `sourcemap` code and save it to the necessary files. First require in the `gulp-sourcemaps` plugin:

```
// mastering-sass-swag/gulpfile.js
'use strict';
var path       = require('path');
var gulp       = require('gulp');
var sass       = require('gulp-ruby-sass');
var sourcemaps = require('gulp-sourcemaps');
```

Then we can pipe our data through it before we output our `css`:

```
// mastering-sass-swag/gulpfile.js
gulp.task('sass:compile', () => {
    return sass(glob.sass, {
        style: 'expanded',
        lineNumbers: true,
        sourcemap: true
    })
    .pipe(sourcemaps.write())
    .pipe(gulp.dest(pathto.css));
});
```

Now, when you run `gulp sass:compile` you'll notice we still don't get the *style.css.map* file we're used to. This is because by default `gulp-sourcemaps` write them into your `css` files. If you open *style.css* you'll see the `sourceMappingURL` at the bottom of the file:

```
/*# sourceMappingURL=data:application/json;base64,eyJ2ZXJ ... */
```

Personally, I prefer to have `sourcemaps` in their own files. So to do this you need to pass at least once parameters to `sourcemaps.write()`, the location where you want to place your `sourcemaps` relative to the `gulp.dest()` location. So, to place them in the same folder as your `css` you would use a dot which means this folder:

```
// mastering-sass-swag/gulpfile.js
gulp.task('sass:compile', () => {
    return sass(glob.sass, {
        style: 'expanded',
        lineNumbers: true,
        sourcemap: true
    })
    .pipe(sourcemaps.write('.'))
    .pipe(gulp.dest(pathto.css));
});
```

You could also have them in a separate folder for maps:

```
// mastering-sass-swag/gulpfile.js
gulp.task('sass:compile', () => {
    return sass(glob.sass, {
        style: 'expanded',
        lineNumbers: true,
        sourcemap: true
    })
    .pipe(sourcemaps.write('maps'))
    .pipe(gulp.dest(pathto.css));
});
```

Personally I prefer to just keep them in the same folder as the `css`. We'll be creating a completely separate folder for our minified "production ready" CSS, HTML, and JavaScript anyways so the *assets* folder is only for us throughout the development.

So we can now compile our Sass and we have `sourcemaps`. The last thing we need to be able to do is watch for changes and recompile the CSS each time we save our SCSS files.

Gulp watch

This is one of the things I really liked straightaway with Gulp. It has a built-in "file watcher" which you can use in any task straight away…and it's really simple.

Grunt had a plugin `grunt-contrib-watch` which does the same thing, but I always wondered why it wasn't just built-in. Having to install it and configure it every time just annoyed me.

So let's just dive right in and create a new task called `sass:watch` (always makes me think of Sasquatch):

```
// mastering-sass-swag/gulpfile.js
gulp.task('sass:watch', () => {

});
```

Next we call `gulp.watch()`. This takes two parameters (actually it can take three, but we'll only use two here). The first is a glob pattern for the files to watch. This can be a string with a simple glob pattern or an array of globs to specify multiple directories or combinations of files to watch and files to exclude. The second parameter can be an array of tasks to run on those files when a change is detected, or you can use a callback where you can do more complex operations. We'll be using the array of tasks in this example:

```
// mastering-sass-swag/gulpfile.js
gulp.task('sass:watch', () => {
    gulp.watch(glob.sass, ['sass:compile']);
});
```

Now run `gulp sass:watch` from the command line and our CSS will update whenever we make a change. This is all well and good, but so far we've just replaced what Sass was able to do anyway with Gulp. Where Gulp really starts to save us time is when we use it to automatically reload our browser when our files change.

BrowserSync

I've tried pretty much all of the `livereload` plugins for Gulp. The most reliable by far is BrowserSync. It also doesn't require you to set up any extensions in your browser unlike Live Reload. `Gulp-connect` is a good option also, and I was all set to use that for this example because it doesn't require you to manually insert the live-reload script tag into the HTML. However, a few days ago after an update from 2.2.3 to 3.x it has stopped working completely and a solution hasn't been found as of yet. I would say check it out though, if you want the least amount of setup.

So, first we'll need a simple HTML page. Let's create a simple homepage for our Mastering Sass Swag project. For now, we'll just show a `Coming Soon` message.

```html
<!-- mastering-sass-swag/index.html ->
<!DOCTYPE html>
<html lang="en">
<head>
    <meta charset="UTF-8">
    <title>Mastering Sass Swag - Covering developers front-ends since
    2016</title>

    <link rel="stylesheet" href="assets/css/style.css">
</head>
<body>
    <main>
        <h1>Mastering Sass Swag</h1>
        <h2>Coming soon</h2>
    </main>
</body>
</html>
```

With that done we can install `browserSync` and require it into our `gulpfile`. From the command line:

```
npm install --save-dev browser-sync
```

Once that's installed you'll need to require it in your *gulpfile.js*:

```js
// mastering-sass-swag/gulpfile.js
'use strict';
var path        = require('path');
var gulp        = require('gulp');
var sass        = require('gulp-ruby-sass');
var sourcemaps  = require('gulp-sourcemaps');
var sync        = require('browser-sync').create();
```

Then we need to create a task which creates a server, watch for changes, and then run the necessary tasks and reload the browser.

Browser `sync` can be one of the more complicated tasks to set up in Gulp, so I'll add comments to explain what we're doing. First, we need to process and place browser sync at the end of any streams in relevant tasks. For example the `sass:compile` task should refresh the browser once it's done. So we need to place `sync.stream` at the end of the stream so it knows when the `css` changes, not the `scss` files.

```js
// mastering-sass-swag/gulpfile.js
gulp.task('sass:compile', () => {
```

```
    return sass(glob.sass, {
        style: 'expanded',
        lineNumbers: true,
        sourcemap: true
    })
    .pipe(sourcemaps.write('.'))
    // Output the files to CSS
    .pipe(gulp.dest(pathto.css))
    // To use browser sync it needs to process the stream AFTER gulp.dest
    .pipe(sync.stream());
});
```

This on its own won't do anything but place browser sync in the stream so it can be made aware of changes. Next we need to create the server and the task which runs the actual reload.

```
// mastering-sass-swag/gulpfile.js
// Creates a server at http://localhost:3000
gulp.task('serve', ['log'], () => {
    // Set up the options for the server
    sync.init({
        server: {
            // set the root of your server relative to this file
(gulpfile.js)
            baseDir: './'
        }
    });

    // Watch for changes and run any task we need
    gulp.watch(glob.sass, ['sass:compile']);
    // We can also manually run reload on files that aren't
    // in a gulp stream (files not processed by a Gulp task)
    gulp.watch('./*.html').on('change', sync.reload);
});
```

You'll notice I've placed the log task in an array as the second parameter of the serve task. This is so I could mention an important feature of Gulp. If you want a task to run before this task you can place it in an array as the second parameter. When we run gulp serve now it will first log our paths and glob patterns and then run the serve task:

gulp serve

You should see something like the following in your command line:

```
[17:54:24] Using gulpfile ~\Documents\MASTERING
SASS\BOOK\Ch06\code\mastering-sass-swag\gulpfile.js
[17:54:24] Starting 'log'...
C:\mastering-sass-swag\assets\scss
```

```
C:\mastering-sass-swag\assets\css
C:\mastering-sass-swag\assets\scss\**\*.{scss,sass}
[17:54:24] Finished 'log' after 545 µs
[17:54:24] Starting 'serve'...
[17:54:24] Finished 'serve' after 41 ms
[BS] Access URLs:
-----------------------------------
    Local: http://localhost:3000
    External: http://123.456.7.89:3000
-----------------------------------
       UI: http://localhost:3001
UI External: http://123.456.7.89:3001
-----------------------------------
[BS] Serving files from: ./
```

Another interesting thing about browser-sync is you can send the external address to someone and they can view it from anywhere...as long as you're connected to the Internet and have the browser-sync server running. Good for quickly demonstrating a new design tweak to a client or co-worker without having to put everything up on an actual server.

So open up your browser of choice and visit http://localhost:3000 and you'll see the coming soon page. Let's test it's working and actually refreshing automatically. Let's edit our HTML and add a better message:

```
<!-- mastering-sass-swag/index.html ->
<h1>Mastering Sass Swag</h1>
<h2>Coming soon</h2>

<p>Sorry! Our front-end is a little exposed right now...</p>
<p>We'll find something to cover it up with real soon!</p>
```

Keep an eye on the browser, and when you save your changes everything should refresh and show the new changes. Now let's try our Sass. We've already hooked up our *assets/css/style.css* so we should be able to make changes to our SCSS and see the updates immediately. Let's center all the text:

```
// mastering-sass-swag/assets/scss/style.scss
h1, h2, p {
    text-align: center;
}
```

Summary

In this chapter we've begun setting up our main project, Mastering Sass Swag, which we'll work on from here on out. We also set up the main directory structure we'll use for this project. We took a quick look at using `npm` and `node` to compile and watch Sass using `node-sass`, which is a `LibSass` wrapper for node-based projects.

Then we looked at installing and configuring Gulp for our project. We saw how to install and set up numerous Gulp plugins, each with a specific purpose such as `gulp-ruby-sass`, `gulp-sourcemaps`, and `browsersync` to live reload our browser on changes to our files.

In the next chapter, we'll finally look at `sourcemaps` so you can see what the big deal is and why we put in the effort to get them working in this chapter.

7
Sourcemaps – Editing and Saving in the Browser

We've mentioned source maps a lot already, and even did a considerable amount of work in the last chapter to ensure we could generate them with our current Gulp workflow. So surely you've been asking questions like *Why?* and maybe *What?*. So, in this chapter we'll look at the *What, why, and how* of source maps.

I'll explain what source maps are and why you should care. We'll then look at setting up source maps to work in Firefox and Chrome, with a few short examples of how this can be really useful when designing in the browser or simply making small changes and tweaks to your styles.

What are source maps and why should you care?

In modern web development, we use many languages on a daily basis. At the frontend especially, many of these languages aren't as terse as we would like. For example, JavaScript and CSS both have similar drawbacks. Both can have odd, non-intuitive behavior which can catch almost every developer out at some point. Both have times where new features are in limbo due to slow browser support for much-desired features. Both benefit from minification to reduce the final file size(s), and both can be a nightmare to manage as the codebase grows and as multiple developers get their idle hands on the code. For these reasons, JS/CSS transpilers and preprocessors came about.

The goals of these **preprocessors** are always the same:

- Abstract away the difficult or verbose syntax in favor of terse, clean, intuitive syntax
- Reduce common repetition in writing the language
- Offer immediate use of new features for the underlying language, minification and easy management of code or file structure on large projects.

These features are the reason CoffeScript, Babel, Sass, Stylus, Less, TypeScript, and many others have become so popular. The only drawback is that when you try to debug the output (JS/CSS) in your browser's dev tools, you're looking at the final output. You're looking at plain JS or CSS. You then need to switch back to your source files (which are often spread out into numerous files) and try to figure out where to make appropriate changes based on the final output.

How often have you been working on a Sass project and jumped over to your browser to find something out of place? Let's say your navigation menu items are too far apart. Happens all the time. So you inspect the element, then you edit the CSS in the style editor of your browser's dev tools until it looks right. All good so far. However, this is where Sass becomes a problem. You look at the file and the line number given by Firefox/Chrome for that CSS rule, and it's *style.css* (Line 506) or something. However we know that that's in *navbar-layout.scss* somewhere. So we jump back over to our IDE or text editor and find/open the appropriate file and then we're faced with:

```
.nav {
    width: 100%;
    line-height: 3;

    &-menu {
        margin: 0;
        padding: 0;

        &-list-item {
            display: inline-block;
            padding: 0.5em 1em;
            margin: {
                top: 0;
                right: 0.5em;
                bottom: 0
                left: 0;
            }
        }
    }
}
```

This is a small example, and the trained eye will probably quickly see we have padding and a margin-right so we can do without the margin most likely. However, in a large file with media queries thrown in, and perhaps parent selectors scattered throughout that someone else wrote, it can be a slow, trial and error process of finding the relevant line of Sass.

This is where **source maps** come in. Source maps allow your browser to understand the original Sass, CoffeeScript Stylus, Less, or whatever, and show you the exact file and the line that is responsible for the piece of CSS in question. If this was all that source maps did, they would still be incredibly useful. However, source maps and browsers have another trick up their proverbial sleeves. Not only can you see the relevant file and line of Sass you need to edit, but with a little bit of set up you can also edit the Sass file right in the browser as you would the CSS, and then save it from the browser. As long as Sass or Gulp is watching the Sass files for changes, the changes happen without needing to reload.

This is really handy for those situations where you simply need to tweak something to get it looking right. If you can get out of the habit of jumping back to your text editor to make those small changes this can really start to save you time when used in conjunction with Gulp and BrowserSync. So now you know the "what" and the "why" of Sourcemaps, now let's look at the "how".

Setting up Source Maps in Firefox

Before I continue I want to say one thing to Firefox users: PLEASE STOP USING FIREBUG!!! The built-in Firefox `dev` tools have been far better than anything Firebug has had to offer for at least 6 years. Also give Firefox Developer Edition a go, it's really nice. For me Firefox Developer Edition is my development browser of choice. Overall, I'm a long time Firefox fan boy. I just think Firefox makes everything look nicer than Chrome/Safari and other browsers. Text looks better in Firefox, animations are smoother (especially animating SVG paths), and overall performance is better in Firefox, especially when multiple tabs are open (Open in **New Tab** is my friend). Also, the built-in `dev` tools are as good as Chrome's `dev` tools for the most part. That's just me.

My issue is not with Chrome, it's Webkit. Chrome is great for development. Their source map support is really nice. It should be, Google proposed the original source map specification. My problem is entirely with Webkit. I don't like Webkit at all. Never have. When Opera switched to Webkit, I was not happy. I really liked Opera. They're reasons for moving to Webkit, however, for the greater good. They wanted to remove themselves from the vendor prefix hell we were all in at that time. Some of you will remember the -o- prefix. I guess that wasn't really that long ago.

I just think Webkit makes the web look terrible. Don't get me started on Safari! So if you're like me and you like Firefox, then this section is for you. If you're good with Chrome, I'll cover that in the next section.

So before we enable source maps we'll need to have something to work with. In our *mastering-sass-swag* folder we have a pretty bare coming soon page. Let's start our `gulp serve` task so we can watch our SCSS, generate the source map, and start a server. So from the root of the `mastering-sass-swag` project, open a command line and run:

`gulp serve`

This will automatically open the homepage in your default browser (I'm assuming that's Firefox) with the URL `http://localhost:3000/`. Now open the **Inspector**. You can do this by right-clicking and going to **Inspect Element** and making sure you're on the **Inspector** tab. Or you can simply press *Ctrl+Shift+C/Cmd+Shift+C*.

You'll notice I'm using Firefox Developer Edition. The only difference (other than how cool it looks) is that you have quicker access to the developer tools from the top menu bar. Everything else is the same. You can even make the developer tools have the dark color scheme if you want. So I'm not using anything here which you can't use in a normal version of Firefox. I mainly just like the dark color scheme.

Now, make sure the <h1> element is highlighted so we can see the relevant styles in the panel on the right:

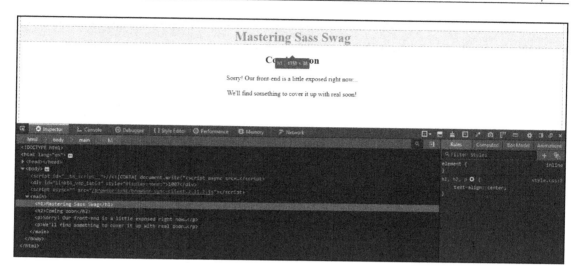

Depending on your version of Firefox you may see `style.css:2` or you might already see the `style.scss:1`. If you see *style.scss* then you're almost done. If you see the *style.css* file, then you need to right-click somewhere in that rules panel and check **Show Original Sources**.

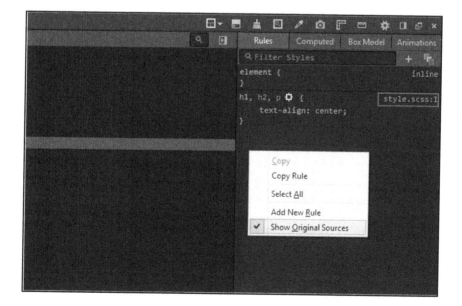

You can also get to it by clicking the gear icon near the top right and selecting **Show original sources** under **Style Editor**.

Or you can go straight to the style editor using *Shift+F7* and clicking the gear icon and check **Show original sources** there. You've got options.

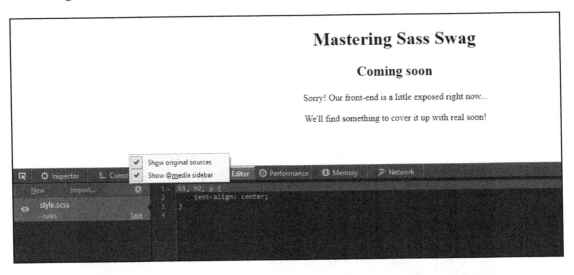

Once you've done that and you see **style.scss:1** click on that to go to the **Style Editor** panel (if you're not already there). From the **Style Editor** you can make edits and then press *Ctrl + S/Cmd + S* to save (or click the **Save link**). You will then be asked where to save the file. Overwrite the existing *style.scss* file.

Minor Gulp, Source Maps and BrowserSync issue

If we were simply using Sass to watch our files and generate the source maps then this would all just work at this point. However, because we are using Gulp and refreshing the browser when any file in the *css* directory changes, we have a problem. Not a big problem, but a problem nonetheless. When you saved, you probably noticed the entire page refreshed and then the styles disappeared from the **Style Editor** and a big red error came up saying *Style sheet could not be loaded*.

This is because currently we are watching all files in the *css* directory for changes. This means when we make a change the CSS files change and that causes a browser to refresh, and the source map changes, and that causes a browser refresh. That's what breaks the "link" so to speak. The refreshes happen almost at the same time, so you won't notice, but it is essentially refreshing twice.

So to fix this we simply need to tell BrowserSync in our `sass:compile` task to only watch CSS files. We do this by passing the `match` option to the stream function:

```
/**
 * Compile Sass to CSS
 */
gulp.task('sass:compile', () => {
    /**
     * Compil Sass and generate sourcemaps
     * @param   glob.sass    Glob pattern we defined above
     * @param   options for gulp-ruby-sass
     */
    return sass(glob.sass, {
        style: 'expanded',
        lineNumbers: true,
        sourcemap: true
    })
    // Generate sourcemaps using gulp-sourcemaps
    .pipe(sourcemaps.write('.'))
    // Output tot files in pathto.css
    .pipe(gulp.dest(pathto.css))
    // To use browser sync it needs to process the stream AFTER gulp.dest
    // To work properly with sourcemaps we need to only
    // watch CSS files and not .css.map files.
    .pipe(sync.stream({match: pathto.css + '/*.css'}));
});
```

Remember, all our tasks are built on top of the `sass:compile` task. Even though we don't call it explicitly, all of our other tasks are calling it. It's a good practice to create small, specialized tasks which can be used by other tasks. Then changes will only need to be made to this one task in most cases and all of our other tasks will be fixed or improved as a result.

With that done, cancel the current `gulp serve` task (*Ctrl + C / Cmd + C*) and rerun `gulp serve`. Now in Firefox you will be able to make changes and save them without things breaking. Let's add some padding to the top of the main element just to see it working:

```
main {
    padding-top: 2em;
}

h1, h2, p {
    text-align: center;
}
```

Save with *Ctrl + S / Cmd + S* and navigate to the correct folder at */mastering-sass-swag/assets/scss/* and overwrite *style.scss*. You should see the changes happen and the message in the top right will now say `Injected: style.css` instead of *Connected to BrowserSync*. This means your source maps are no longer refreshing the browser and everything is good to go. That's it for setting up source maps in Firefox!

Setting up Source Maps in Chrome

To set up source map support in **Chrome** you will first need to check if support is enabled. Open up the Chrome **DevTools**. You can do this with *Ctrl + Shift + I / Cmd + Shift + I* or right click anywhere on the current page and select **Inspect** (or just press *F12)*. From here you will need to navigate to **Settings**. The easiest way to get to the settings is just to press *F1* while the **DevTools** are open. Otherwise, to find the **DevTools** settings, look for an icon of three dots at the top right of your **DevTools** (sometimes jokingly called a *Kebab menu icon*, brother to the Hamburger menu icon). From there you'll see settings.

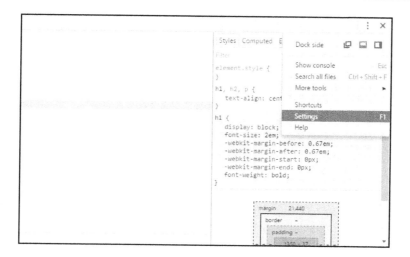

From here you'll need to make sure **Enable CSS source maps** and **Auto-reload generated CSS** are checked under the **Sources** section of the **General** tab.

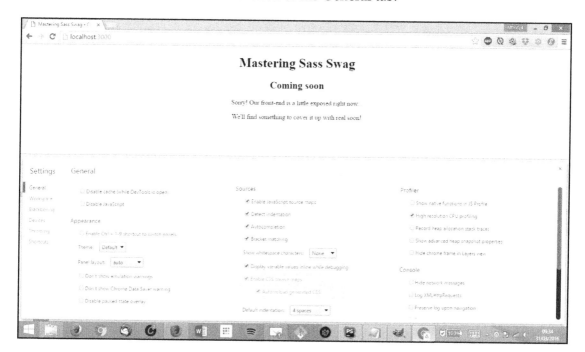

Close settings, and while on the Elements panel select the `<h1>...</h1>` element. Beside the styles for the h1 element you'll see `style.css:1`. Click this to be brought to the **Sources** panel.

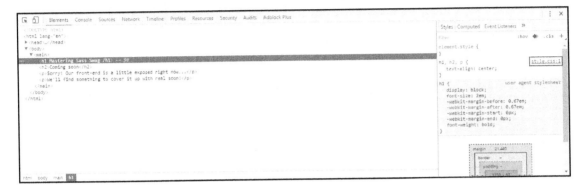

Let's add some `padding-top` to the main element to push all the text down slightly.

```
main {
    padding-top: 2em;
}

h1, h2, p {
    text-align: center;
}
```

Now hit *Ctrl + S / Cmd + S* to save the file. At this point, chances are that the panel goes pink/red and a small "Attention" symbol shows up in the title tab for this file.

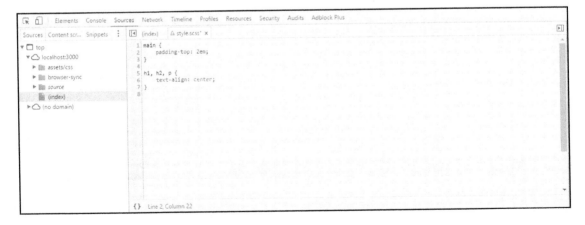

This is because, by default, you need to tell Chrome where your project is. Chrome does this using something it calls **workspaces**. To add this project to workspaces you can right-click somewhere inside the *style.scss* panel and choose **Add Folder to Workspaces.**

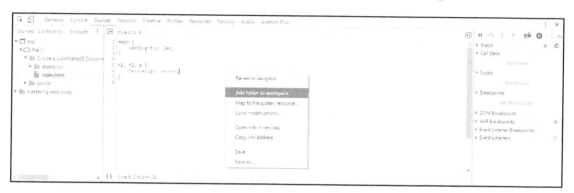

Navigate to the root of your project `mastering-sass-swag` and select that. This will allow Chrome to edit your HTML and save the changes. Chrome will then ask for permission to access your filesystem. Click **Allow**. Chrome will then ask to map the project to workspaces. Click **More** and click the configuration link which will automatically sync your project in Chrome. With that done you'll see the folders on the left will change to match what you actually have on your local filesystem.

Another nice feature in Chrome Workspaces is that you can press *Ctrl + P / Cmd + P* to bring up a quick search to navigate to a file. Simply start typing and the list will filter down to the file you want. Really useful on large projects with many files.

Now you'll need to make those changes again to see if everything is working. So let's add the padding again to the main element:

```
main {
    padding-top: 2em;
}

h1, h2, p {
    text-align: center;
}
```

Hit *Ctrl + S / Cmd + S* to save and you should see the changes happen. There is one last thing we need to do to get this working at its best. Right now, when we save BrowserSync will actually refresh for every changed file it finds in the *assets/css* folder. This currently include the *style.css.map* file. This means the browser actually refreshes twice. It's not such an issue right now but with more files it can slow things down and even break the process. So to fix this we simply need to tell BrowserSync in our `sass:compile` task to only watch CSS files. We do this by passing the `match` option to the stream function:

```
/**
 * Compile Sass to CSS
 */
gulp.task('sass:compile', () => {
    /**
     * Compil Sass and generate sourcemaps
     * @param  glob.sass    Glob pattern we defined above
     * @param  options for gulp-ruby-sass
     */
    return sass(glob.sass, {
        style: 'expanded',
        lineNumbers: true,
        sourcemap: true
    })
    // Generate sourcemaps using gulp-sourcemaps
    .pipe(sourcemaps.write('.'))
    // Output tot files in pathto.css
    .pipe(gulp.dest(pathto.css))
    // To use browser sync it needs to process the stream AFTER gulp.dest
    // To work properly with sourcemaps we need to only
    // watch CSS files and not .css.map files.
    .pipe(sync.stream({match: pathto.css + '/*.css'}));
});
```

Remember, all our tasks are built on top of the `sass:compile` task. Even though we don't call it explicitly, all of our other tasks are calling it. This is a good practice for this reason. Changes will only need to be made to this one task in most cases and all of our other tasks will be fixed or improved as a result.

Now when you make changes and save them from within Chrome you should notice the message on the top right says **Injected: CSS** instead of **Connected to BrowserSync**. This means it is no longer doing a full refresh when it encounters source maps. So that's how to set up Firefox and/or Chrome to use source maps.

Summary

In this chapter we set up the last piece in our "optimized workflow" puzzle. We learned what Source maps are and what problems they're designed to overcome. Problems such as having to manually find the line of SCSS among dozens of files because your browser only shows you the filename and line number of the CSS file. Or needing to copy and paste the changes you make in the browser to your text editor and save them there to make changes permanent.

We looked at setting up support for source maps in Firefox and Chrome and the slight differences between those. Mainly workspaces to sync an entire folder as opposed to Firefox's method of only syncing files as you save them.

We looked at how to solve an issue which can arise if you do not tell BrowserSync to be more selective about the files it watches. By default, BrowserSync will try match a file to a linked file in your HTML. If it finds a matching file it simply updates that one file and "injects" the changes. However, when it finds files it can't match to something or it doesn't understand it simply refreshes the entire page. This can break the link between your browser, source maps, and the compiled CSS.

While it's entirely possible to get by without using source maps I guarantee if you take the time to set them up for each project and get in the habit of using them you'll notice they will save your hours on each project. From this point on I'll leave it up to you as to when to work in the browser and when to work in your text editor/IDE. Next we'll start building our Mastering Sass Swag homepage starting with the wireframe, concept and the layout of our main elements such as the header, footer, and some other important components.

8

Building a Content-Rich Website Components

In this chapter we'll continue with our Mastering Sass Swag website. This chapter will focus on setting up our initial file adding useful mixins and functions which we wrote in previous chapters and creating our main components. We'll improve our Gulp file slightly, as well as include jQuery. jQuery will allow us to manipulate the DOM easier than plain JavaScript. I'll mainly use it to add and remove CSS classes from certain elements.

We'll add some functions and mixins which we've created in previous chapters and make some improvements on them for our specific needs in this project.

We'll add *normalize.css* to fix some common browser issues and then we'll add some base styles of our own to setup styles which we'll be commonly using. We'll also add a class for "screen reader only" text. This improve accessibility for users who require the use screen readers, seeing as our design will have a lot of icons, which are not screen reader friendly.

We'll then add the aforementioned icon font before moving onto some basic grid styles and some of the actual elements of the design. These elements include a top navigation, header with the site logo, and a search bar, main navigation, footer and a slide-out cart panel to show currently selected items.

Setting up our project

First we need to copy all the work we did in our previous chapter into this one. That will be our starting point. You should have the following files and folder structure:

```
mastering-sass-swag
|-- gulpfile.js
|-- index.html
|-- package.json
|-- assets
    |-- css
        |-- style.css
        |-- style.css.map
    |-- scss
        |-- style.scss
|-- dist
    |-- assets
        |-- css
            |-- style.min.css
```

You may need to run:

```
npm install
```

Run this from the command line to re-install the project's dependencies for Gulp.

Gulp

The Gulp tasks we have at the moment are `gulp sass:compile`, which compiles our Sass, `gulp sass:watch`, which compiles our Sass and watches for changes, and finally `gulp serve`, which boots up a server, opens a tab in the browser and loads our project into it (if there is not already a tab open on `localhost:3000`), and then watches for changes to our SCSS files and html files and compiles our Sass and refreshes the browser.,

This is the task that we'll use the most. So let's make it our default task. Open the *gulpfile.js* and add the following task:

```
/**
 * Default Task
 *
 * Runs `gulp serve`
 */
gulp.task('default', ['serve']);
```

Now we only need to use the command:

```
gulp
```

Run it from the command line and our `serve` task will be run.

Adding jQuery

We'll require some small amount of JavaScript for some UI improvements for our design over the next few chapters. To ease some of this work we'll use **jQuery**. The easiest way is to simply link to it from a **Content Delivery Network (CDN)**. I use `https://cdnjs.com/` whenever possible.

So, at the bottom of your *index.html* file just above the closing body tag add the following:

```
<!-- FOOTER SCRIPTS -->
<script
src="https://cdnjs.cloudflare.com/ajax/libs/jquery/2.2.3/jquery.min.js"></script>
<script>
    // Use jQuery in noConflict mode...
    jQuery(document).ready(function ($) {
        alert('jQuery!');
    });
</script>
```

You should see a popup dialog with `jQuery!` which means jQuery is loaded working properly. You can then remove the line seeing as it was just for testing purposes following:

```
alert('jQuery!');
```

We'll place our project's jQuery here as we progress.

Helpers

We'll place all of our functions and mixins in a folder called `helpers`. We'll place our mixins in a folder called *mixins* and functions in a folder called, you guessed it, *functions*. We'll then create a file in the root of the *helpers* directory called *all.scss* which will include all of our functions and mixins in the correct order. This will help avoid cluttering up our *style.scss* file with functions and mixins.

Your folder structure should be like so:

```
scss
|-- helpers
    |-- _all.scss
    |-- mixins
    |-- functions
```

Function – get

We'll be working with maps quite a bit. So we'll add our `get` function from Chapter 5, *Advanced Sass*, which allows us to do away with the verbose `map-get` syntax in favor of a much simpler, cleaner syntax. Create a file called *get.scss* in the *scss/helpers/functions* directory. Inside that place the following code:

```
// Function for retrieving deeply nested map values
@function get($map, $arglist...)
{
    $m: $map;
    @each $item in $arglist {
        @if $m != null {
            $m: map-get($m, $item);
        }
    }
    @return $m;
}
```

I've modified this slightly from the example in Chapter 5, *Advanced Sass*. Here, I've added an if statement to check if our $m is not null:

```
// Function for retrieving deeply nested map values
@function get($map, $arglist...)
{
    $m: $map;
    @each $item in $arglist {
        @if $m != null {
            $m: map-get($m, $item);
        }
    }
    @return $m;
}
```

This prevents `gulp` from showing an error in the console about the variable $m being a value of null. This error happens because once every key/value has been iterated over, the loop returns the final value as expected, however the loop runs one last time but $m is now a null value. This won't stop Sass from compiling, however I'd still prefer not to see the error constantly.

Now import _get.scss in our *scss/helpers/_all.scss* :

```
@import "functions/get.scss";
```

Now import the *scss/helpers/_all.scss* file as the first import in our *scss/style.scss* file:

```
@import "helpers/all.scss";
```

Mixin – hover links

Next, I'm going to create a simple mixin for creating hover links. This is the same as the one you'll find in the Compass utilities; however, I feel it's a waste to require Compass just for the few mixins I want. I also might want modify this mixin or change it somehow in the future.

Create a file called *_hover-link.scss* in *scss/helpers/mixins*. Inside that place the following:

```
@mixin hover-link {
    text-decoration: none;

    &:hover, &:focus {
        text-decoration: underline;
    }
}
```

Now open *scss/helpers/_all.scss* and import our hover-link mixin:

```
@import "functions/get.scss";
@import "mixins/hover-link.scss";
```

Mixin – bp (breakpoint)

I don't know about you, but writing media queries always seems like bit of a chore to me. I just don't like to write (min-width: 768px) all the time. So for that reason I'm going to include the bp mixin, the same as the media mixin in Chapter 5, *Advanced Sass*, but with one minor update. I'd like to default it to (min-width: 768px) seeing as that is where the main breakpoint of our design will be.

Let's write our mixin:

```
$default-breakpoint: medium !default;
$breakpoints: (
    small: 480px,
    medium: 768px,
    large: 980px
) !default;

@mixin bp($size: unquote($default-breakpoint), $breakpoints: $breakpoints)
{
    @media (min-width: map-get($breakpoints, $size)) {
        @content;
    }
}
```

Now import this file in our *scss/helpers/_all.scss* file:

```
@import "functions/get.scss";
@import "mixins/hover-link.scss";
@import "mixins/bp.scss";
```

Next place the `$default-breakpoint` variable and `$breakpoint` map in *scss/style.scss* before our imports:

```
$default-breakpoint: medium;$breakpoints: (
    small: 480px,
    medium: 768px,
    large: 980px);

@import "helpers/all.scss";
```

Let's add a quick test to make sure it works. At the end of *style.scss* add the following:

```
body {
    background-color: red;

    @include bp {
        background-color: green;
    }
}
```

Now resize the browser and you should see a red background on screens below 766px wide and a green background on screens 768px and above.

Mixin – media (based on the OOCSS media component)

The product component we created before will be very useful throughout this project. We'll use it not only for displaying products in various places but also to display blog posts, perhaps portfolio items, and maybe even testimonials. If we're creative with our styling later we can extend it to look completely different for each purpose to hide the fact we're reusing one component over and over again. This isn't cheating, it's just saving us time and work.

We'll call our component `media` (from the media component in OOCSS on which it's based). Create a file called *media.scss* in *scss/helpers/mixins* and inside place the following mixins:

```scss
// Mixin for creating the media-container. Simply adds padding and a
clearfix.
@mixin media-container($spacing: 1em) {
    padding: $spacing;
    overflow: hidden;
}

// Mixin for creating the media-image.
@mixin media-image($img-align: left, $spacing: 1em) {
    display: block;
    float: $img-align;

    @if ($img-align == unquote(right)) {
        margin-left: $spacing;
    } @else if ($img-align == unquote(left))   {
        margin-right: $spacing;
    } @else {
        margin: 0 auto;
    }
}

// Mixin for creating the media-title and link style. Useful if we need to
modify the defaults for more control
@mixin media-title($color: black, $link-color: inherit, $link-hover-color:
inherit, $text-transform: uppercase) {
    margin-top: 0;
    text-transform: $text-transform;
    color: $color;

    a {
        @include hover-link;
```

```scss
        color: $link-color;

        &:hover {
            color: $link-hover-color;
        }
    }
}

// Mixin for creating the media-button. Useful if we need to modify the
defaults for more control
@mixin media-button($img-align: left, $spacing: 1em, $background-color:
black, $text-color: white, $border-width: 1px, $text-transform: uppercase)
{
    padding: ($spacing * 0.25) ($spacing * 0.5);
    text-transform: $text-transform;
    text-decoration: none;
    color: $text-color;
    background-color: $background-color;
    border: $border-width solid transparent;

    @if ($img-align == unquote(none)) {
        float: none;
    } @else if ($img-align == unquote(left) or $img-align ==
unquote(right)) {
        float: if($img-align == left, right, left);
    } @else {
        @warn 'First parameter of `media-button` mixin must be `left` or
`right`. `#{$img-align}` given.';
    }

    &:hover {
        color: $background-color;
        background: transparent;
        border: $border-width solid;
    }
}

// ------------------------------------------------------------
// MEDIA COMPONENT
// ------------------------------------------------------------
// We will create a reusable mixin based loosely on the media
// mixin from OOCSS.
@mixin media($img-align: left, $spacing: 1em, $color: black) {
    @include media-container($spacing);

    &-image {
        @include media-image($img-align, $spacing);
    }
```

```
    &-title {
        @include media-title($color);
    }

    &-button {
        @include media-button($img-align, $spacing, $color);
    }
}
```

As you can see I've abstracted out each part into its own mixin. The container, title, image, and button each are in their own specialized mixin now. This will allow us to use them in various combinations and have more control of each part if needs be. For example, we may not always need a button, or the title, or either, so using the full media component would create a lot of unnecessary CSS bloat. With each part in its own mixin we can take what we need when we need it.

I've also added some error handling to the `media-image` and `media-button` mixins, as well as some additional conditions to allow for a centered layout which would allow for a full width image or a rounded image. We'll use these when we create our centered media component later.

Now open *scss/helpers/_all.scss* and simply import `mixins/media.scss`:

```
@import "functions/get.scss";
@import "mixins/hover-link.scss";
@import "mixins/bp.scss";
@import "mixins/media.scss";
```

normalize.scss

Now that we have our helpers imported, one of the first things we need to do is go and get `normalize.css` which was created by Nicholas Gallagher and Jonathan Neal. You can find the file on Github at `https://github.com/necolas/normalize.css`. Simply download the *normalize.css* file and save it in the directory *assets/scss/base*. Then rename it to *_normailize.scss* and import it into *style.scss*:

```
$default-breakpoint: medium;
$breakpoints: (
    small: 480px,
    medium: 768px,
    large: 980px
);

@import "helpers/all.scss";
```

```
@import "base/normalize.scss";
```

You should see the text change from sans-serif to sans. This is due to *normalize.scss*.

Global base styles

Now that we have *normalize.scss* laying down a good base foundation we still need a file to add our own, more opinionated base styles. For example, more often than not, if I have a list (such as a <ul>) within a nav (<nav>) element I don't want bullets. I also don't want margin or padding on any <ul> elements within a nav element. Also, the first level of list items (<li>) in the first unordered list (<ul>) should be in a row. Also, I want everything to use the border-box box-sizing property.

Create a file in the *scss/base* directory called *_global.scss* and inside that place the following:

```
*, *::before, *::after {
    box-sizing: border-box;
}

body, html {
    overflow-x: hidden;
}

nav {
    ul {
        margin: 0;
        padding: 0;
        list-style: none;
    }

    > ul > li,
    > div > ul > li {
        display: inline-block;
    }
}

p, h1, h2, h3, h4, h5, h6 {
    margin-top: 0;
}
```

The overflow-x: hidden is to prevent a scrollbar on the bottom of the page when we create our cart element, which will be off screen and will slide in when we click a button to see the cart.

The selector `> div > ul > li` is in there for when we have a `div` around the `ul` in order to constrain the menu to a `max-width`. This could be using a container `div` or a row or a column or any `div` really.

I also don't like paragraphs and headings to have a margin on the top and bottom, only the bottom. I think this looks better overall, especially when you have images with text beside them.

Now we just need to import the *scss/base/global.scss* at the top of our *scss/style.scss* file, just after where we imported *base/normalize.scss*:

```
$default-breakpoint: medium;
$breakpoints: (
    small: 480px,
    medium: 768px,
    large: 980px
);

@import "helpers/all.scss";
@import "base/normalize.scss";
@import "base/global.scss";
```

At this point also, it would be a good idea to remove the styles from the previous chapter for the main element and h1, h2, and paragraphs. Remove the following from *style.scss*:

```
main {
    padding-top: 2em;
}

h1, h2, p {
    text-align: center;
}
```

Screen reader text

Our design will make use of a lot of icons in place of text, on buttons, and links. For this reason, we need a way for screen readers to still be able to understand what those buttons are for. To do this we'll need to create elements of text which are hidden visually from sighted users, but still "technically" part of the DOM so screen readers and other assistive technology and search engines can still read them. To do this we'll create a class of `screen-reader-text`. This class can be applied to elements to hide them visually without using `display: none` or `visibility: hidden`. The reason for this is screen readers will not read text in hidden elements.

Instead, we need to simply mask the text by making its containing element as small as possibly using clip, height, width, and a few other properties to hide the text from view:

```scss
.screen-reader-text {
    // Dimensions
    // make our element as small as possible
    clip: rect(1px, 1px, 1px, 1px);
    height: 1px;
    width: 1px;

    // Positioning
    // This lifts our element out of it's container to prevent it
interfering
        with our layout
    position: absolute !important;

    // Visibility
    overflow: hidden; // This stop scroll bars appearing

    // Theme
    // Some screen reader and browsers read broken/hyphenated words as they
     would appear visually
    word-wrap: normal !important;
}
```

Place this inside a file called *_typography.scss* inside *scss/base* and then import it into *style.scss*:

```scss
$default-breakpoint: medium;
$breakpoints: (
    small: 480px,
    medium: 768px,
    large: 980px
);

@import "helpers/all.scss";
@import "base/normalize.scss";
@import "base/global.scss";
@import "base/typography.scss";
```

As you can see, creating a `screen-reader-text` class for accessibility is very easy so there is no reason not to do it. Accessibility is important and should always be part of the process from the very beginning. No exceptions.

Layout – grid

Now, we need a `container` class which will constrain any element inside it or any element with that class to our `max-width`. We'll set this to `1160px`.

Create a file in *scss/layout* called *_grid.scss*. Inside that let's define our container class and a `$grid` configuration map:

```scss
$grid: (
    max-width: 1160px
) !default;

.container {
  // Dimensions
  max-width: get($grid, max-width);

  // Positioning
  margin: 0 auto;

  // Clearfix
  overflow: hidden;
}
```

Now let's import it in our *scss/style.scss* file and add the `$grid` map before our imports:

```scss
$default-breakpoint: medium;
$breakpoints: (
    small: 480px,
    medium: 768px,
    large: 980px
);

$grid: (max-width: 1160px);

@import "helpers/all.scss";
@import "base/normalize.scss";
@import "base/global.scss";
@import "base/typography.scss";
@import "layout/grid.scss";
```

Ionicons

Next we need to download our icon font. My current preference is **Ionicons** from the **Ion Framework**. You can get them from the Github repository at `https://github.com/drifty co/ionicons`.

However, if you prefer another font family such as Font Awesome or something else you can simply replace Ionicons with your preference instead.

To install Ionicons, we'll need a folder called *theme* inside the *assets/scss* directory. Inside the *theme* directory, create a folder called *ionicons* (or replace with your own icon font). Inside here we'll place the *scss* files from the Ionicon *github* repository. These files are *_ionicons-font.scss*, *_ionicons-icons.scss*, *_ionicons-variables.scss*, and *ionicons.scss*.

Next we need to rename *ionicons.scss* to *_ionicons.scss* so it doesn't compile to its own CSS file. Then we import it to our main *style* .scss file:

```
@import "theme/ionicons/ionicons.scss";
```

You'll notice I've left out the underscore before our filename, *ionicons.scss*. Sass is actually smart enough to import a file if you leave out the underscore. You can even leave out the extension if you want! This will work just the same:

```
@import "theme/ionicons/ionicons";
```

The *scss* directory structure should now be as follows:

```
scss
|-- base
    |-- _normailize.scss
|-- theme
    |-- ionicons
        |-- _ionicons.scss
        |-- _ionicons-fonts.scss
        |-- _ionicons-icons.scss
        |-- _ionicons-variables.scss
```

Next we need the actual font files contained within the *fonts* directory. Remember we need the paths to be relative to the *css* directory and not the *scss* directory. I like to keep fonts and background images and anything with paths relative to CSS files inside the *css* directory. This means if I move the *css* directory up or down a level it won't affect the paths.

To accomplish this for Ionicons we first need to override a variable $ionicons-font-path by defining it at the top of our *style.scss* file (anywhere before where we imported the *ionicons.scss* file):

```
$default-breakpoint: medium;
$breakpoints: (
    small: 480px,
    medium: 768px,
    large: 980px
```

```
);

$grid: (
    max-width: 1160px
);

$ionicons-font-path: "fonts/ionicons";

@import "helpers/all.scss";
@import "base/normalize.scss";
@import "base/global.scss";
@import "base/typography.scss";
@import "layout/grid.scss";
@import "theme/ionicons/ionicons.scss";
```

This is because in the *_ionicons-variables.scss* file the variable was defined with the *!default* flag which we covered in a previous chapter. Therefore, if we define that variable anywhere before that definition it will be used instead. For that reason, we never need to modify the *ionicons.scss* files directly, which means we can update the *ionicons.scss* files in future without worrying about losing our customizations.

Now we can place the files from the *fonts* directory in Ionicons inside the directory *asset/css/fonts/ionicons*.

The *css* directory structure should now be:

```
css
|-- style.css
|-- style.css.map
|-- fonts
    |-- ionicons
        |-- ionicons.eot
        |-- ionicons.svg
        |-- ionicons.ttf
        |-- ionicons.woff
```

Top nav

Next, we'll need a top navigation bar which will contain two unordered lists. One will contain our contact-related links and info, such as phone number, e-mail, and social links. The other will contain links where users will access their account and cart. The cart link will open our cart `slide-out` component, which we will get to later in this chapter.

Place the following markup after the opening `<body>` tag:

```
<!-BEGIN .top-nav -->
<nav class="top-nav">
    <div class="container">
        <ul class="top-nav-menu top-nav-contact-menu">
            <li class="top-nav-menu-item top-nav-contact-menu-item">
                <span class="ion-android-phone-portrait"></span>
                <a href="tel:+0123456789">
                    <span class="top-nav-menu-text top-nav-contact-menu-
text">
                        +0123456789
                    </span>
                </a>
            </li>
            <li class="top-nav-menu-item top-nav-contact-menu-item">
                <span class="ion-email"></span>
                <a href="mailto:your@email.here">
                    <span class="top-nav-menu-text top-nav-contact-menu-
text">
                        your@email.here
                    </span>
                </a>
            </li>
            <li class="top-nav-menu-item top-nav-contact-menu-item">
                <span class="ion-social-facebook"></span>
                <a href="javascript:;" target="_blank">
                    <span class="top-nav-menu-text top-nav-contact-menu-
text">
                        Facebook
                    </span>
                </a>
            </li>
            <li class="top-nav-menu-item top-nav-social-menu-item">
                <span class="ion-social-twitter"></span>
                <a href="javascript:;" target="_blank">
                    <span class="top-nav-menu-text top-nav-contact-menu-
text">
                        Twitter
                    </span>
                </a>
            </li>
        </ul>
        <ul class="top-nav-menu-item top-nav-shop-menu">
            <li class="top-nav-menu-item top-nav-shop-menu-item">
                <span class="ion-filing"></span>
                <a href="#">
                    <span class="top-nav-menu-text top-nav-shop-menu-text">
```

```
                    Account
                </span>
            </a>
        </li>
        <li class="top-nav-menu-item top-nav-shop-menu-item">
            <span class="ion-ios-cart"></span>
            <a href="javascript:;" id="cart-button">
                <span class="top-nav-menu-text top-nav-shop-menu-text">
                    Cart
                </span>
            </a>
        </li>
        <li class="top-nav-menu-item top-nav-shop-menu-item">
            <span class="ion-ios-locked"></span>
            <a href="javascript:;">
                <span class="top-nav-menu-text top-nav-shop-menu-text">
                    Login
                </span>
            </a>
        </li>
    </ul>
</div>
</nav>
<!-- END .top-nav -->
```

There's nothing too fancy going on here. There are two separate unordered lists contained within the `nav` element as I explained before. Each has a definite purpose. One is contact info and the other is account/shop related.

Each menu (`<ul>`) has a class of `top-nav-menu` so styles can easily be applied to both equally. Then each has a unique class which identifies them separately and allows us to override the `top-nav-menu` styles if need be. We'll use these to float each menu left or right accordingly. This is also useful if the client wants one to stand out from the other.

Each list item inside those unordered lists will also have a general class of `top-nav-menu-item` applied to them. Also, each will have a more specific class relating to which unordered list they are in, contact or shop. This is for the same reasons as mentioned previously.

Now let's apply some styles to it and lay everything out correctly. Create a file in *scss/components* called *_top-nav.scss*. Inside that place our styles:

```scss
.top-nav {
  overflow: hidden;

  &-contact-menu {
```

```
    @include bp {
      float: left;
    }
  }

  &-shop-menu {
    @include bp {
      float: right;
    }
  }
}
```

That's all we need for now to get everything in place. The assumption we made before; that any unordered list inside a nav element would be inline, means we have less CSS when creating nav menus.

Now simply import the *components/top-nav.scss* file into *style.scss*:

```
$default-breakpoint: medium;
$breakpoints: (
    small: 480px,
    medium: 768px,
    large: 980px
);

$ionicons-font-path: "fonts/ionicons";

@import "helpers/all.scss";
@import "base/normalize.scss";
@import "base/global.scss";
@import "base/typography.scss";
@import "layout/grid.scss";
@import "components/top-nav.scss";
@import "theme/ionicons/ionicons.scss";
```

Grid – container

Next we'll create our header area where our title and search bar will be. The title will be to the left and search bar to the right. We'll wrap each in their own div so we can better control where they go.

Place the following markup just after the top-nav element:

```
<!-- BEGIN .main-header -->
<header class="main-header">
    <div class="main-header-inner container">
```

```
            <div class="two-thirds column">
                <h1 class="main-header-title">Mastering Sass Swag</h1>
            </div>
            <div class="one-third column">
                <!-- TODO: Search bar to go here -->
            </div>
        </div>
    </header>
<!-- END .main-header -->
```

Now open up *scss/layout/_grid.scss* and add a `gutter` property to the `$grid` map and the column, a `one-third` class and `two-thirds` classes.

 A `gutter` is generally the space between columns in a grid. It's padding or margin added to the left, right or both sides of columns, rows or containers.

The *_grid.scss* file should now look like this:

```
$grid: (
    max-width: 1160px,
    gutter: 1em
) !default;

.container {
    // Dimensions
    max-width: get($grid, max-width);

    // Positioning
    margin: 0 auto;

    // Clearfix
    overflow: hidden;
}

.column {
    // Dimensions
    padding-left: get($grid, gutter) / 2;
    padding-right: get($grid, gutter) / 2;
    // Positioning
    float: left;
    &:first-child {
        padding-left: 0;
    }
    &:last-child {
        padding-right: 0;
```

```
        }
    }
    .one-third {
        width: 100%;
        @include bp {
            width: (100% / 3);
        }
    }
    .two-thirds {
        width: 100%;
        @include bp {
            width: (100% / 3) * 2;
        }
    }
```

We use the `column` class to apply padding and floats, while the `one-third` and `two-thirds` classes set the width. We'll add more in the next chapter but this will be enough to get us started for now.

It's also important you remember to add the `gutter` property to the `$grid` map in *scss/style.scss*:

```
$grid: (
    max-width: 1160px,
    gutter: 1em
);
```

Search component

In the rightmost column of our `main-inner-header` we're going to place a `search` component. Once again we want to be able to use this anywhere we might want, so it needs to be independent of where we put it on the page.

Here's our markup for the `search` component:

```
<!-- BEGIN search-bar -->
<form class="search-bar" action="#" method="get">
    <label for="search">
        <span class="screen-reader-text">Search for:</span>
    </label>
    <input id="search" class="search-bar-input" type="search"
placeholder="Search...">
    <button class="search-bar-button" type="submit">
        <span class="screen-reader-text">Search</span>
        <span class="ion-android-search"></span>
    </button>
```

```
</form>
<!-- END search-bar -->
```

Next we need to create a file in *scss/components* called *_search.scss*. Inside that place the following:

```scss
.search-bar {
    position: relative;

    &-input {
        // Dimensions
        width: 100%;
        line-height: 1.4;
        max-height: 2em;

        // Positioning
        padding: 0.25em 2em 0.25em 0.25em;
    }

    &-button {
        // Dimensions
        line-height: 1.4;
        max-height: 2em;
        padding: 0.25em 0.5em;

        // Positioning
        position: absolute;
        right: 0;
        top: 0;
    }
}
```

Here, we are setting the `search-bar` element to `position: relative`. This will allow us to then set the button to `position: absolute` so we can position it inside (or above) the search input. Then we set the button to `top: 0` and `right: 0` to place it in the top right of the `search-bar` element. It's also important to set both the `line-height` and the `max-height` on the input element and the button to eliminate browser inconsistencies due to font-sizing.

Now let's import *components/search.scss* in *style.scss* just after *components/top-nav.scss*:

```scss
$default-breakpoint: medium;
$breakpoints: (
    small: 480px,
    medium: 768px,
    large: 980px
);
```

```
$ionicons-font-path: "fonts/ionicons";

@import "helpers/all.scss";
@import "base/normalize.scss";
@import "base/global.scss";
@import "base/typography.scss";
@import "layout/grid.scss";
@import "components/top-nav.scss";
@import "components/search.scss";
@import "theme/ionicons/ionicons.scss";
```

Main nav

Next, we need to add our `main-nav`, just below our header. Add the following markup:

```
<!-- BEGIN .main-nav -->
<nav class="main-nav">
    <ul class="main-nav-menu container">
        <li class="main-nav-menu-item"><a href="#">Home</a></li>
        <li class="main-nav-menu-item"><a href="#">Our Swag</a></li>
        <li class="main-nav-menu-item"><a href="#">Our Blog</a></li>
        <li class="main-nav-menu-item"><a href="#">Our Customers</a></li>
        <li class="main-nav-menu-item"><a href="#">Who We Are</a></li>
        <li class="main-nav-menu-item"><a href="#">Contact</a></li>
    </ul>
</nav>
<!-- END .main-nav -->
```

We don't need to apply any styling to this seeing as we already defined enough in our *base/_global.scss*. We're also using the class of container on the `<ul>` which will keep it centered and at a `max-width` of 1160px.

Cart slide-out component

Next we need to create the `cart` element which will contain the list of currently selected items along with prices, (VAT, subtotal, total, and so on) and a link to go to the checkout page. The cart will be the most important component in many ways. It will be the gateway to the checkout page and will need to be powerful but also subtle. To achieve this, and in the interest of `mobile-first`, we'll make it a `slide-out` panel which will be activated by clicking the `cart` link in the `top-nav`. This will require a simple piece of jQuery which will add an `is-opened` class to the `cart` element.

Our `cart` component will consist of a container, and inside that will be a header, body, and footer section. First we'll add the `div` which will container the sections of our cart. It will have an `id` of cart, which we will target with jQuery to open and close the cart when the cart link is clicked. Just inside that we'll have our `cart-header`.

Let's add the markup just before our main (`<main>`) element and after our header:

```
<!-- BEGIN .cart -->
<div id="cart" class="cart">
    <!-- BEGIN .cart-header -->
    <header class="cart-header">
        <a href="javascript:;" id="cart-close-button"
        class="cart-close-button">
            <span class="ion-close"></span>
        <span class="screen-reader-text">
            Close
        </span>
        </a>
        <h3 class="cart-title">
            Cart
        </h3>
    </header>
    <!-- END .cart-header -->
```

Our `<header>` contains a link called `cart-close-button`. This will be used to close our cart. On small screens the cart slides over the `cart` link in the menu. Therefore we can't use that link to close the cart. So we need a close button. It's also just a good idea to give the user options about how to open/close an interactive component, such as a modal or `slide-out` panel.

Next, just after our `cart` header, we have our `cart` body. This will contain a list of our cart items with an image, the product title, price, and a link to remove the item from the cart:

```
<!-- BEGIN cart-body -->
<div class="cart-body">
    <ul class="cart-list">
        <li class="cart-list-item">
            <img src="http://placehold.it/150x150" alt="Image of
Product" class="cart-list-item-image"/>
            <div class="cart-list-item-details">
                <h4 class="cart-list-item-title">
                    <a href="#" class="cart-list-item-title-link">
                        Mastering Sass T-shirt (Medium)
                    </a>
                </h4>
                <span class="cart-list-item-price">
```

```
                        <span class="cart-list-item-price-label">Item
Price:
                        </span>
                        &euro;40
                    </span>
                    <a href="#" class="cart-list-item-remove">Remove
&times;
                    </a>
                </div>
            </li>
            <li class="cart-list-item">
                <img src="http://placehold.it/150x150" alt="Image of
Product" class="cart-list-item-image"/>
                <div class="cart-list-item-details">
                    <h4 class="cart-list-item-title">
                        <a href="#" class="cart-list-item-title-link">
                            Mastering Sass Hat (Black)
                        </a>
                    </h4>
                <span class="cart-list-item-price">
                    <span class="cart-list-item-price-label">Item Price:
                    </span>
                    &euro;10
                </span>
                    <a href="#" class="cart-list-item-remove">Remove
&times;
                    </a>
                </div>
            </li>
        </ul>
    </div>
    <!-- END .cart-body -->
```

We then have the `footer` of our cart component. This will contain our subtotal, VAT, and total price of all our items in the cart:

```
    <!-- BEGIN .cart-footer -->
    <footer class="cart-footer">
        <div class="cart-totals">
            <div class="cart-subtotal">
            <span class="cart-totals-title cart-subtotal-title">
                Subtotal:
            </span>
            <span class="cart-totals-value cart-subtotal-value">
                €50.00
            </span>
            </div>
            <div class="cart-vat">
```

```
                <span class="cart-totals-title cart-vat-title">
                    VAT:
                </span>
                <span class="cart-totals-value cart-vat-value">
                    %23
                </span>
                </div>
                <div class="cart-total">
                <span class="cart-totals-title cart-total-title">
                    Total:
                </span>
                <span class="cart-totals-value cart-total-value">
                    €
                </span>
                </div>
            </div>
            <div class="cart-checkout">
                <a href="#checkout" class="cart-checkout-button">
                    Go to Checkout &rarr;
                </a>
            </div>
        </footer>
        <!-- END .cart-footer -->
    </div>
    <!-- END .cart -->
```

Our `cart` element consists of three main sections; a header, body, and a footer. We can use the header and footer elements here also to reflect this semantically.

The header will contain the title and the close button (`#cart-close-button`), which when clicked will remove the `is-opened` class, thus causing the cart component to slide off screen once more.

The body will contain an unordered list with the current products contained within the user's cart. This will consist of an image, the product name, the price, and a button to remove the product from the cart.

The `cart` footer will contain the totals, such as the subtotal, VAT, and total price of the products in the cart. We'll also add a link/button here to go to the checkout page.

Next, we'll add the jQuery to our script section to add the `is-opened` class when the `cart` link is clicked, and remove it when the `#cart-close-button` is clicked:

```
<script>
    jQuery(document).ready(function ($) {
        $cartButton = $('#cart-button');
        $cartCloseButton = $('#cart-close-button');
```

```
        $cart = $('#cart');
        $cartButton.on('click', function () {
            $cart.toggleClass('is-opened');
        });
        $cartCloseButton.on('click', function () {
            $cart.removeClass('is-opened');
        });
    });
</script>
```

So first, we're creating variables to easily access the element with an ID of cart-button and cart-button-close. From there we're simply saying when the $cartButton is clicked we want to toggle the is-opened class on the cart element. This means the cart-button can open and close the cart. However, on a mobile the cart element will cover the entire page. So we also need a way to close it from within the panel itself. This is where the cart-close-button comes in. We set this to simply remove the class of is-opened, thus closing the cart.

With the markup and jQuery in place, let's add our SCSS. Create a file in the *scss/components* called *_cart.scss*. Inside it, we'll have all of our styles for the cart component:

```
$cart: (
    slide-in: right,
    height: 100vh,
    width: (
        small: 100vw,
        medium: 20em
    ),
    spacing: 1em,
    bg-color: white,
    transition-speed: 350ms
) !default;

.cart {
    // Dimensions
    height: get($cart, height);
    width: get($cart, width, small);

    // Positioning
    position: absolute;
    padding: get($cart, spacing);
    top: 0;
    bottom: 0;
    z-index: 9999;

    // What side will the panel slide in from
    @if (get($cart, slide-in) == 'right') {
```

```scss
        right: -#{get($cart, width, small)};
    } @else {
        left: -#{get($cart, width, small)};
        @warn 'The `slide-in` property must be left or right in the
        $cart map.';
    }

    // State
    transition: transform get($cart, transition-speed);

    // Theme
    background-color: get($cart, bg-color);

    @include bp {
        width: get($cart, width, medium);

        // What side will the panel slide in from
        @if (get($cart, slide-in) == 'right') {
            right: -#{get($cart, width, medium)};
        } @else {
            left: -#{get($cart, width, medium)};
        }
    }

    &-list {
        margin: 0;
        padding: 0;
        list-style: none;
        overflow: hidden;

        &-item {
            @include media-container((get($cart, spacing) get($cart,
spacing) get($cart, spacing) 0));

            &-image {
                @include media-image(left, get($cart, spacing));

                max-width: 50px;
                height: auto;
            }

            &-title {
                @include media-title();
            }

            &-price {
                float: left;
```

```scss
                    &-label {
                        font-weight: bold;
                    }
                }

                &-remove {
                    @include hover-link;

                    float: right;
                }
            }
        }
    }
}

.cart.is-opened {
    // What side will the panel slide in from
    @if (get($cart, slide-in) == 'right') {
        transform: translateX(-#{get($cart, width, small)});
    } @else {
        transform: translateX(#{get($cart, width, small)});
    }

    @include bp {
        @if (get($cart, slide-in) == 'right') {
            transform: translateX(-#{get($cart, width, medium)});
        } @else {
            transform: translateX(#{get($cart, width, medium)})
        }
    }
}
```

First, we need to create a container which will be full width on small screens with a height of 100vh (viewport height). Then at 768px wide and above it will be 20em wide.

Viewport-percentage units are similar to in concept to percentages. However, if you were to create a div with a height and width of 100% it would be 100% of its containing element. Viewport-percentage units (vw and vh) are relative to the viewport (browser window). You can read more about them here https://developer.mozilla.org/en/docs/Web/CSS/leng th.

We'll also need to hide the cart element just off to the right (or left) of the screen by default using the translateX transform property. Then, when the class of is-opened is applied using jQuery it will slide in from the right. We use a transition to create the slide in/slide out effect. Otherwise, it would simply appear and disappear. It's important to place this on the default element and not the is-opened state.

You can see the last piece of SCSS is the `.is-opened` rules for both small and medium to large screens. The `if` statements are to allow us to switch from left to right by simply changing the slide-in property in our `$cart` configuration map. Setting it to left will mean the panel slides in from the left. Setting it to right means it will slide in from the right.

The slide in effect is achieved by first placing the element off the screen by setting it to absolute positioning. We then use the left (or right) property to push off screen the exact width so it sits just off screen. We do this using a negative value. Right or left zero would of course place the element `flush` with the side of the screen. Then, in the `.cart.is-opened` rule we use `translateX` to move the element in the other direction, bringing it back on screen.

We're also using the `media-container`, `media-title`, and `media-image` mixins to easily achieve our layout for product items in the list. However, we don't need the button element which is included with the default `media` mixin so using the individual mixins will save a few lines of CSS. We ensure they match our styles by using the values of the `$cart` map to set our padding.

Now simply import our file in *style.scss* and also copy the configuration to the top of *style.scss* so we can configure it from there:

```scss
$default-breakpoint: medium;
$breakpoints: (
    small: 480px,
    medium: 768px,
    large: 980px
);

$cart: (
    slide-in: right,
    height: 100vh,
    width: (
        small: 100vw,
        medium: 20em
    ),
    spacing: 1em,
    bg-color: white,
    transition-speed: 350ms);

$ionicons-font-path: "fonts/ionicons";

@import "helpers/all.scss";
@import "base/normalize.scss";
@import "base/global.scss";
@import "base/typography.scss";
```

```
@import "layout/grid.scss";
@import "components/top-nav.scss";
@import "components/cart.scss";
@import "theme/ionicons/ionicons.scss";
```

Remember our components go after the layout but before our theme, so we can theme them independently. That way we can take the component and drop it into another project if needs be, or replace the theme files in this project and our component will have a brand new look to it.

Mixin – media centered

Next, we're going to create a variation on the media component that will have the image centered as well as the text. Rather than being in a column layout this will be in rows.

Open the file *scss/helpers/mixins/_media.scss* and below our media mixin add a mixin called media-centered:

```
@mixin media-centered($img: fullwidth, $spacing: 1em, $color: black) {
    @include media-container($spacing);

    text-align: center;

    &-image {
        @include media-image(none, $spacing);

        @if ($img == unquote(fullwidth)) {
            width: 100%;
            height: auto;
        } @else if ($img == unquote(rounded)) {
            border-radius: 9999px;
        } @else {
            @warn 'First parameter of `media-centered` mixin must be
`fullwidth` or `rounded`. `#{$img}` given.';
        }
    }

    &-title {
        @include media-title($color);

        margin-top: $spacing;
    }

    &-button {
        @include media-button(none, $spacing, $color);
```

```
        }
    }
```

Here, we are using our `media-container` mixin to the set the properties of our container, which are padding and a clearfix. We then set `text-align: centered` which will cascade down through our component.

We use the `media-image` mixin, but we set the `$img-align` property to none, which will remove the float and center the image. We then check if the image is **fullwidth** or **rounded** and apply the appropriate styles. If the value passed in is neither fullwidth or rounded we show a warning to let the user know they've entered an invalid value.

The only change to the title is to add some margin to the top to give some space after the image. Our button uses a `$img-align` value of none also to center it instead of floating it left or right.

Footer

Next, we'll add our `footer` for the page. The `footer` will have our copyright text on the left and a `footer` menu to the right.

Here's our markup:

```
<!-- BEGIN header -->
<footer class="footer container">
    <div class="footer-copyright">
        <span class="footer-copyright-text">
            &copy; Since 2016. Mastering Sass Swag. All rights reserved
        </span>
    </div>
    <nav class="footer-nav">
        <ul class="footer-nav-menu">
            <li class="footer-nav-menu-item"><a href="#">Terms and
Conditions</a></li>
            <li class="footer-nav-menu-item"><a href="#">Privacy
Policy</a></li>
            <li class="footer-nav-menu-item"><a href="#">FAQ</a></li>
        </ul>
    </nav>
</footer>
<!-- END footer -->
```

In *scss/components* create a file called *_footer.scss* and inside, place the following:

```
.footer {
    overflow: hidden;
    &-copyright, &-nav {
        @include bp {
            width: 50%;
            float: left;
        }
    }

    &-nav-menu {
        float: right;
    }
}
```

Now import *scss/components/footer.scss* into *style.scss*:

```
@import "helpers/all.scss";
@import "base/normalize.scss";
@import "base/global.scss";
@import "base/typography.scss";
@import "layout/grid.scss";
@import "components/top-nav.scss";
@import "components/search.scss";
@import "components/cart.scss";
@import "components/footer.scss";
@import "theme/ionicons/ionicons.scss";
```

The last thing I want to do is add a minimum height to the main element (`<main>`) on medium to large screens so the `footer` is at the bottom of the page at least until we have some content to fill the page. In *style.scss* add the following below our imports:

```
main {
    @include bp {
        min-height: 800px;
    }
}
```

The preceding solution is temporary. We'll remove it in the next chapter once there is more on our page.

Summary

In this chapter we set out to create a practical starting point for the next phase. We have created modular components rather than a strict, grid layout. With this in place, we can be more flexible when it comes to laying things out on the page and making choices regarding typography, color, and the overall look.

We focused on creating a base using some simple, but useful, mixins, `normalize.css`, and some of our own more opinionated rules. We created the main components of the page, which are the top navigation area, header, main nav and footer, as well as a few independent components which we could perhaps use on other projects.

Even though our focus was on components, we did need to create some styles for layout and even theming, such as icons. We also added jQuery to assist us in creating some animations for a smoother UI.

In the next chapter we'll focus on layout. We'll look at Susy grids to create our own grid for our exact purposes, and we'll add breakpoint to improve our `bp` mixin.

9
Building a Content-Rich Website – Layout

In this chapter, we will focus on creating our layout. This means positioning our elements, setting up a grid system, and deciding what sections and components should go where. We won't be worrying about choosing fonts, or setting font sizes, colors, or other aesthetic styling at this stage. Here, it's all about the structure.

We'll be using the **Susy Sass library** throughout this chapter. We'll install it through **Bower** and import it into our project. Once that is done, we'll examine some of the basic features of Susy. I'll explain how to use the container and `span` mixins to create a basic layout before moving on to creating a complete grid system.

The grid system we will generate using Susy and our previous breakpoint (bp) mixin will take aspects of Bootstrap, Foundation, and Breakpoint. It will have a container and columns which can be set for our major sizes as defined in our `$breakpoints` map. Using these mixins we will be able to use loops to generate a configurable grid system with less than 30 lines of Sass.

After that, we'll create the various sections of our design and look at how Susy can also help us maintain semantic HTML easily. Combined with our media mixins and our bp mixin you'll be amazed at how quickly you can get the bones of a web page laid out.

Installing Susy

I find the most straightforward way to install **Susy** is to use *Bower*. Bower is also a *package manager*, however, while npm mostly manages JavaScript packages and Node-based projects, Bower manages non-JavaScript packages and libraries (including many JavaScript libraries). These happen to include some Sass libraries such as Susy. If you are unsure if you have Bower installed, you can run the following command:

```
bower -v
```

Run this from the command line. If you see a version number you're good to go. If not, simply run the following:

```
npm install bower -g
```

This installs Bower globally so you can use it in all your NPM projects without needing to install it as a dependency of that project.

Once you have Bower installed, you'll need to create a *bower.json* file to manage the projects bower components. To do so you can run this command:

```
bower init
```

You can simply accept all the defaults for now. Your *bower.json* file should look similar to the following:

```
{
  "name": "mastering-sass-swag",
  "description": "Front-end for Mastering Sass Swag",
  "main": "gulpfile.js",
  "authors": [
    "Luke Watts"
  ],
  "license": "ISC",
  "homepage": "",
  "ignore": [
    "**/.*",
    "node_modules",
    "bower_components",
    "test",
    "tests"
  ]
}
```

Then you're ready to install Susy from the command line by running this command:

```
bower install susy --save
```

From there, you can import Susy by referencing the *bower_components/susy/sass/_susy.scss* file (remember to properly "go up" as many levels to the root before entering the path):

```
@import '../../bower_components/susy/sass/susy';
@import "helpers/all";
@import "base/normailize";
@import "base/global";
@import "base/typography";
@import "layout/grid";
@import "components/top-nav";
@import "components/main-header";
@import "components/search";
@import "components/cart";
@import "components/footer";
@import "theme/ionicons/ionicons";
```

Setting up a basic grid

Now that we have Susy installed we can replace our current grid styles using some of the mixins Susy provides. We'll then add a basic grid, similar to that of Bootstrap or Foundation. This will be for the end user to add columns when they need.

We'll then use the built-in Susy mixins and functions to add containers and columns to our layout. This will remove the need for presentational classes within our HTML.

The container mixin

Next, let's replace our container with Susy's `container` mixin. The container mixin sets the `max-width` of the containing element, which right now is our `.container` element. However, later in this chapter we will use this to semantically restrict certain parts of the design to our maximum width.

The container element takes a width argument, which will be the `max-width`. It also automatically applies the *micro clearfix* hack. This prevents the containers height from *collapsing* when the elements inside it are floated. I prefer the `overflow: hidden` method myself, but they do the same thing essentially.

By default, the container will be set to `max-width: 100%`. However, you can set it to be any valid unit of dimension, such as 60em, 1160px, 50%, 90vw, or whatever. As long as it's a valid CSS unit it will work.

So let's replace our current properties in the `.container` rule in *scss/layout/_grid.scss* with the container mixin:

```
.container {
    @include container(1160px);
}
```

The preceding code will give the following CSS output:

```
.container {
    max-width: 1160px;
    margin-left: auto;
    margin-right: auto;
}

.container:after {
    content: " ";
    display: block;
    clear: both;
}
```

Due to the fact the container uses `max-width` we don't need to specify different dimensions for various screen sizes. It will be 100% until the screen is above `1160px` and then the max-width value will kick in. The `.container:after` rule is the micro clearfix hack.

The span mixin

Next we'll need to replace the properties of our one-third and two-thirds with the span mixin. This will be temporary just so we can see how the span mixin works. Later, we'll create a grid system like that of Bootstrap, Foundation, or Breakpoint. We'll also use the Susy mixins in to allow for more semantic markup. This means we'll keep the use of special classes such as `container` or `col-6-sm` to a minimum.

With our current styles we used a class of `.column` to apply properties which would be needed for all our columns, regardless of their width. These properties include padding on the left and right, float, and then removing the float on the left or right if the column was the first or last column. The span mixin is diverse enough to handle all of these traits. Therefore, we can simply remove the following from *scss/layout/_grid.scss*:

```scss
.column {
    // Dimensions
    padding-left: get($grid, gutter) / 2;
    padding-right: get($grid, gutter) / 2;

    // Positioning
    float: left;

    &:first-child {
        padding-left: 0;
    }

    &:last-child {
        padding-right: 0;
    }
}
```

Now replace the `.one-third` property with the following:

```scss
.one-third {
    @include span(12 of 12);

    @include bp {
        @include span(4 of 12);
    }
}
```

What we are saying here is we want the `.one-third` element to take up 12 columns of 12 columns. So essentially one full width column. Then, on 768px wide screens and above, we want it to take up 4 of 12 columns, which is `one-third`.

Now let's do the same for two-thirds:

```scss
.two-thirds {
    @include span(12 of 12);

    @include bp {
        @include span(8 of 12);
    }
}
```

Here, we've done almost the same as we did for the `one-third` class, however this time at 768px and above we want our width to be two-thirds of 12, which is 8. Therefore, we use `span(8 of 12)`.

That's essentially how we use the span mixin. However, if you check the page in the browser now, you'll notice we have a problem:

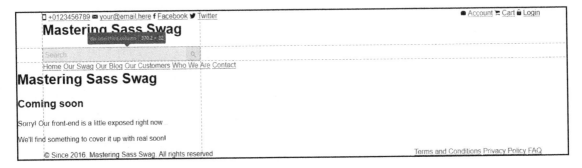

The last keyword

Remember we had our .column class, which not only handled floats and padding, it also removed the padding from the last column in a row The span mixin doesn't do this by default. Instead, you need to implicitly specify this behavior. We can do this by adding a :last-child pseudo-selector and using the keyword last after our values:

```
.one-third {
    @include span(12 of 12);

    @include bp {
        @include span(4 of 12);

        &:last-child {
            @include span(4 of 12 last);
        }
    }
}

.two-thirds {
    @include span(12 of 12);

    @include bp {
        @include span(8 of 12);

        &:last-child {
            @include span(8 of 12 last);
        }
    }
}
```

By default, the `span` mixin works by calculating the width and also applying a gutter (margin or padding) to the right of *each* column. This makes the last column too wide and therefore it drops down out of place. The `last` keyword removes the gutter from the right to fix this problem. We apply it to the `:last-child` pseudo-selector which means regardless of the combination the last column will never have the right gutter.

The $susy configuration map

Right now, we're mostly using the default settings of Susy. However, Susy allows for a lot of configuration through its configuration map, which is called `$susy`. The settings in the `$susy` map allow us to set how wide the container should be, how many columns our grid should have, how wide the gutters are, whether those gutters should be margins or padding, and whether the gutters should be on the left, right, or both sides of each column. Actually, there are even more settings available depending on the type of grid you'd like to build.

Let's define our `$susy` map with the container set to 1160px in *scss/style.scss* in place of our `$grid` map:

```
$susy: (
    container: 1160px
);
```

Now we can go back to our *scss/layout/_grid.scss* file and remove the `1160px` value from the `container` mixin because it will use the value in the `$susy` container property:

```
.container {
    @include container;
}
```

You'll also notice we needed to specify of `12` in each span to let Susy know we are working in a 12 column grid. This is called the **context**. The reason we need to specify it every time is because Susy is extremely customizable and flexible (perhaps too much for the majority of situations). This means you could have one row of columns be 12-column layout and the next be 16, or 24, or 18, and so on. This is cool…but we only want one grid system of 12 columns. So we can specify that in the `$susy` map also.

In *scss/style.scss* add the column property to the `$susy` map to set the default number of columns to 12:

```
$susy: (
    container: 1160px,
    columns: 12
);
```

Now you can remove the of 12 from all the spans in *scss/layout/_grid.scss*:

```
.one-third {
    @include span(12);

    @include bp {
        @include span(4);

        &:last-child {
            @include span(4 last);
        }
    }
}

.two-thirds {
    @include span(12);

    @include bp {
        @include span(8);

        &:last-child {
            @include span(8 last);
        }
    }
}
```

Next, we can specify the width we want our gutters to be. Remember, gutters are set using a ratio of an overall column width, such as 1/4 or .25. By default, Susy uses a value of 1/4, so let's set it to .33 or 1/3:

```
$susy: (
    container: 1160px,
    columns: 12,
    gutters: 1/3
);
```

That's about all we need to set for our purposes, however, Susy has a lot more to offer. In fact, to cover everything in Susy, I would need to write an entirely separate book. If you want to explore more of what Susy can do you should read the documentation at `http://s usydocs.oddbird.net/en/latest/`.

Setting up a grid system

Our previous example using two-thirds and one-third was more academic than practical. A grid based on halves, quarters, thirds, and so on would be more complex and less intuitive than a strictly column-based grid.

We've all used a 12 column grid which has various sizes (small, medium, large) or a set breakpoint (or breakpoints). These are the most popular methods for two reasons...it works, and it's easy to understand. Furthermore, with the help of Susy we can achieve this with less than 30 lines of Sass! Don't believe me? Let's begin.

The concept of our grid system

Our grid system will be similar to that of Foundation and Bootstrap. It will have three breakpoints and will be mobile first. It will have a container, which will act as both `.container` and `.row`, therefore removing the need for a `.row class`.

The breakpoints

In the previous chapter we defined three sizes in our `$breakpoints` map. These were as follows:

```
$breakpoints: (
    small: 480px,
    medium: 768px,
    large: 980px
);
```

So our grid will have `small`, `medium`, and `large` breakpoints.

The columns naming convention

Our columns will use a similar naming convention to that of Bootstrap. There will be four available sets of columns:

- The first will start from 0px up to the 399px .col-12
- The next will start from 480px up to 767px .col-12-small
- The medium will start from 768px up to 979px .col-12-medium
- The large will start from 980px .col-12-large

Having four options will give us the most flexibility.

Building the grid

Using the same method we used for the .one-third and .two-thirds rules we can use a for loop and our bp mixin to create our four sets of classes. Each will go from 1 through 12 and will use the breakpoints we defined for small, medium, and large.

In *scss/layout/_grid.scss*, replace the .one-third and .two-thirds rules with the following:

```
@for $i from 1 through get($susy, columns) {
    .col-#{$i} {
        @include span($i);

        &-last {
            @include span($i last);
        }
    }
}
```

These nine lines of code are responsible for our mobile first set of column classes. This loops from one through 12 (which is currently the value of the $susy columns property) and creates a class for each. It also adds a class which handles removing the final columns right margin so our last column doesn't wrap onto a new line. Having control of when this happens will give us the most control. The preceding code would create:

```
.col-1 {
  width: 6.38298%;
  float: left;
  margin-right: 2.12766%;
}
```

```
.col-1-last {
  width: 6.38298%;
  float: right;
  margin-right: 0;
}

/* 2, 3, 4, and so on up to col-12 */
```

That means our nine lines of Sass will generate 144 lines of CSS! Now let's create our three breakpoints. We'll use an @each loop to get the sizes from our $breakpoints map. This will mean if we add another breakpoint, such as extra-large it will automatically create the correct set of classes for that size:

```
@each $size, $value in $breakpoints {
    // Breakpoint will go here and will use $size
}
```

Here we're looping over the $breakpoints map and setting a $size variable and a $value variable. The $value variable will not be used, however the $size variable will be set to small, medium, and large for each respective loop. We can then use that to set our bp mixin accordingly:

```
@each $size, $value in $breakpoints {
    @include bp($size) {
        // The @for loop will go here similar to the above @for loop...
    }
}
```

Now, each loop will set a breakpoint for small, medium, and large, and any additional sizes we might add in the future will be generated automatically. Now we can use the same @for loop inside the bp mixin with one small change, we'll add a size to the class name:

```
@each $size, $value in $breakpoints {
    @include bp($size) {
        @for $i from 1 through get($susy, columns) {
            .col-#{$i}-#{$size} {
                @include span($i);

                &-last {
                    @include span($i last);
                }
            }
        }
    }
}
```

That's everything we need for our grid system. Here's the full *scss/layout/_grid.scss*:

```scss
.container {
    @include container;
}

@for $i from 1 through get($susy, columns) {
    .col-#{$i} {
        @include span($i);

        &-last {
            @include span($i last);
        }
    }
}

@each $size, $value in $breakpoints {
    @include bp($size) {
        @for $i from 1 through get($susy, columns) {
            .col-#{$i}-#{$size} {
                @include span($i);

                &-last {
                    @include span($i last);
                }
            }
        }
    }
}
```

That's 27 lines of SCSS. And how many lines of CSS does that generate? Nearly 600 lines of CSS!

Also, like I've said, if we wanted to create another breakpoint it would only require a change to the $breakpoint map. Then, if we wanted to have 16 columns instead, we would only need to the $susy columns property. The *grid.scss* would automatically loop over each and create the correct amount of breakpoints and the correct amount of columns.

Testing the grid

So let's test it all by creating a few rows of columns which will apply a different number of spans for each column at each breakpoint. Let's say we want a section of four columns. On a mobile, each column will be full width. We'll leave out the col-n-medium class so our col-n-small styles will carry on up through to the large breakpoint. And finally, on large screens we will have four columns. You'll also see how using the `col-n-size-last` classes will give us full control of our columns at every possible size and number of columns.

Add the following markup just before the closing `</main>` tag in *index.html*:

```
<section class="services container">
    <article class="col-12 col-6-small col-3-large">
        <h3>Service One</h3>
        <p>
            Lorem ipsum dolor sit amet, consectetur adipisicing elit. A
consequatur consequuntur dignissimos
            dolores eius impedit incidunt soluta voluptatum. Deserunt
dolore mollitia placeat quam rerum. Amet
            dolorum exercitationem modi porro voluptates?
        </p>
    </article>
    <article class="col-12 col-6-small-last col-3-large">
        <h3>Service Two</h3>
        <p>
            Lorem ipsum dolor sit amet, consectetur adipisicing elit. Animi
dicta dignissimos est ex, expedita
            illum impedit incidunt modi mollitia nam? Asperiores
consequuntur dicta eligendi error facilis,
            fuga incidunt quo voluptatem.
        </p>
    </article>
    <article class="col-12 col-6-small col-3-large">
        <h3>Service Three</h3>
        <p>
            Lorem ipsum dolor sit amet, consectetur adipisicing elit.
Accusantium aspernatur, atque autem
            blanditiis commodi debitis dicta doloribus, ducimus eius eos
laudantium magni molestias mollitia
            pariatur quod repellendus unde, voluptate voluptatum?
        </p>
    </article>
    <article class="col-12 col-6-small-last col-3-large-last">
        <h3>Service Four</h3>
        <p>
            Lorem ipsum dolor sit amet, consectetur adipisicing elit.
Accusantium atque commodi dolore labore
            obcaecati! Accusantium delectus dignissimos doloremque fugiat
inventore maiores possimus quaerat
            quia, rerum sint, totam veritatis voluptates! Quas!
        </p>
    </article>
</section>
```

You can see we have `col-12` on each which will make each column full-width on very small screens up to our "small" breakpoint. We don't need to specify the `col-12-last` class because full-width columns don't have a left or right gutter. Our mobile columns will look like this:

Service One

Lorem ipsum dolor sit amet, consectetur adipisicing elit. A consequatur consequuntur dignissimos dolores eius impedit incidunt soluta voluptatum. Deserunt dolore mollitia placeat quam rerum. Amet dolorum exercitationem modi porro voluptates?

Service Two

Lorem ipsum dolor sit amet, consectetur adipisicing elit. Animi dicta dignissimos est ex, expedita illum impedit incidunt modi mollitia nam? Asperiores consequuntur dicta eligendi error facilis, fuga incidunt quo voluptatem.

Service Three

Lorem ipsum dolor sit amet, consectetur adipisicing elit. Accusantium aspernatur, atque autem blanditiis commodi debitis dicta doloribus, ducimus eius eos laudantium magni molestias mollitia pariatur quod repellendus unde, voluptate voluptatum?

Service Four

Lorem ipsum dolor sit amet, consectetur adipisicing elit. Accusantium atque commodi dolore labore obcaecati! Accusantium delectus dignissimos doloremque fugiat inventore maiores possimus quaerat quia, rerum sint, totam veritatis voluptates! Quas!

Then we specify `col-6-small` with `col-6-small-last` on the second and fourth column. This will create a two over two column layout on small screens upwards. Here's what it will look like:

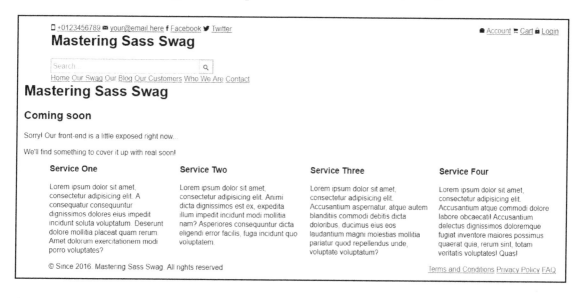

Finally, we have `col-3-large` with `col-3-large-last` on the fourth column. This will make four columns on large screens up. Here's what that will look like:

So our grid system works as expected. However, Susy also allows for a completely semantic approach, which means we can achieve any layout we want without requiring additional classes. So let's move on to finalizing our layout using Susy along with our previous mixins.

The header

The first section we need to finish laying out is the header. This includes the `top nav` and the `main nav`. First let's add some padding to each list item in the top nav. We'll also add some styles to make each list item stack on mobile screens and then go inline on small screens up.

We're going to add a `$spacing` variable, which we'll reuse a lot in our layout for properties such as padding and margin. We'll set the default padding/margin to 1em, however for the `nav-menu-items` 0.5em will look better.

At the very top of *scss/style.scss* add the `$spacing` variable set to 1em:

```
$spacing: 1em;
```

Now open the *scss/components/_top-nav.scss* file and add the following:

```scss
.top-nav {
  overflow: hidden;

  &-menu-item {
      padding: $spacing / 2;
      display: block;

      @include bp(small) {
          display: inline-block;
      }
  }

  &-contact-menu {
    @include bp {
      float: left;
    }
  }

  &-shop-menu {
    @include bp {
      float: right;
    }
  }
}
```

Main header inner

Next, we can remove the `one-third`, `two-thirds`, and `column` classes from the `divs` in our `main-header-inner` element and replace them with `main-header-inner-left` and `main-header-inner-right`, like so:

```html
<div class="main-header-inner container">
    <div class="main-header-inner-left">
        <h1 class="main-header-title">Mastering Sass Swag</h1>
    </div>
    <div class="main-header-inner-right">
        <!-- BEGIN search-bar -->
        <form class="search-bar" action="#" method="get">
            <label for="search">
                <span class="screen-reader-text">Search for:</span>
            </label>
            <input id="search" class="search-bar-input" type="search"
placeholder="Search...">
            <button class="search-bar-button" type="submit">
                <span class="screen-reader-text">Search</span>
                <span class="ion-android-search"></span>
            </button>
        </form>
        <!-- END search-bar -->
    </div>
</div>
```

Now in *scss/components/_main-header.scss* we can use Susy's span mixins and the bp mixin to achieve the best layout for each size. First, let's add our mobile styles:

```scss
.main-header-inner {
    &-left {
        @include span(12);
    }

    &-right {
        @include span(12);
    }
}
```

Let's also add some padding to `main-header-inner` to move everything off the edges of the screen and prevent the search bar from sitting right on top of the main `nav` on mobile:

```scss
.main-header-inner {
    padding: $spacing / 2;

    &-left {
```

```
        @include span(12);
    }

    &-right {
        @include span(12);
    }
}
```

Now let's add our spans for medium screens up, which we'll just make span(8) and span(4). We'll also need to use "last" on the &-right rule:

```
.main-header-inner {
    padding: $spacing / 2;

    &-left {
        @include span(12);

        @include bp {
            @include span(8);
        }
    }

    &-right {
        @include span(12);

        @include bp {
            @include span(4 last);
        }
    }
}
```

Main nav

Our main-nav is much like our top-nav. It needs some padding to space everything out. It also needs to stack on mobile and then go inline on small screens and up.

Create a file scss/components called _main-nav.scss and inside place the following:

```
.main-nav {
    &-menu-item {
        padding: $spacing / 2;
        display: block;

        @include bp(small) {
            display: inline-block;
        }
```

```
        }
    }
```

Then import it just after the `main-header` import in *scss/style.scss*:

```scss
@import '../../bower_components/susy/sass/susy';
@import "helpers/all";
@import "base/normailize";
@import "base/global";
@import "base/typography";
@import "layout/grid";
@import "components/top-nav";
@import "components/main-header";
@import "components/main-nav";
@import "components/search";
@import "components/cart";
@import "components/footer";
@import "theme/ionicons/ionicons";
```

That's our `top-nav`, `header`, and `main-nav` all laid out. So on a mobile, the header should look like so:

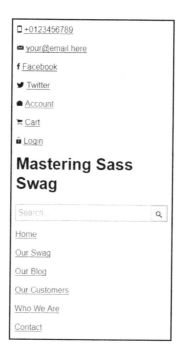

On desktop it should look like:

Next, we'll make both the `top nav` and the `main-nav` collapse down and expand when a button is clicked for small screens.

Mobile menus

Next, we need to do something about both the `top-nav` and the `main-nav` on mobile. Right now they're simply taking up too much screen space on mobile. For this reason, we'll need to hide them by default on mobile to medium sizes screens and have a button for each which, when clicked, reveals/hides that menu.

Top nav

So, the first thing we need to do is hide the *container* inside the `top-nav` on small to medium screens. Then we'll add a button just before the container which will open and close the container using jQuery's `slideDown` and `slideUp` built in animations.

First let's add the button just inside the `top-nav` markup in *index.html*:

```
<nav class="top-nav">
    <a href="javascript:;" class="top-nav-menu-button" id="top-nav-menu-
button">        <span class="ion-navicon">
</span>
        <span class="screen-reader-text">
            Top Nav Button
        </span>
    </a>
    <div class="container">
        ...
    </div>
</nav>
<!-- END .top-nav -->
```

Here, we've added a link with a class and id of `top-nav-menu-button`. The class is for styling and the id is for jQuery. I prefer to set the `href` to `"javascript:;"` instead of using a hash (#) symbol. The hash symbol, when clicked, will cause the page to jump back to the top. Using `"javascript:;"` prevents such behavior. It also lets me know this link has some custom JavaScript behavior associated with it.

Inside the anchor tag are two spans. The first is simply the hamburger menu icon. The second is the text for screen readers. Remember phones, have screen readers too!

Next, let's add some styles to the button. We'll add some padding and also make sure it doesn't show on screens from 480px up. In *scss/components/_top-nav.scss* add the following:

```scss
.top-nav {
    overflow: hidden;

    &-menu-button {
        padding: $spacing / 2;

        @include bp(small) {
            display: none;
        }
    }

    ...
}
```

Next, we need to hide the element after the `top-nav-menu-button` and all of its contents on screens below our small breakpoint, currently at 480px.

In *scss/components/_top-nav.scss* insert the following:

```scss
&-menu-button {
    padding: $spacing / 2;

    @include bp(small) {
        display: none;
    }

    ~ * {
        display: none;

        @include bp(small) {
            display: block;
        }
    }
}
```

This will select the next sibling, which is the container, and hide it up until the small breakpoint where we use display: block to ensure the menu is visible.

Now, we're ready to add some jQuery. In the footer script section of *index.html* after the previous cart jQuery add the following:

```
jQuery(document).ready(function ($) {
    ...

    // Top Nav Button
    $topNavButton = $('#top-nav-menu-button');
    $topNavButton.on('click', function (e) {
        e.preventDefault();
        $(this).next().slideToggle();
    });
});
```

That's it. Now the page should look like this on a mobile:

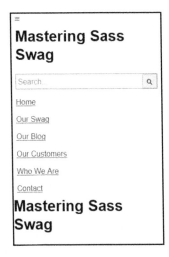

Then when you click the button the menu should open to reveal:

Main nav

Now, we can do almost the exact same thing for the `main-nav`. Add the markup to *index.html*:

```
<!-- BEGIN .main-nav -->
<nav class="main-nav">
    <a href="javascript:;" class="main-nav-menu-button" id="main-nav-menu-
button">
        <span class="ion-navicon-round"></span>
        <span class="screen-reader-text">
            Main Menu Button
        </span>
    </a>
    <ul class="main-nav-menu container">
        ...
    </ul>
</nav>
<!-- END .main-nav -->
```

Note that I've changed the class and id to `main-nav-menu-button`. I've also changed the icon to `"ion-navicon-round"` to add some distinction between the two.

Once that is done, we can add the necessary styles to *scss/components/_man-nav.scss*:

```
.main-nav {
    &-menu-button {
        padding: $spacing / 2;
```

```
        @include bp(small) {
            display: none;
        }

        ~ * {
            display: none;

            @include bp(small) {
                display: block;
            }
        }
    }
}


    ...

}
```

Finally, we can add the jQuery to *index.html*. The full jQuery should now look like this:

```
jQuery(document).ready(function ($) {
    $cartButton = $('#cart-button');
    $cartCloseButton = $('#cart-close-button');
    $cart = $('#cart');

    $cartButton.on('click', function () {
        $cart.toggleClass('is-opened');
    });

    $cartCloseButton.on('click', function () {
        $cart.removeClass('is-opened');
    });

    // Top Nav Button
    $topNavButton = $('#top-nav-menu-button');

    $topNavButton.on('click', function (e) {
        e.preventDefault();

        $(this).next().slideToggle();
    });

    // Main Nav Button
    $mainNavButton = $('#main-nav-menu-button');

    $mainNavButton.on('click', function (e) {
        e.preventDefault();

        $(this).next().slideToggle();
    });
```

```
    });
```

Image banner

Next, we'll add a full width image banner. I'm not a fan of sliders or carousels. I think they're bad for performance, pointless on mobile devices, and generally a bad user experience. I much prefer one image that is carefully chosen along with a short catchy call to action.

For this website we'll simply use placeholder images throughout, so we'll do the same here. However, the text should be catchy. It should set the tone of the website for the visitor.

First let's add the following markup just before the `<main>` element in *index.html*:

```html
<!-- BEGIN .image-banner -->
<div class="image-banner" style="background-image:
url('http://placehold.it/1280x400');">
    <div class="image-banner-overlay">
        <div class="image-banner-caption">
            <h2 class="image-banner-caption-title">
                Mastering Sass Swag
            </h2>
            <p class="image-banner-caption-body">
                You bring the Sass...we'll bring the swag!
            </p>
            <a href="#products" class="image-banner-button">View our Swag
&rarr;</a>
        </div>
    </div>
</div>
<!-- END .image-banner -->
```

I prefer to add the `background-image` inline so it can be added from a database, or from an external API. The overlay will simply allow us to darken or lighten the image to make light or dark text more legible. There's nothing worse than a bright image with white text over it. Then there is some text and a button.

First let's add the `image-banner` styles to position the image correctly and make sure it's full-full width. Create a new file in *scss/components* called *_image-banner.scss* and inside place the following:

```scss
.image-banner {
    background-position: center center;
    background-repeat: no-repeat;
    background-size: cover;
```

```
}
```

As with our cart component let's create a map for the image banner settings. Place the following at the top of the *scss/components/_image-banner.scss* file:

```
$image-banner: (
    height: 400px,
    overlay-color: hsla(0, 0%, 0%, 0.5)
) !default;
```

Then place the same map in *scss/style.scss* (without the `!default` flag). This will be where we will make our changes:

```
$image-banner: (
    height: 400px,
    overlay-color: hsla(0, 0%, 0%, 0.5)
);
```

Now, back in *scss/components/_image-banner.scss*, we'll add our styles for the overlay:

```
.image-banner {
    ...

    &-overlay {
        height: get($image-banner, height) / 2;
        background-color: get($image-banner, overlay-color);

        @include bp(large) {
            height: get($image-banner, height);
        }
    }
}
```

Here we are saying we want the height to be half of the specified height on small to large screens. We're then setting the background color and giving it some opacity using `hsla`.

Next, add the styles for the caption container, text and button. Here, we can use our media mixins to easily add some layout and styles. We'll also use the Susy container mixin to keep inside our max width:

```
.image-banner {
    ...

    &-caption {
        @include container;
        @include media-container($spacing / 2);
        @include bp(large) {
            position: relative;
```

```
            top: get($image-banner, height) / 4;
        }
        &-title {
            @include media-title(white);
        }
    }
    &-button {
        @include media-button(none);
    }
}
```

So first, we're setting the container mixin to add the `max-width`, and also the `media-container` mixin to give the caption some spacing. On large screens we set the position to relative so we can place the caption somewhere near the vertical center of the banner. We're using the `media-title` mixin and also the media-button mixin to add styles to the h2 and to style the link as a button.

The homepage should now look something like this:

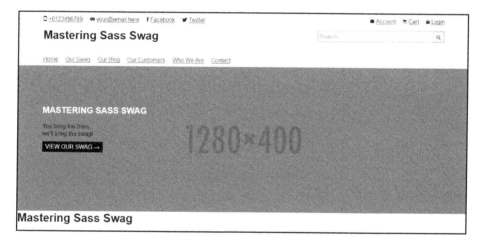

Featured products

The next section will be the featured products section. This will replace what is currently our `Coming soon` message in the `<main>` element.

The featured products section will consist of a row of four products. We'll use the Susy span mixin to achieve the columns, while we use the media mixin to lay out each product correctly.

Let's start with the markup. In *index.html* replace the current h1 and the coming soon text below that with the following:

```
<section class="featured-products">

    <h2 class="featured-product-title">Featured Products</h2>

    <article class="featured-product product-centered">
        <img src="http://placehold.it/300x400" alt="Image Placeholder"
class="product-centered-image featured-product-image">
        <h3 class="featured-product-title product-centered-title">
            <a href="#" class="featured-product-title-link product-
centered-title-link">Produc</a>
        </h3>
        <div class="featured-product-description product-centered-
description">
            <p>
                &euro;60.00
            </p>
        </div>
        <a href="#" class="featured-product-button product-centered-
button">View Product &rarr;</a>
    </article>

    . . .

</section>
```

Where the three dots (…) are, you should duplicate the .featured-product three more times so there are four in total.

Now, create a file called *_featured-product.scss* in the *scss/components* folder. Inside that we'll place all of our styles for the layout of the .featured-product elements:

```
.featured-product {
    @include span(12);

    padding-left: $spacing;
    padding-right: $spacing;

    &-title {
        padding-top: $spacing;
    }
```

```scss
        &s {
            @include container;

            padding: $spacing ($spacing / 2);
        }
    }

    // 480px up
    @include bp(small) {
        .featured-product {
            @include span(6);

            &:nth-child(2), &:nth-child(4) {
                @include span(6 last);
            }
        }
    }

    // 768px up
    @include bp(medium) {
        .featured-product {
            @include span(3);

            // We need to explicitly override the span(3 last)
            // from the small breakpoint
            &:nth-child(2) {
                @include span(3);
            }

            &:nth-child(4) {
                @include span(3 last);
            }
        }
    }
}
```

Here we are simply creating our columns for each of our predefined breakpoints. On extra small screens we'll have one full-full width column. Then on small to medium screens we'll have two columns. This will require us to use span(6 last) on the second and fourth columns. Finally, we have four columns on screens larger than 768px. For this, we'll need to explicitly set span(3) on the nth-child(2). Otherwise, it will float right and break our layout.

Don't forget to add the newly created file to *scss/styles.scss*:

```scss
@import '../../bower_components/susy/sass/susy';
@import "helpers/all";
@import "base/normailize";
```

```scss
@import "base/global";
@import "base/typography";
@import "layout/grid";
@import "components/top-nav";
@import "components/main-header";
@import "components/main-nav";
@import "components/search";
@import "components/cart";
@import "components/image-banner";
@import "components/featured-product";
@import "components/footer";
@import "theme/ionicons/ionicons";
```

There is also a class of `product-centered` on each `featured-product`. We'll use this to apply our `media-centered` mixin. This will allow us to reuse that class throughout our design. We can then use the `featured-product` class to add styles specifically for featured products.

Create a file called *_product-centered.scss* in *scss/components* and inside that place the following styles:

```scss
.product-centered {
    @include media-centered(fullwidth);

    padding-left: 0;
    padding-right: 0;

    &-title {
        margin-top: 0
    }
}
```

Now we can import it in *scss/style.scss*:

```scss
@import '../../bower_components/susy/sass/susy';
@import "helpers/all";
@import "base/normailize";
@import "base/global";
@import "base/typography";
@import "layout/grid";
@import "components/top-nav";
@import "components/main-header";
@import "components/main-nav";
@import "components/search";
@import "components/cart";
@import "components/image-banner";
@import "components/featured-product";
@import "components/product-centered";
```

```
@import "components/footer";
@import "theme/ionicons/ionicons";
```

After all of that, the featured-products section should look like:

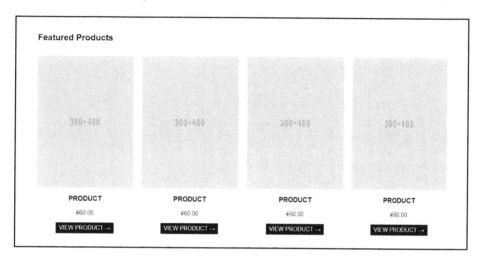

Testimonial

Next, let's add a fullwidth section which will be for a message or a testimonial. We'll use our `media-centered` mixin again, this time with a round. The section will have a full width background image with an overlay to darken or lighten it, the same as our image banner. In fact, they are very similar.

Here's our HTML. Place this after the featured products section:

```
<section class="testimonials" style="background-image:
url('http://placehold.it/1280x300');">
    <div class="testimonials-overlay">
        <article class="testimonial">
            <img src="http://placehold.it/75x75" alt="Image of Testimonial
Author" class="testimonial-image" />
            <h2 class="testimonial-title">
                Amazing!!!
            </h2>
            <blockquote class="testimonial-body">
                Amazing products! Amazing prices!
            </blockquote>
            <cite class="testimonial-author">&mdash; John Doe</cite>
        </article>
```

```
        </div>
    </section>
```

Next, we'll need to create a file called *_testimonials.scss* and place that in the *scss/components* directory. Inside the *_testimonials.scss* file place the following:

```scss
$testimonials: (
    height: 300px,
    overlay-color: hsla(0, 0%, 0%, 0.5)
) !default;

.testimonial {
    max-width: 20em;
    margin: 0 auto;

    @include media-centered(rounded);

    &s {
        background: {
            position: center center;
            size: cover;
            repeat: no-repeat;
        }

        &-overlay {
            min-height: get($testimonials, height); // So container can
 grow for long testimonials
            padding-top: $spacing * 2;
            padding-bottom: $spacing * 2;
            background-color: get($testimonials, overlay-color);
        }
    }
}
```

So, here we are setting the `background-position`, `background-size`, and `background-repeat` properties using property nesting. This will set our background image to be full width and responsive. We're using the media-centered mixin once again, this time with a rounded image. We also set a configuration map for our testimonials component called `$testimonials`.

We should also add the `$testimonials` map to the *scss/style.scss* file:

```scss
$image-banner: (
    height: 400px,
    overlay-color: hsla(0, 0%, 0%, 0.5)
);
```

```
$testimonials: (
    height: 300px,
    overlay-color: hsla(0, 0%, 0%, 0.5));

$ionicons-font-path: "fonts/ionicons";
```

The testimonials section should now resemble:

Subfooter and footer

At this point we could keep adding more sections. However, I hope at this point you see that we are simply reusing the mixins we already have in various combinations to create new components. While in truth these new components are simply variations on our core components, the media component and the media-centered component. Coupled with Susy grids, we can achieve any layout we can imagine.

That said, we still need a subfooter. A content-heavy website needs somewhere for additional links and info to go.

The markup

There's quite a bit of HTML so I'm going to break it up so it makes more sense before we look at styling it. We currently have a footer and inside that a div with a class of "footer-inner container".

Just above that we'll add another footer-inner div. We'll add a class of subfooter to that so we can style it. Inside the subfooter element we'll have three columns where our widgets will go:

```
<div class="footer-inner subfooter container">
    <div class="subfooter-widget">
        <!-- 1 -->
    </div>
```

```
        <div class="subfooter-widget">
            <!-- 2 -->
        </div>
        <div class="subfooter-widget">
            <!-- 3 -->
        </div>
    </div>
```

Now inside the first `subfooter-widget` column we will have a text widget and below that a social media links widget. Replace `<!-- 1 -->` with the following:

```
<div class="subfooter-widget-section">
    <h3 class="subfooter-widget-section-title">Mastering Sass Swag</h3>
    <div class="subfooter-widget-section-text">
        <p>Lorem ipsum dolor sit amet, consectetur adipisicing elit.
Delectus dolore impedit officia?</p>
    </div>
</div>
<div class="subfooter-widget-section">
    <h3 class="subfooter-widget-section-title">
        Where the Swag is at
    </h3>
    <ul class="subfooter-widget-section-socials">
        <li>
            <a href="#" target="_blank">
                <span class="ion-social-facebook-outline"></span>
                <span class="screen-reader-text">
                    Facebook
                </span>
            </a>
        </li>
        <li>
            <a href="#" target="_blank">
                <span class="ion-social-twitter-outline"></span>
                <span class="screen-reader-text">
                    Twitter
                </span>
            </a>
        </li>
        <li>
            <a href="#" target="_blank">
                <span class="ion-social-instagram-outline"></span>
                <span class="screen-reader-text">
                    Instagram
                </span>
            </a>
        </li>
    </ul>
```

```
    </div>
```

Next, replace `<!-- 2 -->` with our `Best Selling Swag` widget:

```
<div class="subfooter-widget-section">
    <h3 class="subfooter-widget-section-title">Top Selling Swag</h3>
    <ul class="subfooter-widget-section-list">
        <li class="subfooter-widget-section-list-item">
            <div class="subfooter-widget-product">
                <img src="http://placehold.it/50x50" class="subfooter-
widget-product-image" />
                <div class="widget-product-details">
                    <h4 class="subfooter-widget-product-title">
                        <a href="#" class="subfooter-widget-product-title-
link">
                            Product
                        </a>
                    </h4>
                    <div class="subfooter-widget-product-description">
                        <p>
                            Lorem ipsum dolor sit amet.
                        </p>
                    </div>
                </div>
            </div>
        </li>
        <li class="subfooter-widget-section-list-item">
            <div class="subfooter-widget-product">
                <img src="http://placehold.it/50x50" class="subfooter-
widget-product-image" />
                <div class="widget-product-details">
                    <h4 class="subfooter-widget-product-title">
                        <a href="#" class="subfooter-widget-product-title-
link">
                            Product
                        </a>
                    </h4>
                    <div class="subfooter-widget-product-description">
                        <p>
                            Lorem ipsum dolor sit amet.
                        </p>
                    </div>
                </div>
            </div>
        </li>
    </ul>
</div>
```

This will have two products in a similar layout as the items in our slide-out cart component. Next, replace `<!-- 3 -->` with our `Swag Tags` widget:

```
<div class="subfooter-widget-section">
    <h3 class="subfooter-widget-section-title">Swag Tags</h3>
    <ul class="subfooter-widget-section-tagcloud">
        <li class="md"><a href="#">Tag 1</a></li>
        <li class="xs"><a href="#">Tag 2</a></li>
        <li class="xl"><a href="#">Tag 3</a></li>
        <li class="md"><a href="#">Tag 4</a></li>
        <li class="lg"><a href="#">Tag 5</a></li>
        <li class="sm"><a href="#">Tag 6</a></li>
        <li class="md"><a href="#">Tag 7</a></li>
        <li class="md"><a href="#">Tag 8</a></li>
        <li class="xs"><a href="#">Tag 9</a></li>
    </ul>
</div>
```

This is simply a list of tags. We'll make them into a tag cloud in the next chapter.

The SCSS

Next, we need to lay out our columns. Create a file called *_subfooter.scss* in the *scss/components* folder. Inside that place:

```
.subfooter {
    padding: $spacing ($spacing / 2);

    ul {
        padding: 0;
        margin: 0;
        list-style: none;
    }

    &-widget {
        @include span(12);
    }
}

@include bp(medium) {
    .subfooter {
        &-widget {
            @include span(4);

            &:last-child {
                @include span(4 last);
```

```
                }
            }
        }
    }
```

This will give use full width stacked columns on all screens below 768px. The subfooter should now look like:

Our subfooter is already looking fairly good. Next, lets apply some of our media mixins to our `subfooter-widget-products`:

```scss
.subfooter {
    padding: $spacing ($spacing / 2);

    ul {
        padding: 0;
        margin: 0;
        list-style: none;
    }

    &-widget {
        @include span(12);

        &-product {
            @include media-container;

            padding: 0 0 ($spacing / 2) 0;

            &-image {
                @include media-image(left, $spacing);
            }

            &-title {
                @include media-title();
                margin: 0;
```

```
                }
            }
        }
    }
```

Now our subfooter should look like:

Lastly, we'll make our socials tagcloud lists display inline:

```
.subfooter {
    ...

    &-widget {
        ...

        &-section {
            &-socials, &-tagcloud {
                li {
                    display: inline-block;
                }
            }
        }
    }
}
```

That's it for our subfooter layout. The subfooter will now look like this:

Let's also add some padding to the bottom footer elements. At the moment they're a bit squashed. In the *scss/components/_footer.scss* file add the following:

```
.footer {
    overflow: hidden;

    &-copyright, &-nav {
        @include bp {
            width: 50%;
            float: left;
        }
    }

    &-copyright {
        padding: $spacing ($spacing / 2);
    }

    &-nav-menu {
        float: right;

        &-item a {
            display: inline-block;
            padding: $spacing ($spacing / 2);
        }
    }
}
```

Finishing touches

The last thing we need to do is fix the section just above the footer. We used this as an example of our grid classes. However, we want our layout to be semantic before we hand it over to the client. They'll use those classes once they take control of adding content, but for us to use those classes would be lazy.

First, let's fix our markup:

```
<section class="services">
    <h3 class="services-title">Swag Services</h3>
    <div class="container">
        <article class="service">
            <h3 class="service-title">Service One</h3>
            <p>
                Lorem ipsum dolor sit amet, consectetur
                adipisicing elit. A consequatur consequuntur
```

```
dignissimos
                dolores eius impedit incidunt soluta voluptatum. Deserunt
dolore mollitia placeat quam rerum. Amet
                dolorum exercitationem modi porro voluptates?
            </p>
        </article>
        <article class="service">
            <h3 class="service-title">Service Two</h3>
            <p>
                Lorem ipsum dolor sit amet, consectetur adipisicing elit.
Animi dicta dignissimos est ex, expedita
                illum impedit incidunt modi mollitia nam? Asperiores
consequuntur dicta eligendi error facilis,
                fuga incidunt quo voluptatem.
            </p>
        </article>
        <article class="service">
            <h3 class="service-title">Service Three</h3>
            <p>
                Lorem ipsum dolor sit amet, consectetur
                adipisicing elit. Accusantium aspernatur, atque
                autem blanditiis commodi debitis dicta doloribus,
                ducimus eius eos laudantium magni molestias
                mollia pariatur quod repellendus unde, voluptate
                voluptatum?
            </p>
        </article>
        <article class="service">
            <h3 class="service-title">Service Four</h3>
            <p>
                Lorem ipsum dolor sit amet, consectetur
                adipisicing elit. Accusantium atque
                commodi dolore labore
                obcaecati! Accusantium delectus dignissimos
                doloremque fugiat inventore maiores possimus
                quaerat quia, rerum sint, totam veritatis
                voluptates! Quas!
            </p>
        </article>
    </div>
</section>
```

Now we'll need to create a file called *_services.scss* in the *scss/components* folder. You should already know what layout we're aiming for so I shouldn't need to explain the SCSS:

```
.service {
    @include span(12);
```

```
    &s {
        padding: $spacing ($spacing / 2);
    }
}

@include bp(small) {
    .service {
        @include span(6);

        &:nth-child(2), &:nth-child(4) {
            @include span(6 last);
        }
    }
}

@include bp {
    .service {
        @include span(3);

        &:nth-child(2) {
            @include span(3);
        }

        &:nth-child(4) {
            @include span(3 last);
        }
    }
}
```

Summary

In this chapter we focused on layout. In essence, layout is the positioning, size, and spacing of our elements on the page. By focusing on these topics without getting distracted by color, or look and feel we can better structure our codebase. It also means from here we have full freedom over styling our page. We could apply numerous different themes (or skins) to what we have now.

We used Susy grids as well as our breakpoint mixin (bp) to create a solid, flexible grid system. With just 27 lines of Sass we generated our grid system which consists of almost 600 lines of CSS. We then used our media mixins and Susy to create a semantic layout, with the minimal amount of code.

In the next chapter, we'll focus on the colors, fonts, icons, and adding the finishing touches to our site.

10
Building a Content-Rich Website – Theme

In this chapter, we'll wrap up our design. We'll focus mainly on typography, color, and some other aesthetic elements; however, we'll also need to revisit our layout as we go along. Increasing or decreasing font sizes and adding new elements could potentially show us areas of our layout that need to be improved or modified to accommodate our theme. This is usually limited to adding or removing padding and margin here or there.

For our typography we'll decide upon at least two fonts which complement each other and represent the overall brand correctly. Typography is one of the most important aspects of a design's aesthetic. The right font will lay the foundation for the rest of the design.

We'll choose a font for the body text and also a font for accentuation, such as the logo, dropcaps, and other stand out typographical elements. We'll also use a loop to import our fonts from Google fonts to make it very easy for us to add or remove fonts in future from one place.

We'll create a mixin to generate a dropcap using the `:first-of-type:first-letter` pseudo-selector. We'll also write a mixin which will generate our CSS for the tag-cloud in our footer. It's simpler than you may think.

Once that's done we'll move onto creating our color scheme. We'll use a map called `$theme` to insert our colors throughout our design. This will allow us to change our entire color scheme in one place if we need to.

We have a lot to cover so let's get into it!

Typography

The first part of our theme we'll look at is typography. We'll choose a minimum of two fonts and set our font families with sensible fallback fonts. We may also need to make some layout tweaks while we do this. This is because we'll be increasing and decreasing our font sizes in places and this can affect the layout and uncover areas that need to be laid out differently.

We need to create a file called *_typography.scss* in the *scss/theme* directory. We'll add our main fonts and font family defaults here. We'll also use a list and an @each loop to import all the necessary fonts from Google Fonts:

```
$fonts: (
    'Bilbo+Swash+Caps',
    'Roboto'
) !default;

$main-font: 'Verdana' !default;
$secondary-font: 'Roboto' !default;
$tertiary-font: 'Bilbo Swash Caps' !default;

$body-font-family: ($main-font, Geneva, sans-serif) !default;
$heading-font-family: ($secondary-font, Helvetica, Arial, sans-serif)
!default;
$accent-font-family: ($tertiary-font, cursive) !default;

@each $font in $fonts {
    @import url('http://fonts.googleapis.com/css?family=#{$font}');
}
```

Here we've created a list called $fonts, which we can now add any Google font to and instantly have access to it. This also means we don't need to add them to our HTML which will keep our number of HTTP requests to a minimum.

We've also added our main font, secondary font, and an accent font. We're going to be using Bilbo Swash Caps for dropcaps and accents, due to its similarity to the Sass logo.

We then set up our font families for the body text, heading text, and accents. The @each loop is simply importing all of our fonts from the $fonts list.

Now, add *themes/typography* to *scss/styles.scss* and add our typography variables:

```
// Typography
$fonts: (
    'Bilbo+Swash+Caps',
    'Roboto'
```

```
);

$main-font: 'Verdana';
$secondary-font: 'Roboto';
$tertiary-font: 'Bilbo Swash Caps';

$body-font-family: ($main-font, Verdana, Geneva, sans-serif);
$heading-font-family: ($secondary-font, Helvetica, Arial, sans-serif);
$accent-font-family: ($tertiary-font, cursive);

@import '../../bower_components/susy/sass/susy';
@import "helpers/all";
@import "base/normailize";
@import "base/global";
@import "base/typography";
@import "layout/grid";
@import "components/top-nav";
@import "components/main-header";
@import "components/main-nav";
@import "components/search";
@import "components/cart";
@import "components/image-banner";
@import "components/featured-product";
@import "components/product-centered";
@import "components/testimonials";
@import "components/services";
@import "components/subfooter";
@import "components/footer";
@import "theme/ionicons/ionicons";
@import "theme/typography";
```

Now we need to implement our fonts. We're going to add our `$main-font-family` to our body and our `$heading-font-family` to all of our headings. Back in *scss/theme/_typography.scss* add the following:

```
body {
    font-family: $body-font-family;
}

h1, h2, h3, h4, h5, h6 {
    font-family: $heading-font-family;
}
```

We're going to use a similar font to the one used in the Sass website logo. We'll use this on the word "Sass" in the site title in the header. We'll also increase its size. This will most likely mean we'll need to adjust the search bar also. Let's add a span to the site title so we can style the word "Sass" separately. In *index.html* modify the `.main-header-title` like so:

```
<h1 class="main-header-title">Mastering <span>Sass</span> Swag</h1>
```

Now, let's reduce the `font-size` of the `.main-header-title` to `1.75em`. We'll also style the span we added to `.main-header-title`. We'll set it to use the `$accent-font-family`, increase its size, and make it `italic`:

```
.main-header-title {
    font-size: 1.75em;

    > span {
        font-family: $accent-font-family;
        font-size: 2em;
        font-style: italic;
    }
}
```

Now our header should look like:

As you can see we now need to add some top padding to the `.main-header-inner-right` div to push the search element down in line with our `.main-header-title`. Open *scss/components/_main-header.scss* and add the following line:

```
.main-header-inner {
    ...

    &-right {
        @include span(12);

        @include bp {
            @include span(4 last);

            padding-top: $spacing * 1.25;
        }
```

```
        }
    }
```

Dropcaps

I quite like **dropcaps**. I feel they can make a boring chunk of text instantly more interesting and visually appealing. Therefore, I'm going to add a mixin which we can use in various places in our design to add dropcaps. Prime candidates for dropcaps are the services sections and the text widget in the footer.

There are a number of methods for creating a dropcap. You can use an image, however, this means the first letter is invisible to screen readers, and therefore the text makes no sense. So that option is out of the question. You can wrap the first element in a span with a class of `dropcap` and simply add the dropcap styling to that class. However, this involves more markup and I usually try my best to avoid this.

For these reasons, my preferred approach is to use the `:first-letter` pseudo-class. We could use `:first-child:first-letter`, however, this would not work if we are trying to target a paragraph tag in an element where the paragraph is not the first child. Take this markup for example:

```
<article class="service">
    <h3 class="service-title">Service One</h3>
    <p>
        Lorem ipsum dolor sit amet, consectetur adipisicing elit. A
consequatur consequuntur dignissimos dolores eius impedit incidunt soluta
voluptatum. Deserunt dolore mollitia placeat quam rerum. Amet dolorum
exercitationem modi porro voluptates?
    </p>
</article>
```

We could try and use the following CSS:

```
.service > p:first-child:first-letter {
    /* Styles for dropcap here... */
}
```

However, this won't work. This is because the `:first-child` in `.service` is actually the h3. So instead we need to use the `:first-of-type` pseudo-selector:

```
.service > p:first-of-type:first-child {
    /* Styles for dropcap here... */
}
```

This correctly targets the first <p> tag in the `.service` element. With that in mind, let's create our `dropcap` mixin. Create a file in *scss/helpers/mixins* called *_dropcap.scss*. Inside that we'll create our mixin:

```
@mixin dropcap($size: 4.5em, $color: black, $font-family: $accent-font-
family) {
    min-height: $size;

    &:first-of-type:first-letter {
        // Positioning
        float: left;
        padding-top: #{($size * 0.02)};
        padding-right: #{($size * 0.05)};

        // Theme
        font-size: $size;
        font-family: $font-family;
        color: $color;
    }
}
```

Now import the `dropcap` mixin in *scss/helpers/_all.scss*:

```
@import "functions/get";
@import "mixins/hover-link";
@import "mixins/bp";
@import "mixins/media";
@import "mixins/dropcap";
```

The mixin could then be used, like so:

```
.service > p {
    @include dropcap;
}
```

We set a `min-height` to ensure we only have one or two sentences and the next element won't overlap our dropcap. We use float left to allow the remaining text to wrap around the first letter. The `padding-top` pushes the element down so it is flush with the first line. The `padding-right` keeps our text from overlapping the dropcap. Our dropcap can be configured to use whatever size, color, or font-family we want. That way we could have numerous dropcap styles if we wanted.

Let's add it to our services section and also the subfooter text widget. Let's first modify the services section markup in our *index.html* file:

```
<section class="services">
    <h3 class="services-title">Swag Services</h3>
```

```
<div class="container">
<article class="service">
    <h3 class="service-title">Service One</h3>
    <p>
        Lorem ipsum dolor sit amet, consectetur adipisicing elit. A
consequatur consequuntur dignissimos dolores eius impedit incidunt soluta
voluptatum. Deserunt dolore mollitia placeat quam rerum. Amet dolorum
exercitationem modi porro voluptates?
    </p>
</article>
<article class="service">
    <h3 class="service-title">Service Two</h3>
    <p>
        Ipsum dolor sit amet, consectetur adipisicing elit. Animi
dicta dignissimos est ex, expedita illum impedit incidunt modi mollitia
nam? Asperiores consequuntur dicta eligendi error facilis, fuga incidunt
quo voluptatem.
    </p>
</article>
<article class="service">
    <h3 class="service-title">Service Three</h3>
    <p>
        Dolor sit amet, consectetur adipisicing elit. Accusantium
aspernatur, atque autem blanditiis commodi debitis dicta doloribus, ducimus
eius eos laudantium magni molestias mollitia pariatur quod repellendus
unde, voluptate voluptatum?
    </p>
</article>
<article class="service">
    <h3 class="service-title">Service Four</h3>
    <p>
        Sit amet, consectetur adipisicing elit. Accusantium atque
commodi dolore labore obcaecati! Accusantium delectus dignissimos
doloremque fugiat inventore maiores possimus quaerat quia, rerum sint,
totam veritatis voluptates! Quas!
    </p>
</article>
</div>
</section>
```

All I've done here is removed some words from the beginning of each paragraph so each one doesn't start with L. Next, in *scss/theme/_typography.scss*, add our styles for the dropcaps:

```
.service > p {
    @include dropcap;
}
```

I've also just realized that we need to place the `container` mixin on the `.services` element to keep the `.services-title` in line with everything else. Let's do that now. Open *scss/components/_services.scss* and add the following line:

```
.service {
    @include span(12);

    &s {
        @include container;

        padding: $spacing ($spacing / 2);
    }
}
```

With that, our services section should look like so:

Now let's do the same for the `.subfooter-widget-section-text` element. First, let's remove some words from the beginning so we have a unique letter for the dropcap:

```
<div class="subfooter-widget-section-text">
    <p>Amet consectetur adipisicing elit. Delectus dolore impedit
officia?</p>
</div>
```

Now, in `scss/theme/_typography.scss` add the following:

```
.subfooter-widget-section-text > p {
    @include dropcap;
}
```

Our `subfooter` should now look like:

Tagcloud

The next section of the page I want to look at is the tag cloud in the footer. We've already added an unordered list containing list items with classes for each size such as `xs`, `sm`, `md`, and so on. Now let's create a mixin which we can apply to the unordered list which will automatically add all of our font sizes accordingly.

Create a file in *scss/helpers/mixins* called *_tag-cloud.scss*. Inside, we'll create our mixin:

```
@mixin tag-cloud($base: 1em) {
    .xs {
        font-size: ($base * 0.5);
    }

    .sm {
        font-size: ($base * 0.75);
    }

    .md {
        font-size: $base;
    }

    .lg {
        font-size: ($base * 1.25);
    }

    .xl {
        font-size: ($base * 1.5);
    }
}
```

As you can see, we've set a base font size of `1em`. The `md` class will be the default size. The `sm` class will be one quarter of our `$base` value, and the `xs` class will be half the `font-size` of the `$base` value. Likewise, `lg` will be one quarter larger and `xl` will be one half larger.

Next you'll need to import the `tag-cloud` mixin in *scss/helpers/_all.scss*:

```
@import "functions/get";
@import "mixins/hover-link";
@import "mixins/bp";
@import "mixins/media";
@import "mixins/dropcap";
@import "mixins/tag-cloud";
```

Now let's use the `tag-cloud` mixin in our *scss/theme/_typography.scss* file:

```
// Tagcloud
.subfooter-widget-section-tagcloud {
    @include tag-cloud;
}
```

That should be it. The `footer` should now look like this:

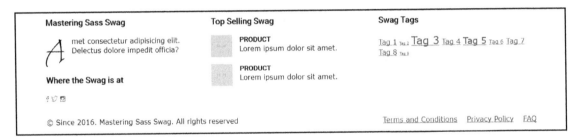

Color scheme

The next part of our theme is creating a color scheme. We'll use two to three main colors which we'll place in variables. We'll then create a `$theme` map which we will use throughout our colors Sass file. This will allow us to easily switch **themes** by simply modifying our `$theme` map in future.

Let's first add a file called *_color.scss* in the *scss/theme* directory. Inside that we'll start to add our variables:

```
$red: hsl(0, 57%, 60%) !default;
$dark-grey: hsl(0, 3%, 22%) !default;
```

```scss
$theme: (
    color: (
        primary: $red,
        secondary: $dark-grey
    )
) !default;
```

You should also place them at the beginning of the *scss/style.scss* file as we've been doing with all of our variables so far:

```scss
// scss/style.scss
$red: hsl(0, 57%, 60%);
$dark-grey: hsl(0, 3%, 22%);

$theme: (
    color: (
        primary: $red,
        secondary: $dark-grey
    )
);
```

Now let's add some color to our header. We're going to make the top bar background, the primary color (the red) with white text and icons. We'll then make the span in our `site-title-header` the primary color also. Our main `nav` will use the secondary color (dark grey) for the background, with white text which will turn red on hover:

```scss
.top-nav, .main-nav {
    a, [class^="ion-"] {
        color: white;
    }
}

.top-nav {
    background-color: get($theme, color, primary);

    a {
        @include hover-link;
    }
}

.main {
    &-nav {
        background-color: get($theme, color, secondary);

        &-menu-item {
            a {
                text-decoration: none;
            }
```

```
            &:hover a {
                color: get($theme, color, primary);
            }
        }
    }

    &-header-title > span {
        color: get($theme, color, primary);
    }
}
```

Search

Next, we'll style the Search field in the header. I want to ensure that the border on the input and the button match. We'll set it to the secondary color by default. The background color of the search button will also be this color with the icon being white. Then when the input or the button is hovered on or active we set the border color to be the primary theme color. The button background color will also change to the primary color. The icon will remain white:

```
// Search
.search-bar {
    &-input, &-button {
        border: 1px solid get($theme, color, secondary);

        &:active, &:focus, &:hover {
            border: 1px solid get($theme, color, primary);
        }
    }

    &-button {
        background-color: get($theme, color, secondary);
        color: white;

        &:active, &:focus, &:hover {
            background-color: get($theme, color, primary);
        }
    }
}
```

At this point I'm also realizing that our logo and search bar aren't vertically centered perfectly. So to address this, we'll need to add some margin-top and a line-height to our .header-main-title and increase the padding-top on the .main-header-inner-right on screens from 768px upwards using our bp mixin:

```
.main-header {
    overflow: hidden;

    &-title {
        @include bp {
            margin-top: ($spacing * 0.4);
            line-height: ($spacing * 1.5);
        }
    }
}

.main-header-inner {
    ...

    &-right {
        @include span(12);

        @include bp {
            @include span(4 last);

            padding-top: ($spacing * 1.4);
        }
    }
}
```

With that, our header should now look the following:

Image banner

The image banner doesn't need much alteration. Mainly, we'll want to make all the text white because the overlay over the background image is dark. However, this isn't actually part of our theme, rather this should be a feature of our component itself. By that I mean if we change the color of our overlay to be a lighter color, the text in the caption should turn dark and vice versa.

For this we're going to use the built-in `lightness` function in Sass to check if the lightness is above or below 50% and make the text white if the overlay is dark or black if the overlay is light. To do this we'll create a function called `abs-contrast-color`.

First, create a file in *scss/helpers/functions* and call it *_abs-contrast-color.scss*. Inside that file we'll write our function:

```
@function abs-contrast-color($color) {
    @if (type-of($color) == color) {
        @if (lightness($color) <= 50%) {
            @return white;
        } @else {
            @return black;
        }
    } @else {
        @error 'Type of `$color` must be a valid color. Type of `' +
type_of($color) + '` given.';
    }
}
```

First we're checking if the value entered for `$color` is a valid type of color. If it's not a valid color, we show an error. Otherwise we check if the lightness of the color is above or below `50%`. If it is less than `50%` the color is dark and therefore we return white, which is the absolute contrast color of any dark color. Otherwise the color must be a light color and we return black.

Now let's improve our image-banner component by adding our function to the caption and title elements. Open *scss/components/_image-banner.scss* and modify it as follows:

```
.image-banner {
    ...

    &-caption {
        @include container;
        @include media-container($spacing / 2);

        color: abs-contrast-color(get($image-banner, overlay-color));

        @include bp(large) {
            position: relative;
            top: get($image-banner, height) / 4;
        }

        &-title {
            @include media-title(abs-contrast-color(get($image-banner,
overlay-color)));
        }
```

```
    }

    . . .
}
```

Finally, we'll set the button to use our primary theme color also so it stands out:

```
.image-banner {
    . . .

    &-button {
        @include media-button($img-align: none, $background-color:
get($theme, color, primary));
    }
}
```

The image banner should now look like:

Featured products

Before we move on to the testimonials I want to add our primary color to the buttons and product titles in the Featured Products section. After all, we want the products to stand out.

Once again, a color can be passed into our media mixins to set the title and button colors. Therefore, we should apply our color using those mixins. That way we prevent unnecessary duplication in our final CSS output.

Open *scss/components/_product-centered.scss* and make one simple modification:

```
.product-centered {
    @include media-centered($img: fullwidth, $color: get($theme, color,
primary));

    padding-left: 0;
```

```
        padding-right: 0;

        &-title {
            margin-top: 0
        }
    }
```

Our **Featured Products** section should now be much more eye-catching:

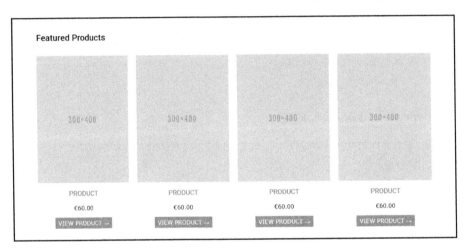

Testimonials

The testimonials component is very similar to our image banner component. That means we can use the exact same function to ensure our text color is always the absolute contrast of the overlay color.

Open the *scss/component/_testimonials.scss* file and add the following:

```
.testimonial {
    max-width: 20em;
    margin: 0 auto;

    @include media-centered($img: rounded, $color: abs-contrast-color(
    get($testimonials, overlay-color)));
    blockquote, cite {
        color: abs-contrast-color(get($testimonials, overlay-color));
    }

    &s {
        ...
```

```
        }
    }
```

As you can probably guess, the text will all be white now seeing as the overlay is dark:

Services

The **services** section seems a bit boring, to be honest. Even with the dropcaps. I think we need some icons to make everything a bit more visually appealing. This will require us to add some elements for our icons. We'll also make the `.services-title` an h2 element instead of h3 so it matches Featured Products.

Open *index.html* and add the following:

```html
<!-- BEGIN .services -->
<section class="services">
    <h2 class="services-title">Swag Services</h2>
    <div class="container">
        <article class="service">
            <div class="ion-clock"></div>
            <h3 class="service-title">Fast Delivery</h3>
            <p>
                ...
            </p>
        </article>
        <article class="service">
            <div class="ion-earth"></div>
            <h3 class="service-title">Worldwide Shipping</h3>
            <p>
                ...
            </p>
        </article>
        <article class="service">
            <div class="ion-help-buoy"></div>
            <h3 class="service-title">24/7 Support</h3>
```

```
            <p>
                . . .
            </p>
        </article>
        <article class="service">
            <div class="ion-cash"></div>
            <h3 class="service-title">Money Back Guarantee</h3>
            <p>
                . . .
            </p>
        </article>
    </div>
</section>
<!-- END .services -->
```

Now let's center the icons and the `service-titles`. Open *scss/theme/_typography.scss* and add the following above where we placed our `tag-cloud` styles:

```
.service {
    text-align: center;

    [class^="ion-"] {
        font-size: 2em;
        padding-bottom: 0.5em;
    }
}
```

I've also increased the size of the icon to 2em because it was too small at 1em. Now, however, the dropcaps look completely out of place. So I think we should simply remove them and center all of the text in the services columns.

Once again, in the *scss/theme/_typography.scss* file, remove the following:

```
// Dropcaps
.service > p {
    @include dropcap;
}
```

The last step is to color the icons using the primary theme color. Open *scss/theme/_color.scss* and add the following:

```
.service [class^="ion-"] {
    color: get($theme, color, primary);
}
```

We'll do more with the section title in a while, but for now that will do. The services section looks much better now:

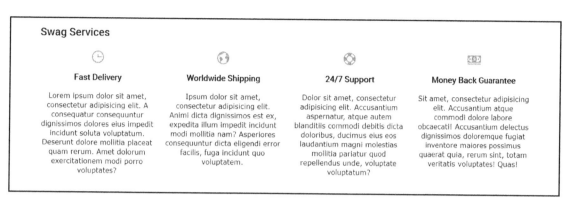

Footer

One of the final steps for our homepage is to color the footer. We'll use the secondary color as the background and the primary color for all the links, as well as the dropcap. Open *scss/theme/_color.scss* and add the following to the end of the file:

```
.footer {
    background-color: get($theme, color, secondary);
    color: white;

    a,
    a:hover,
    .subfooter a,
    .subfooter a:hover {
        @include hover-link;
        color: get($theme, color, primary);
    }

    .subfooter-widget-section-text > p:first-of-type::first-letter {
        color: get($theme, color, primary);
    }

    .footer-inner:last-child {
        border-top: 1px solid hsla(0, 0%, 100%, 0.1);
    }
}
```

Lastly, we'll increase the size of the social icons in the *_typography.scss* file in our *scss/theme* folder. While we're here we'll also tidy up all of our `.subfooter-section-widget` rules. Right now we have three separate rules which could instead be nested under one `.subfooter-widget-section`, including our socials `font-size`:

```scss
// scss/theme/_typography.scss
.subfooter-widget-section {
    &-text > p {
        @include dropcap;
    }

    &-tagcloud {
        @include tag-cloud;
    }

    &-socials {
        font-size: 2em;
    }
}
```

With that, the `subfooter` should look like:

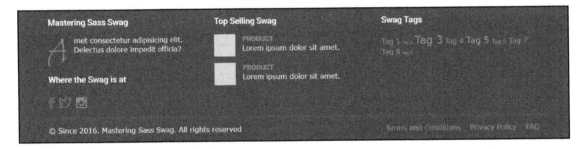

Section titles

There's only two things left to do and we're finished! Both are to do with our section titles. First, we want to center them to match the content better, and lastly, we'll add an *underline* using the `::after` pseudo element for that extra touch. After all, as the old saying goes *God is in the detail.*

So the first thing we will need to do is add a common class to our section titles so we can style them all together. We'll call this class `section-title`. Open *index.html* and modify the `.featured-product-title` and the `.services-title` like so:

```html
<h2 class="featured-product-title section-title">Featured Products</h2>
```

. . .

```
<h2 class="services-title section-title">Swag Services</h2>
```

We're actually going to create a mixin to handle both our alignment and generating our underline. Create a file called *_underline.scss* in the *scss/helpers/mixins* folder. Inside that add our mixin:

```scss
@mixin underline($align: left, $color: black, $height: 3px, $width: 3em,
$spacing: 0.75em) {
    text-align: unquote($align);

    &::after {
        display: block;
        content: " ";
        position: relative;
        height: $height;
        background-color: $color;
        top: 0;
        width: $width;
        margin-top: $spacing;

        @if ($align == center) {
            left: 50%;
            margin-left: -#{($width / 2)}
        } @else if ($align == right) {
            right: 0;
        } @else {
            left: 0;
        }
    }
}
```

We've added parameters for any value which we (or the client) may want to change in future. These are $align, $color, $height, $width, and $spacing. The align will not only align the text, it will also align the underline using relative position and the left or right property. If we choose center, the line will be centered by moving it 50% from the left and then pulling it back half the width of the element using a negative left margin. Without the negative left margin, the underline would not be dead in the center.

Before moving on, let's import the underline mixin in the *scss/helpers/_all.scss* file:

```scss
@import "functions/get";
@import "functions/abs-contrast-color";
@import "mixins/hover-link";
@import "mixins/bp";
@import "mixins/media";
```

```
@import "mixins/dropcap";
@import "mixins/tag-cloud";
@import "mixins/underline";
```

Now, once again in the *scss/theme/_typography.scss* file let's apply our mixin:

```
.section-title {
    @include underline(center, get($theme, color, primary));

    padding-top: $spacing;
}
```

The `padding-top` will improve the vertical spacing. However, now the footer looks a bit off. The final touch is to double the padding at the top of the `subfooter`. We can do this by simply making one change to the *scss/components/_subfooter.scss* file:

```
.subfooter {
    padding: ($spacing * 2) ($spacing / 2) $spacing ($spacing / 2);

    ...

}
```

Before we wrap up, I want to do some quick reorganizing of our imports in the *scss/style.scss* file. Right now we are required to have our variables at the top of our file for our theme to work correctly. If we were to remove these variables the components which use our $theme variables would throw up errors because the theme files (*_color.scss* and *_typography.scss*) are imported last.

To fix this we'll need to move them up just before our component imports. Open *scss/style.scss* and modify to be:

```
@import '../../bower_components/susy/sass/susy';
@import "helpers/all";
@import "base/normailize";
@import "base/global";
@import "base/typography";
@import "layout/grid";
@import "theme/ionicons/ionicons";
@import "theme/typography";
@import "theme/color";
@import "components/top-nav";
@import "components/main-header";
@import "components/main-nav";
@import "components/search";
@import "components/cart";
@import "components/image-banner";
@import "components/featured-product";
```

```scss
@import "components/product-centered";
@import "components/testimonials";
@import "components/services";
@import "components/subfooter";
@import "components/footer";
```

Next, let's move all of our config variables into a file called *_config.scss* which we'll place in the *scss* directory alongside our *style.scss* file. The *_config.scss* file should look like:

```scss
// Theme
$ionicons-font-path: "fonts/ionicons";

$red: hsl(0, 57%, 60%);
$dark-grey: hsl(0, 3%, 22%);

$theme: (
    color: (
        primary: $red,
        secondary: $dark-grey
    )
);

// Typography
$fonts: (
    'Bilbo+Swash+Caps',
    'Roboto'
);

$main-font: 'Verdana';
$secondary-font: 'Roboto';
$tertiary-font: 'Bilbo Swash Caps';

$body-font-family: ($main-font, Verdana, Geneva, sans-serif);
$heading-font-family: ($secondary-font, Helvetica, Arial, sans-serif);
$accent-font-family: ($tertiary-font, cursive);

// Layout
$spacing: 1em;

$default-breakpoint: medium;
$breakpoints: (
    small: 480px,
    medium: 768px,
    large: 980px
);

$susy: (
    container: 1160px,
```

```scss
        columns: 12,
        gutters: 1/3
);

// Components
$cart: (
        slide-in: right,
        height: 100vh,
        width: (
                small: 100vw,
                medium: 20em
        ),
        spacing: 1em,
        bg-color: white,
        transition-speed: 350ms
);

$image-banner: (
        height: 400px,
        overlay-color: hsla(0, 0%, 0%, 0.5)
);

$testimonials: (
        height: 300px,
        overlay-color: hsla(0, 0%, 0%, 0.5)
);
```

Then we just need to add it to our *style.scss* file:

```scss
@import "config";
@import '../../bower_components/susy/sass/susy';
@import "helpers/all";
@import "base/normailize";
@import "base/global";
@import "base/typography";
@import "layout/grid";
@import "theme/ionicons/ionicons";
@import "theme/typography";
@import "theme/color";
@import "components/top-nav";
@import "components/main-header";
@import "components/main-nav";
@import "components/search";
@import "components/cart";
@import "components/image-banner";
@import "components/featured-product";
@import "components/product-centered";
@import "components/testimonials";
```

```
@import "components/services";
@import "components/subfooter";
@import "components/footer";
```

Now to prove our theme works as expected, let's pretend we've submitted this to the client for approval.

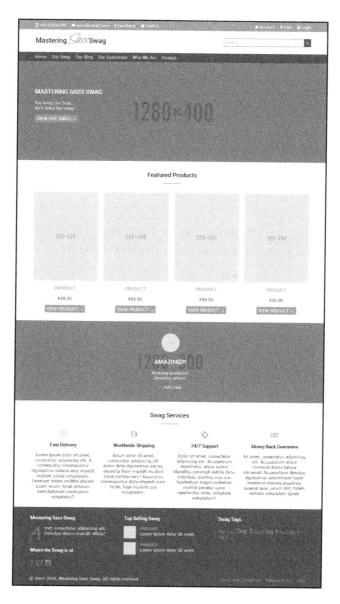

The client likes the majority of it, however they want more "space" in the design overall, and they want to see what the site would be like in a light pastel blue.

In a plain vanilla CSS project (or a poorly conceived Sass project) this would be at least a few hours' work. However, we should be able to simply add a variable of $blue, place that in our $theme map instead of $red and then change our $spacing variable. Let's see what happens. In *scss/_config.scss* make the following modifications:

```scss
$red: hsl(0, 57%, 60%);
$blue: hsl(210, 40%, 60%);
$dark-grey: hsl(0, 3%, 22%);

$theme: (
    color: (
        primary: $blue,
        secondary: $dark-grey
    )
);

// Layout
$spacing: 2em;
```

With those three small changes we have a very different design:

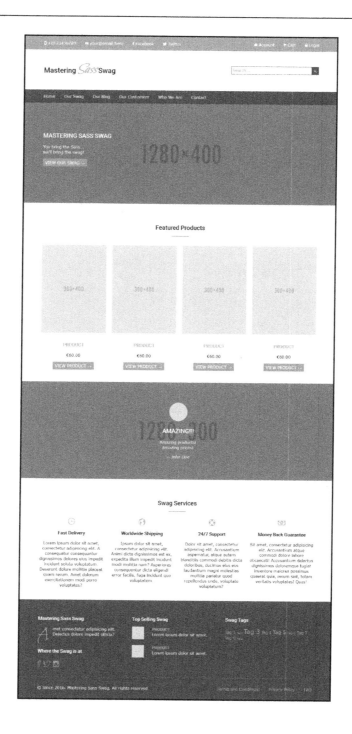

The client was right about the spacing, so we'll keep our $spacing set at 2em. However the blue is much too cold and doesn't give off the correct feel. So we'll go back to the red. Once again this is a small change. We simply change our $theme map to use red as its primary color:

```
$theme: (
    color: (
        primary: $red,
        secondary: $dark-grey
    )
);
```

That's it! We're finished! Our design is complete. This is what you should have after all of that:

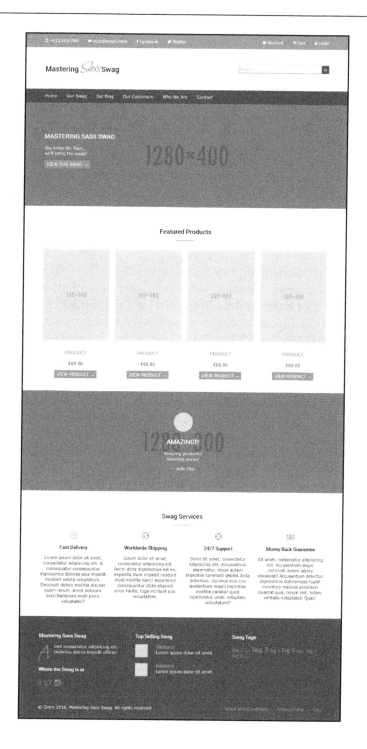

Summary

Over the course of this book I've tried to share more than just code snippets and techniques to write better Sass. I've also tried to share some of the ideas and practices that I believe will help you better organize your projects and therefore, write better, more reusable, future-proof Sass. That in turn, will give you the freedom to design better sites and apps without constantly running into the same issues.

Most, if not all of these practices are based on, or derived from, numerous other practices, techniques, and frameworks such as OOCSS, BEM, SMACSS, Atomic Design, Bootstrap, Foundation, and countless articles and videos across the Internet. All I can hope for is that within this book you found a few tips and techniques which will help you on your future projects.

At this point you may be wondering to yourself *where to next?*, *What should I learn now?* Well, I would certainly recommend you start using the indented Sass syntax if you don't already. Once you've embraced the indented syntax I think you'll enjoy learning Jade (`http://jade-lang.com/`). Jade is a JavaScript language which uses an indented *Sass-like* syntax to generate HTML. Similar to HAML but much, much better! Trust me, you'll never write HTML again once you've tried it.

Also, as I mentioned earlier in this book, your Sass code can only ever be as good as your CSS. By that I mean if you can't build it in plain CSS then you won't be able to build it in Sass. Luckily, there is a huge range of books and videos on Packt to help you with your CSS. So if you still struggle with the idea of mobile first or some part of responsive web design I would recommend you check out *Mastering Responsive Web Design* by Ricardo Zea. Or if you still find you keep running into similar problems in your CSS perhaps *Professional CSS3* by Piotr Sikora would be a logical next step. If you like being on the cutting edge and you'd like to start using the newest CSS features right now, you should check out *Mastering PostCSS for Web Design* by Alex Libby.

In reality you can't go wrong as long as you challenge yourself, and be honest about what skills you need to work on.

That's all from me. You stay Sassy, San Diego!

Index

E

elements
  floating 89
experimental implementation phase 55

F

featured products
  about 255
  testimonial, adding 259
Firefox
  source maps, setting up 183, 184
font-size of headings
  about 32
  if statement 34
  mixin 35, 36
  sizing 33

G

global scope 126
Grunt
  about 161
Gulp
  about 162, 196
  BrowserSync 176
  file watcher 176
  jQuery, adding 197
  setting up 170, 171, 172, 175

H

heading font sizes
  adjusting 68
  CodePen, using 70
  SassMeister, using 70
  setup, obtaining 70
heading line heights
  controlling 39, 41, 42
  different font families for each heading, allowing 42
  error handling 47
  repetition, removing 44, 45
  type validation 47
helpers
  about 197
  bp (breakpoint) 199

cart slide-out component 216, 217
footers, adding 225
get function 198
global base styles 204, 205
grid 207
grid container 212
hover links 199
Ionicons 207
main nav 216
media (based on OOCSS media component) 201
normalize.scss 203
screen reader text 205, 206
search component 214
top navigation bar 209, 211
hex color codes 117
HTML5
  about 15
  command line 17
  programming 17
hue 117
Hue Saturation Brightness (HSB) 119
Hue Saturation Lightness (HSL)
  about 95, 117, 118, 119
  values, obtaining without Photoshop 119
Hue Saturation Vibrancy (HSV) 119

I

image banner
  adding 253
Ion Framework 207
Ionicons
  reference link 208

J

jQuery 197

L

lists
  about 38, 81, 84
  considerations 37
local scope 132

Made in the USA
Middletown, DE
16 January 2019